Costs and outcomes of
non-infant adoptions

Costs and outcomes of non-infant adoptions

Julie Selwyn, Wendy Sturgess,
David Quinton and
Catherine Baxter

BAAF
ADOPTION
& FOSTERING

Published by British Association
for Adoption and Fostering
(BAAF)
Saffron House
6–10 Kirby Street
London EC1N 8TS
www.baaf.org.uk

Charity registration 275689

British Library Cataloguing in Publication Data
A catalogue record for this book is available
from the British Library

ISBN 1 903699 19 3

Editorial project management by Shaila Shah
Cover photos posed by models,
John Birdsall Photography,
www.johnbirdsall.co.uk
Designed by Andrew Haig & Associates
Typeset by Avon DataSet, Bidford on Avon
Printed in Great Britain by Creative Print
and Design Group

BAAF is the leading UK-wide membership
organisation for all those concerned with
adoption, fostering and child care issues.

Contents

Acknowledgements

This research would not have been possible without the considerable help of a number of people. We would like to thank the Department of Health for funding the study and the local authorities for agreeing to participate. We are especially grateful to everyone who gave the information we needed to calculate the unit costs and who helped us identify our sample, access the children's case files and find the families. We have greatly appreciated the help of our advisory group, especially the advice and support given by Caroline Thomas. Most importantly, we would like to say thank you to the families who shared with us their experiences, often at the cost of considerable amounts of their time and emotional energy.

The research was undertaken by Julie Selwyn who was the lead manager and Wendy Sturgess. Catherine Baxter (health economist) advised on the economic evaluation and David Quinton analysed the comparison outcomes of adoptive and foster care. Any errors or deficiencies in this study are the sole responsibility of the lead manager and should not be attributed to any advisers. The views expressed in this publication are those of the authors and are not necessarily those of the Department of Health or the Department for Education and Skills.

April 2006

Notes about the authors

Julie Selwyn is Director of the Hadley Centre for Adoption & Foster Care Studies, in the School for Policy Studies at the University of Bristol. The centre aims to link research, policy, practice and training in all aspects of permanence and planning for looked after children (www.bristol.ac.uk/hadley). Julie qualified as a social worker in 1981 after lengthy residential childcare experience and then worked in local authority children's services until joining the university in 1993.

David Quinton is Emeritus Professor of Psychosocial Development at the University of Bristol. His interest is in continuities and discontinuities in social adaptation, especially following poor parenting experiences, and in interventions and supports for those who experience them. He is the founder of the Hadley Centre for Adoption & Foster Care Studies at Bristol.

Wendy Sturgess was a Research Associate within the School for Policy Studies, University of Bristol. Prior to joining the school, she worked on the ALSPAC (Children of the Nineties) study. Her psychology background informed the development of the instruments and analysis.

Catherine Baxter is a Research Fellow in the Social Policy Research Unit at the University of York. She trained as a health economist and was based previously in the Primary Care Unit at the University of Bristol where she was involved primarily in evaluations of primary health care policy and practice. Her research in SPRU centres on choice and independence across the life-course.

Preface

The "Costs and Outcomes of Non-Infant Adoptions" study was one project in the Department of Health's research initiative on *Costs and Effectiveness of Services to Children in Need*. The purpose of this initiative was to examine variations in the use of resources by local authorities and to develop a better understanding of the costs and effectiveness of different interventions for looked after children and children in need in the community. The research aims were informed by the developing policy context of Quality Protects: in particular, the key objectives of promoting placement stability and improving the life chances of looked after children. Within this policy context, adoption is seen as the placement of choice for younger looked after children who are unable to return to their birth families.

Background, design & methods

1   Background and research issues

Adoption has changed significantly over the last 30 years. Children adopted out of care today are unlikely to share the characteristics or experiences of the infants adopted in the 1960s or earlier. They are older; more likely to have led fractured lives; have often been abused and neglected by their birth parents; and have usually been looked after by local authorities for some while prior to their adoption.

The thrust of recent policy has been greatly to reduce these delays in decision-making and to promote adoption as the best route to a stable family life for children unlikely to return to their birth families. However, most of our knowledge on the long-term success of adoption as placement choice is based on earlier studies of children adopted in early childhood and with less severe experiences. Much less is known about the psycho-social outcomes for older, maltreated children or about the financial and emotional costs to their adoptive families.

Even what we do know about the outcomes for these children can be misleading because most studies examine outcomes *from the point at which an adoptive placement is made*. A more accurate view on the success of adoption as a placement choice can be formed if children are tracked forward from the point of *the best-interests decision*. Unless this is done we do not know how many intended adoptions fall by the wayside before a placement is made, nor to what these failures relate, nor what the outcomes are for those who are not adopted. In short, there is a danger of adoption being seen as more successful than other forms of placement simply because those other forms contain children from unsuccessful adoptions, while the adopted group mostly contains placements that have succeeded, at least for some while.

This study was able to look at many of these issues because it was based upon a complete sample (n = 130) of *all* children for whom an "adoption in best interests" decision was made within one authority over a defined period; it collected data on the children's experiences prior to this decision as well as on what happened to them subsequently; and it

3

was able both to assess the costs of the adoption process and to assess the psychosocial outcomes for children who went down different placement routes. To our knowledge this is the first study to select a sample from the point of the "best interests" decision, to track back through their prior experiences and forward through their subsequent adoptions or other placements. It is only when this is done that true comparisons can be made between adoption and other kinds of "care career".

Legal and policy context

In 1975, only seven per cent of all adoptions were of looked after children. By the year 2003, the picture had changed dramatically – 71 per cent of all adoptions were of children who were looked after. In part, this reflects a change in the way adoption statistics are collected, as relinquished infants had not previously been classified as "in care". It also reflects a policy shift about how the needs of children who cannot return to their birth families should best be met. Although children who have been looked after now make up the largest percentage of all adoptions, this needs to be considered in the context that in 2005 adoption concerned only eight per cent of all looked after children (Department for Education and Skills (DfES), 2005).

During the early 1990s, trends in the adoption statistics and reports from Social Services Inspectorate (SSI) reviews began to raise concerns about adoption policy and practice. In particular, the numbers of children adopted out of care began to drop and three reports – the *Children Act Report 1995– 99* (Department of Health (DH), 2000a), *For Children's Sake* (SSI, 1996) and *Adopting Changes* (SSI, 2000) – raised concerns about the quality of adoption services. Authorities were thought not to be giving adoption sufficient priority and there were wide variations between authorities in the use of adoption that could not be explained by variations in the children's characteristics. These findings came at a time when concern was increasing about the length of time children were remaining looked after and the poor outcomes for children who remained in the care system.

The Department of Health circular (LAC98) *Adoption – Achieving the right balance* (DH, 1998) was a turning point in the way adoption was perceived of and used by local authorities. It stated that adoption should be brought back into the mainstream of children's services and that it should be given a higher priority. The impact of the circular was almost immediate as the numbers of children adopted out of care began to rise and the topic of adoption became more firmly established as a policy issue.

These changes were given further weight when the Prime Minister led a review of adoption (Performance and Innovation Unit (PIU), 2000), which was quickly followed by a White Paper (DH, 2000b) and the Adoption and Children Bill. The Bill passed into law as the Adoption and Children Act in 2002, with a phased introduction of certain provisions. A number of other policy and practice initiatives were introduced to support the increased use of adoption, such as National Standards, the Adoption Register and the Adoption and Permanency Taskforce (see www.dfes.gov. uk/adoption for the most recent information). Policy objectives were translated into Public Sector Agreement (PSA) targets, which encouraged local authorities to make more use of adoption and speed up decision-making.

Since LAC98 there has been a rise in the numbers of children adopted out of care from 2,200 in 1998/9 to 3,800 in year ending 31 March 2005 (DfES, 2005). A Department of Health analysis reported in *The Children Act Report 2001* (DH, 2002) has suggested that the rise in adoption can be attributed to decisions being taken more speedily, and therefore younger children are being placed for adoption.

Research background

Studies of infant adoptions

Long-term outcome studies of children adopted as infants have consistently shown that in adulthood psycho-social outcomes are good (e.g. Bohman and Sigvardsson, 1980; Lambert and Streather, 1980). These studies necessarily follow the practice and the kinds of children placed as infants more than 20 years ago (for general reviews see Brodzinsky and Schechter, 1990; Sellick and Thoburn, 1996; Triselioits *et al*, 1997; Howe, 1998; Maluccio and Anderson, 2000). Not only do these children do better than children from similar socio-economic backgrounds but they compare favourably with the general population (Maughan and Pickles, 1990; Collinshaw *et al*, 1998). The majority of those adopted as infants and

5

their adoptive parents rate their adoption experiences as satisfactory. Disruption rates in these studies are rare, with disruption rates around one per cent (Kadushin, 1970; Holloway, 1997; Castle *et al*, 2000).

However, in comparison with the general population, slightly more children adopted as infants have behavioural difficulties, particularly during adolescence (Fergusson *et al*, 1995), although these problems usually decline to the population level by early adulthood (Maughan and Pickles, 1990). Studies in behaviour genetics (Cadoret, 1990; Plomin, 1995; Rutter *et al*, 1999) have emphasised the importance of considering genetic influences. The most common conclusion is that there is a complex interplay between risk and protective factors, which can result in the expression of inherited vulnerability. The current view is that the key protective/risk factors which are involved in this interplay are: the child's genetic inheritance, early adverse experiences including prenatal trauma such as exposure to drugs/alcohol or maltreatment, later positive re-parenting experiences and nurturing environments, and the meanings the children themselves have attached to life events (Howe, 1998; Peters *et al*, 1999; Rutter, 2000).

Studies of later adoptions

There have been few UK studies of the adoption of maltreated children placed after infancy, even though these now constitute the great majority of those adopted out of care. As Howe (1997) points out, the research emphasis has been on rates of breakdown and disruption rather than on children's developmental and behavioural outcomes. Older children adopted from care generally bring with them a history of neglect and abuse as well as the consequences of time spent in the care system. They have usually come from families where there have been multiple problems in parenting and where parents have mental health and addiction problems, some of which carry genetic risks (Quinton and Rutter, 1988; Howe, 1997; Roy *et al*, 2000). Some authors stress the impact of neurological changes to the developing brain and the impact on "wiring", as the result of pre- and post-natal exposure to trauma and/or parental substance abuse, particularly alcohol (Perry, 1995; Fisher *et al*, 2000; ACE studies, 2005).

Generally, children adopted past infancy do worse on psychosocial measures than children in the general population or those adopted as babies (Seglow *et al*, 1972; Hodges and Tizard, 1989a &b) but do better than those who remain in residential care, foster care or return to their birth families (Hodges and Tizard, 1989a&b; Thoburn, 1990; Triseliotis and Hill, 1990). Howe (1998) in his review of outcome studies combined disruption rates, developmental rates and adopter satisfaction rates to produce a crude measure which suggested that 50–60 per cent of late adoptions are "successful". Taking into account children's histories, even this rate of success should be seen as encouraging.

Most of the USA studies (Kadushin, 1970; Nelson, 1985; Rosenthal and Groze, 1992), while reporting high levels of satisfaction among parents adopting older children, also show the prevalence of persistent behavioural problems. Haugaard and colleagues' review (1999) of outcome studies of children late-placed for adoption concluded that these children were likely to exhibit higher levels of behavioural problems than those adopted as infants, including problems with peer relationships, attachment, conduct difficulties, and over-activity and poor concentration (Rosenthal and Groze, 1992; Quinton *et al*, 1998; Rushton, 1999; Rushton *et al*, 2001).

The extent of the mental health needs of children in the general population, and more recently the extent of problems among children looked after, has recently been acknowledged (Meltzer *et al*, 2000; 2003). These studies report that 39 per cent of children in foster care were assessed as having a psychiatric disorder, with particularly high rates of conduct disorder among five- to ten-year-olds: 36 per cent of looked after children v 5 per cent of children in the general population. Children adopted out of care take these problems with them into their adoptive families and they rarely disappear simply because the child has been adopted (Parker, 1999).

Outcome studies comparing adoption versus long-term foster care

There has been debate about the relative merits of adoption and long-term fostering. In the USA, Barth and Berry (1994) found that adoption had advantages over other sorts of permanency planning in relation to better developmental outcomes, child satisfaction and protection from re-abuse. Rosenthal (1993) has argued that stability may be the greatest advantage of adoption. Even so, it has been argued that, when age at placement is held constant, there is little difference between outcomes of adoption and long-term fostering (Thoburn, 1991). In practice, however, long-term fostering rarely continues after the age of 16 (Sinclair *et al*, 2004) and the instability of the care system is reflected in the statistic that only 65 per cent of long-term looked after children under 16 years of age have been in the same placement for four years or more (DfES, 2005).

Without longitudinal studies examining the outcomes of children placed in long-term foster care, the outcomes for children brought up in this form of care are not known. At present, comparisons between the two systems tend to be comparisons of those who remain in placement. More recently there have been calls to consider long-term fostering as a positive choice for some children (Cleaver, 2000; Lowe *et al*, 2002) and to implement polices that support placements. We know of no comparisons between adoption and long-term foster care in which the placement with particular foster carers was the long-term plan. The weight of evidence is that adoption has clear advantages in terms of stability and continuity of family support into adulthood. Studies (Howe, 1996; 1997; Quinton *et al*, 1998) indicate that adopters are more likely to persevere with children, while foster carers' contractual relationship with social services departments (SSDs) makes it easier for them to request a change of placement. Triseliotis's review (2002) of comparative studies led him to conclude that, compared with long-term fostering, adoption provided a greater sense of belonging and a more enduring psychological base in life.

However, there will always be children for whom long-term fostering is appropriate, e.g. older children, those closely attached to foster carers, or children whose religious beliefs exclude adoption. Growing up in foster care can be a positive experience (Triseliotis, 1980; Schofield, 2003) but, as Rowe remarked, placements were successful "often in spite of rather than because of the system" (Rowe *et al*, 1984). The challenge is how to make foster care more stable. The introduction of Special Guardianship in the Adoption and Children Act 2002 may change the nature of long-term foster care and improve stability for children.

Disruption rates, risks and protective factors

Disruption rates should be treated with caution. Definitions differ from study to study. Some include disruptions occurring after placement, while others include disruptions during the matching process. Most studies have only included children once a placement has been found and therefore the "success" of adoption may be overestimated. The length of follow-up periods also differ. In addition, placements may continue although children and adoptive parents are unhappy (Rushton and Dance, 2004). If disruption is defined as the end of an adoptive placement at any time during the adoption process (Berry and Barth, 1990), rates vary between 15–50 per cent. Studies of the risks for disruption have shown some consistency and also that risks rarely operate independently. The following paragraphs outline the most commonly found risks.

Characteristics of the child: The factor most strongly associated with disruption is older age at placement, probably because as age increases so does the time the child is exposed to adverse environments (Rosenthal, 1993; Rushton *et al*, 1995; Howe, 1997). It has also long been known that previously abused children are at greater risk. Recent studies (Quinton *et al*, 1998; Rushton *et al*, 2001) have indicated that children who have been singled out for rejection by their birth parents are particularly prone to placement instability and poorer outcomes.

Emotional and behavioural difficulties are strong predictors of disruption, especially aggressive, acting out behaviours (Sack and Dale, 1982; Partridge *et al*, 1986; Reid *et al*, 1987; Barth and Berry, 1988; Haugaard *et al*, 1999) including cruelty to others, getting into fights, threatening others, overactivity, restlessness and hanging out with "bad" friends. Some studies have found overt sexualised behaviour to be a strong behavioural predictor of disruption (Smith and Howard, 1991).

On the other hand, developmental and serious health conditions have not been shown to be risk factors but paradoxically minor developmental delays and learning disabilities predict negative outcomes (Rosenthal and Groze, 1992). This may be because such disabilities were not so apparent at the time of the placement and adopters might have been unprepared or had less realistic expectations.

Family characteristics: The associations of ethnicity, family structure, and income and education levels with risk of disruption are weak. The adoption of children by their foster carers has been consistently associated with reduced risk (Nelson, 1985; Rosenthal *et al*, 1988). The role of fathers has been highlighted by Westhues and Cohen (1990) who found that, where fathers were more actively involved in parenting and able to nurture and support the mother in her role, placements were more likely to be sustained.

The placement of children into a family with their own birth children at home has been shown to increase the risk of disruption but the placement of siblings into a home without children appears to be protective (Groze, 1996; Quinton *et al*, 1998; Rushton *et al*, 2001). Few studies have examined adoptive parents' parenting styles. One of the few, Erich and Leung (1998) found that the more successful families were high on problem solving, communication, cohesiveness and future orientation. But as Dance and colleagues (2002) have noted, parents may be unable to sustain their warmth and positive feelings in the face of a rejecting or aggressive child whose behaviour does not improve over time.

Agency characteristics: The contribution of service characteristics has received greater emphasis in the USA than the UK. Failure to disclose all known information on the child and lack of educational support has been consistently shown in the USA to be associated with disruption (Rosenthal and Groze, 1992).

Post-adoption support: The provision of adoption support has been recognised as being crucial to increasing the success of adoption placements (DH, 2003a) but there is still much to be learnt about which services adopters and children find helpful or which work and how needs change across the life span. Research on post-adoption services has been sparse and the literature characteristically describes gaps in services or best practice examples (Rushton and Dance, 2002; Hart and Luckock, 2004).

The SSI report (2000), *Adopting Changes*, found that post-adoption support was underdeveloped and poorly advertised. Significantly, in at least four of the councils inspected, the absence of post-adoption services deterred staff from pursing adoption. The report concluded, 'This is clearly not an acceptable way to support the placement of some very damaged and vulnerable children'. Lack of appropriate support services (in this case financial support) was shown in the USA (Sedlak and Broadhurst,

1993) to have a direct relationship with the length of time children spent waiting for adoption.

There have been no large-scale surveys of adoptive parents' views on support services. Existing studies pre-date the Adoption and Children Act 2002 but give indications of what is needed. The *Supporting Adoption* study (Lowe *et al*, 1999) highlighted how little authorities knew about the post-adoption services they were providing and how adopters also found it hard to find information on what support might be available. Although they found some examples of well-supported placements, they concluded that, 'good-quality adoption services were a lottery'. The only study to examine support beyond the first year of placement in the UK (Rushton *et al*, 1993) found that *none* of the families were receiving a social work service, although some adoptive parents had secured psychiatric, educational or psychological help for their child.

The views of adopted children have rarely been sought. *Adopted Children Speaking* (Thomas *et al*, 1999) is the only study to attempt this, but when asked about support the children often found it hard to remember what had been offered.

There are very few studies (Rushton and Dance, 2002) that examine the effectiveness of interventions but more which indicate that adopters have had difficulty gaining access to appropriate services. Although the links between high-quality post-placement services and reduced disruption rates are not clearly established, there is some evidence that suggests a relationship (Lowe *et al*, 1999; Barth and Berry, 1988). Practice experience also supports this view. An inspection of adoption agencies in 2001 (DH, 2003b) showed that one agency with a high level of services had had no disruptions in the previous three years. Over the last 20 years there has been a growing recognition that agency responsibilities should not end with the making of an adoption order and the Adoption and Children Act 2002 and the National Standards (Adoption) and Guidelines all underline the need for continuing support. However, at the time this study was conducted, the guidance and standards around adoption support had not been issued.

Economic context

Children are not cheap, as every parent knows. Information from insurance companies suggests that, by the time a child in the general population is 18 years old, they will have cost about £100,000, with a typical seven-year-old annually costing their parents £6,255. Children adopted out of care are likely to carry additional costs. Adoption has been viewed as providing better outcomes for children but also substantially reducing SSD costs of providing care. However, little has been known about the costs of adoption, although studies (Lowe *et al*, 1999; Rushton *et al*, 2001) have commented on the sacrifices adoptive families have made. If post-adoption services are to increase, much more needs to be known about what services adopters and children value, which services are effective in which situations and the cost of providing such a service.

In the USA, Sedlak and Broadhurst (1993) and Barth (1997) have estimated the savings to the state generated by adoption. Barth estimated that the savings attached to placing a child in an adoptive home for 15 years in comparison with being raised for the same time in a foster home was $120,654. However, these estimates excluded the cost of recruiting and training families and the costs of families who "drop out". To understand more about the costs of adoption it is necessary to decide which social work activities relate only to adoption and estimate their costs, but as the boundaries between adoption and foster care are fluid this has proved difficult. Allphin and colleagues (2001) tried to address some of these methodological problems by asking workers to keep time and activity diaries to separate foster care and adoption. They estimated that the approximate cost of adoption in California was $19,000 using 1997–8 prices.

The Department of Health's Children in Need census (CiN) came at an opportune moment for this study. For the first time, it provided some information on how SSDs spent their money. Linked to this initiative, Beecham (2000) produced a generic model for calculating unit costs for services provided to children in need. A unit of service may be a one-off item (for example, a visit from a social care professional) or a more complex package of care (for example, day care for a child with learning disabilities) and costs are estimates of providing a "unit" of service to an individual (Netten *et al*, 2001). Estimations of unit costs are important for a number of reasons: to provide local and national data; to support public sector performance assessment by government; to provide the information needed for best value initiatives; and to inform planning and commissioning of services and so that scarce resources can be better allocated.

This study was funded to look at the costs of adoption, both to services and to carers. Unfortunately, a lack of detailed information in case files meant that it was not possible to estimate the full costs of adoption to all agencies. However, unit costs were estimated for social services input and the services provided by other agencies were described, thus giving a full profile of all the help that the children, their families and their carers received.

In sum, there are substantial gaps in our knowledge on the outcomes and costs of adoption on its own or in comparison with other forms of permanence, especially because the population of children now being placed for adoption is very different from the baby adoptions to which all the major cohort studies relate. Adoption is, for good reason, the preferred route to permanence and family stability for children with severely adverse early experiences, but we are at the beginning of the accumulation of evidence on the children who will most benefit from it, what kinds of support for adoptive parents and adopted children will be most helpful and how this support should be organised. This study is a contribution to the body of knowledge on these issues.

2   Study design and methods

Purpose and design

The study capitalised on the opportunity to follow up a complete epidemiologically based sample of children for whom adoption in best interests (AIBI) decisions had been taken. It was therefore possible to look at the costs and outcomes for the children who were adopted and for those who were not. We knew from an early stage that about a quarter of the sample had not been adopted. Thus, the costs and outcomes for children who – in current terminology – had different "careers" in care were examined. The design also made it possible to look at apparent delays in the decision-making process and to arrive at some judgements about the costs of these, both in financial terms and in terms of their effects on the children's longer-term development.

Design

The study followed the care careers of a complete population-based sample of 130 children who were approved for adoption in the early 1990s when they were between the ages of three and 11. The data collection was completed in two parts. In the *first part*, the case files were reviewed in order to collect data on the children's family and experiences up to the best interests decision and from then to the time of the follow-up. In the *second part*, the children were traced and their current carers interviewed.

The follow-up was six to 11 years after the best interests decision. Although all the children had AIBI decisions, only 96 (74 per cent) were placed for adoption and, of these, 80 children were still in adoptive placements at the time of the follow-up. Sixteen adoptive placements had disrupted, 11 before the adoption order was granted and five afterwards. Of the remaining children, 34 (26 per cent) had lived in long-term foster care or other permanent placements and 16 (12 per cent) had not achieved any form of stable placement. We included in this last group children who had had either five or more placement breakdowns, or more than one long-term fostering or adoptive placement breakdown since they had become long-term looked after. This group of children were mostly in residential care at follow-up. These three outcome groups form the basis of many of the analyses presented later in this report. They will be referred to as the *"adopted"*, *"permanently placed"* and *"unstable care career"* groups respectively.

Sample characteristics

The sample was drawn from a former two-tier authority, which later became four unitary authorities. It comprised all children between the ages of three and 11 for whom an AIBI decision was made between 1991–1996. The lower age threshold was chosen to ensure that the sample reflected the age profile of children adopted out of care more generally. The upper age threshold was chosen as there is little use made of adoption for children older than ten years (PIU, 2000). All these children were assessed by the same community paediatrician as part of the adoption process. Checks between her records and those of the local authority confirmed the sample completeness. The characteristics of the sample are shown in Table 2.1.

Table 2.1
Characteristics of the sample

Number of children	130
Gender	73 boys (56%), 57 girls (44%)
Age at best interests decision	Range 3 to 11, Mean 5.7 years (s.d. 2.4)
Age at follow-up	Range 7 to 21, Mean 14.7 years (s.d. 9.3)
Ethnicity	120 white (92%), 10 ethnic minority (8%)
Physical disability	5 (4%) moderate to marked physical disabilities
Siblings	69 children had siblings *in the sample* (53%)

The 130 children came from 90 families. There were 29 sibling groups in the sample: one of five children, two of four children, four of three children and 22 sibling pairs. Five children had no siblings at the time of the best interest decision. Twenty-eight per cent were the oldest child in their family and 61 per cent the only child from the family eligible for inclusion.

Data collection

Stage 1 case file data

The Integrated Children's System and the Children in Need Census were used to inform the development of a *case file review schedule*, which was accompanied by a coding manual with clear rating criteria. This schedule was used to collect basic information on the children and their birth parents and included the children's social and care history. The child's public care career was divided into four stages, each of which related to a decision point in the process leading to the AIBI decision and after it. The first stage covered the period from the child's first referral to social services to the point at which they were looked after for more than six weeks. The second went from the point when the child was first looked after for more than six weeks to the *social work* decision to plan for adoption. The third covered the period from the social work adoption decision to the Adoption Panel's AIBI decision and the last ran from the adoption panel decision to the date of the follow-up.

Access to case files: Access to the children's case files was agreed by social services directors of the four unitary authorities and from a voluntary agency holding one child's files. Permission was also given by the Lord Chancellor's Department to read court papers held by social services departments.

Locating files: Finding the case files and abstracting data from them was a very arduous and time-consuming business. However, all except one of the children's files were eventually found.

Reading the files: All files were read on local authority premises. Reading the case files took a very long time. The average number of files per child was eight but some children had in excess of 20. The majority of files were quite well organised but few contained chronologies. It was not unusual for some to lack a clear order or even to be no more than a pile of papers in an envelope. Some files had been put on to microfiche and this made them quite difficult to navigate.

Case file reviews generally took between one and five days to complete. Following the case file review, a detailed *case summary* was written describing the child's experiences while living with their birth family and summarising their care career, psychosocial outcomes and contacts with other agencies. The same two researchers completed all case file reviews and frequently compared and clarified their coding to ensure inter-rater consistency.

Data collected at stage 2

The purpose of the follow-up was to collect information from the carers of the children who were in adoptive or foster families. This information covered the use of services from the time the child came to the family and was also used to make an assessment of psychosocial outcomes. Since the sampling approach resulted in placements of varying lengths, we did not attempt to collect detailed data for the whole period. Rather, we concentrated on the first year of placement and the year prior to the follow-up interview. These two periods were chosen so that we could look at changes in the children's psychosocial adjustment and because carers' recall would be more accurate if asked about the previous 12 months. However, in order to track major events and service use we developed a time-line technique in order to record *all* major events and service interventions during the whole of the placement.

The interview was the main source of follow-up data but, in order to help with this, we also mailed a *questionnaire to the parents* before we interviewed them. This gave them a chance to think of the health, education and other resources used for the child and the family during the intervening years. It also included Goodman's "Strengths and Difficulties Questionnaire" (Goodman, 1997; 1999) and the "Parent Child Communication Questionnaire" (Skinner *et al*, 1983). The interview followed a well-established approach that uses a "qualitative" approach to questioning but allows a "quantitative" treatment of data. It provides systematic and detailed coverage of topics and numerically analysable data while providing extensive case material (Brown, 1983; Quinton and Rutter, 1988; Quinton *et al*, 1998).

Collecting follow-up data

Contacting the adopters and foster carers: Local authorities sent the adopters and foster carers an information sheet about the study and an invitation to help in the research. If they agreed to participate a researcher explained over the telephone the aims of the study and what participation would entail. A confirmation letter was then sent out along with the study questionnaire for carers to complete. Families who could not be reached by telephone were sent two follow-up letters asking them to contact the researchers regarding their participation in the study.

All except one of the 80 adopted children were traced and the carers of 64 of them (80 per cent) agreed to be interviewed, three refused and the remaining 13 did not reply. Given the difficulties usually reported with collecting samples such as this, this response was extremely pleasing. From the permanently placed group, 31 children had had long-term foster care placements. The current carers of 23 (74 per cent) of these children also agreed to be interviewed but eight either did not respond to our letters or were too busy to be interviewed.

Interviewing carers: Adopters and foster carers were usually interviewed in their homes, often during the evening so that both partners could be seen. For those families who agreed to take part, 99 per cent of female carers and 40 per cent of male carers were interviewed. The interviews took on average three-and-a-half hours. The interviews often raised strong emotions and provision was made for the adopters and the researchers to access support if they needed it. A "help and advice lines" information sheet was compiled for adopters, which listed all the local and national adoption support groups helpline numbers, websites and hours of operation.

Follow-up data on other children: Some children had never had a permanent placement or had not left care, so the social workers or key workers were either interviewed in person or over the telephone and asked for a brief update of the child's care career, resource use and outcomes. The children's case summaries were amended accordingly. The Strengths and Difficulties Questionnaire was also completed as part of this outcome data collection.

Data were completed in this way for six (18 per cent) children who had been permanently placed and for 14 (88 per cent) of the 16 children in the "unstable care career" group. This meant that outcome data were collected for 29 (85 per cent) of the permanently placed group altogether. We were unable to interview the social or key-workers of the remaining seven children (five permanently placed and two unstable care career) because of sickness or work pressures, because the children had left care, because birth parents refused or, in one case, because we couldn't locate anyone who knew the young person well enough to be interviewed.

In total, full interview data were collected for 87 (67 per cent) of the 130 children and outcome interview data for a further 20 children (15 per cent). No outcome data were available for the remaining 23 (18 per cent) children (16 children adopted, five children permanently placed and two children who had unstable care careers).

Costing adoption: The costing element of this study was primarily concerned with three costs. These were the cost of placing children for adoption, the costs of maintaining them in adoptive placements prior to the adoption order and the costs to social services in providing post-adoption support. Three separate adoptive placement unit costs were calculated. An "*adoption process*" *unit cost* – the cost of successfully placing a child for adoption; a *post-placement unit cost per week* – the cost to social services of maintaining a looked after child in an adoptive placement; and a *post-adoption unit cost per week* – the cost to social services of providing post-adoption support.

In addition to these three costs we attempted to put figures on the costs of services to the children and their families prior to the beginning of the adoption process. It was not possible as intended originally to estimate the full cost of delay during this period due to the poor quality of the data in case records. However, SSD costs have been calculated from the time the child became known to SSDs until the AIBI decision. These illustrate the size and range of costs associated with delays. Further details on the costing methodology are given in Appendix A.

Representativeness of the sample

Since this is an epidemiologically-based and substantially complete sample, checks on representativeness are not essential. Nevertheless, it is helpful to examine the extent to which the profile of the sample reflects that of children currently adopted from public care.

Population comparisons: Eight per cent of the children were of minority ethnic origin. No national figures on the ethnicity of children approved for adoption were available but this figure is lower than the 17 per cent in the looked after population nationally (PIU, 2000) and higher than the four per cent population rate for the area from which the sample was drawn (Baker *et al*, 1997). Of the ten minority ethnic children, five were of mixed ethnicity and five were African-Caribbean (including four siblings).

Adoption studies often exclude disabled children from their samples. The best comparison data for this study comes from Lowe and his colleagues (1999) who reported a four per cent rate for physical special needs. The same percentage of this sample had severe physical disabilities at the time they were approved for adoption.

Data analysis

Numerical data

The numerical data were analysed using SPSS, Excel and STATA, with some additional multivariate analyses being conducted using CHAID. Analysis of small samples such as these sometimes needs to go beyond the examination of statistical trends and significances and to make some arguments on the basis of apparent consistencies in the data. This approach allows for a more subtle examination of the data but it has to be recognised that the conclusion are sometimes necessarily speculative. We point this out whenever appropriate.

Qualitative data

Our methods allowed for the collection of the free accounts of the carers' experiences of the adoption process and their experiences with the children. In presenting these data we have tried both to illustrate the carers' experiences and feelings but also to retain the necessary discipline of pointing out how representative these comments were.

SECTION II

Pathways to permanence

3 Life in the birth family

This chapter and the next begin the story of the children's lives from the time a social services department (SSD) receives a referral expressing concern about the child's family up to the time the children entered longer-term care. This chapter presents a picture of the children's early lives assembled through reading all the case files, including the earliest family files. This is as comprehensive a picture as we could bring together, but it is still unlikely to be complete. Case files contain only what was treated as important at the time they were written. For example, risk factors such as parental substance abuse were given less attention in the 1980s and may not have been noted on the files. The full extent of abuse and neglect as reported here was not always known to the social worker at this point in the child's life and only became apparent much later.

There were often only brief details on the case files, although many families (67 per cent) were well known to SSDs either because older children were in their care or because birth parents had already had contact with them for other reasons. Recording was focused on reporting home visits, and children's development was rarely mentioned by social workers.

Characteristics of the birth parents

The records had more information on birth mothers than birth fathers. Data were complete for 85 (94 per cent) of the 90[1] mothers but for only 37 (33 per cent) of the 112 fathers. Sometimes this was because the mother refused to identify him or because it was clear that he had refused to co-operate. But, even when the father was present, basic details such as his date of birth were often missing. By the time the child was born, 34 per cent of fathers were no longer in the picture and, by the time of the best

---

[1] There were 90 mothers for the 130 children in the study. Some information was missing in two cases where mothers had abandoned their children before SSD involvement, one where a mother had died soon after giving birth, and two cases where mothers were suffering from severe mental illness.

interests decision, many more had lost touch and could not be traced. Basic data on the birth parents are given in Table 3.1.

Table 3.1

Birth family characteristics at the time of the child's birth

	Mothers n = 90	Fathers n = 112
Average age (mean)	24 yrs	29 yrs
Ethnicity other than white	9%	5%
Previous teen pregnancy/fatherhood	87%	Not known
Previous adoptions	23%	Not known
Children currently looked after	20%	Not known
Family already known to SSD	67%	

Demographic characteristics

The average age of the mothers at the time of the child's birth was 24, with an age range of 17–38 years. Fathers were older, with an average age of 29 years and a range of 17–51 years. Although there were few very young mothers in this sample, 87 per cent had had a pregnancy in their teens. Eight mothers and six fathers were from minority ethnic groups. Of these, all the fathers and six of the mothers were of African-Caribbean origin, one mother's ethnicity was Black African and another was of mixed ethnicity.

Disabilities

Only three birth parents had significant physical disabilities. These parents all had difficulties that affected their mobility, as a result of injuries, gross obesity or medical conditions. Far more were said to have "learning difficulties". Unfortunately, this term seemed to cover disabilities with a genetic or organic cause as well as cognitive problems that probably arose from very poor childhood experiences or inadequate education. By examining reports that described the functioning and IQ of parents, we estimated that 27 per cent had a moderate to severe learning disability with 12 per cent of these also having severe mental health problems. Even so, these figures are likely to underestimate learning disabilities, since these were rarely discussed in assessments of parenting capacity.

Parents' own histories

The parents' own childhoods often involved abuse, neglect and periods spent in care. Three-quarters of the mothers said they had been physically and/or sexually abused. For a few, sexual abuse was continuing into their adult lives. Many (63 per cent) had spent long periods in care, usually residential care or EBD residential schools (for children with emotional and behavioural difficulties.) Few had any educational qualifications: 14 per cent had GCSEs or equivalent, three per cent had completed some higher education and three per cent had vocational qualifications. Over half of the fathers also gave accounts of abuse (57 per cent) and nearly half had spent time in care (48 per cent).

Mental health

It is not surprising with these histories that many parents had mental health problems. Fifty-nine per cent of mothers and 30 per cent of fathers were said to have moderate to severe mental health difficulties that needed hospital in-patient care. These involved severe depression, suicide attempts, personality disorders or obsessive-compulsive disorders. Other parents (20 per cent) had not received psychiatric care but had mental health difficulties that affected their functioning as a parent. Happier childhoods were recorded for only three parents. Their lives had been changed for the worse by tragic life events.

Parenting history

While the children were being supported in their families, 32 per cent of the families had a child/children currently being looked after or had had a previous child adopted. Some mothers had children removed serially and placed for adoption. Sometimes, all but the youngest child had been removed in the hope that the mother would be able to cope with just the one.

Counselling

It is widely acknowledged (Howe *et al*, 1992) that mothers who have children adopted should be offered counselling. There were, however, few accounts of support services being made available to mothers even though their distress – and that of their social workers – was often evident from case file recording.

Characteristics of the children and their early experiences

There were 78 boys and 52 girls in the sample. Only 10 of these were from a minority ethnic group.

Age at first referral

At the time of the first referral to an SSD, all the children were age four or younger, with the average age being six months. In 63 per cent of cases social services were involved with the family at or before the child's birth: a quarter because of concerns about the mental health of the mother and/ or her ability to parent the expected baby. These mothers had accepted little if any ante-natal care and hospital staff often expressed concern shortly after the child was born, as some mothers seemed unable to care for their baby. There were reports of mothers walking out of the hospital and forgetting they had a child to care for, or of them interfering with other children on the ward. Ten per cent of mothers and babies – and occasionally fathers too – went on to a mother and baby home for a period of assessment and/or to learn parenting skills. For 19 per cent of all the children no further action was taken as a result of the initial referral but, of course, further referrals eventually led to intervention.

Children's experiences at home

While they were still at home, 38 per cent of the children lived with a single parent and a further 30 per cent had a step-parent. These homes contained many risks for them. Parental mental illness and substance misuse were common and parental relationships were rarely stable, with high levels of conflict and domestic violence. Only one child who became looked after shortly after birth was not exposed to any of these circumstances. Many of the children were exposed to multiple risks.

Parental discord and violence: Domestic violence was recorded for 86 per cent of the families. The children witnessed shouting and violence and some mothers were hospitalised because of their injuries. Women often had very dependent relationships with these violent men. Partners left and returned, mothers were re-housed and spent time in refuges and support was received from SSDs. Even so, a quarter of women were unable to cut these ties. Parents could be so preoccupied with their own relationships that they seemed unable to provide the care their children needed. These women commented that they believed they could not live without the partner to the extent, that given a choice between leaving their partner and keeping their children, they chose their partner.

Parental mental illness and substance misuse: Eleven per cent of children also had a parent who was sectioned under the Mental Health Act and a further five per cent of parents were admitted as voluntary patients. Adult mental health services were providing services to 28 (31 per cent) of the children's parents.

Parental misuse of alcohol was a risk factor for 46 per cent of the children. Twenty-eight per cent had at least one parent diagnosed as an alcoholic. Case files contained reports of heavy drinking resulting in violence or of mothers going on drinking binges and leaving the children alone. Where alcohol was being misused there was often drug abuse also. Drug misuse by parents was known about in 28 per cent of cases with three-quarters of these also heavily dependent on alcohol.

Poverty and poor environments: Most of the families (94 per cent) were dependent on benefits and 66 per cent of children were living in households where the families had significant debts. At times, gas and electricity supplies were cut off despite very young children living in the house. These events were taken as commonplace by some social workers. Case file recording did not include planning for any additional support families might need e.g. how were mothers going to make up bottles without being able to add hot water or sterilise bottles?

Debts accumulated for a number of reasons. Some mothers' learning difficulties were such that they could not manage money, or the level of parental addiction ensured that all money coming in was used to finance their addiction. Environments were frequently unpredictable, chaotic and often unsafe, with burglaries and house fires experienced by 20 per cent of the children.

Criminality: Just over half the children (54 per cent) lived in families where there had been police involvement for criminal activities. In 22 per cent of the families, a parent was under the supervision of a probation officer.

Case summary: An example of an early entry to care

Carol was born to Meg and Ian. Meg had been sexually abused when at home and was an alcoholic with a chaotic lifestyle. She ran away as a teenager and met Ian, who was illiterate and had 20 previous convictions for violence. Pre-birth, the SSD plan was for the immediate removal of the newborn baby, but the parents disappeared and moved to another authority where they were given the chance to see if they could parent Carol. A few months later the police took out an emergency protection order (EPO) as Ian had run off with Carol without food, clothes or money. He thought that if he had the baby he would not get a prison sentence for his latest offence. The baby was checked at hospital and returned home. Family support workers visited the family but were refused entry when they asked to see the food cupboard. Throughout this period, Meg claimed she was receiving hate mail and death threats. Letters also arrived at the SSD claiming the baby was being abused. The police found that Meg had been writing the letters herself. Ian went to prison again and Meg's parenting became even more inadequate. Carol was admitted to hospital with further bruising and entered care aged eight months.

Housing instability: The majority of families remained in the local area throughout the period children were supported in their families, with 77 per cent of families having no more than one house move. Some of these families (19 per cent) did experience a period of homelessness.

A smaller number of 15 families (17 per cent) moved frequently within the local authority or around the country. This was because the family thought that the children were about to be removed and sometimes because they had themselves made their homes uninhabitable or were forced to move as neighbours ganged up to have them removed from the area. This group of unstable families moved between five and 13 times and nearly all (13) also experienced a period of homelessness. Ninety-five per cent of all the children who experienced homelessness were also living in families where domestic violence, substance misuse and criminal activity were taking place.

Changes of carer: Many children experienced additional instability through changes of carer. Thirty-four per cent lived with members of their extended families at least once, and five per cent of children moved more frequently between different family members or back and forth between their grandparents and their own parents. Nearly two-fifths (39 per cent) also spent short periods in foster care. Just under half of these had only one placement but the remainder had between three and 16 placements.

The children with the most admissions to care were the ones who also spent most time with relatives. A small number (8 per cent) of children experienced between 10 and 28 different moves either because of a house move or a change in their main carer.

Case summary: An example of a multi-problem family who moved frequently

Tom was the second of three brothers, born while his mother's partner was in prison for sexual offences and violence. Tom's mother was an alcoholic and had been in prison for violent behaviour. She had been, and still was being sexually abused by her own father. Tom was a result of this abuse. The family moved around the UK when her partner was released, moving through B&Bs or in and out of refuges. Tom was hated by his stepfather and suffered numerous injuries from beatings. Other Schedule 1 offenders visited the home and his mother's mental health deteriorated, culminating in a serious suicide attempt. When Tom was four an EPO was taken out after his mother came home drunk and attacked him.

Abuse

Most of the children were extremely poorly parented. Children were left at home alone, left in the care of minors or received inappropriate punishments, such as being smacked for "deliberate" wetting or soiling. Only three children did not meet common definitions of having been abused. Two of these were removed within weeks of being born. Even so, one of these was born to a mother who had been subjected to extremely violent assaults by her partner throughout her pregnancy, including being stabbed in the stomach. The other child's mother's lifestyle put the baby at grave risk. The third child was the most unusual. His parents were accused of physical abuse and he was removed from home on the basis of medical evidence, which was later disproved. These three children are not included in our abuse statistics. Had we used different definitions – including mothers' problems before the birth or repeated medical examinations of the child afterwards – all the children would have been included. The extent and type of abuse experienced by the children is presented in Table 3.2.

Table 3.2
Suspected and confirmed maltreatment

	Neglect	*Physical abuse*	*Sexual abuse*	*Rejection*
Confirmed	75%	49%	15%	38%
Suspected	16%	19%	20%	13%

n = 130

Neglect: Neglect was closely associated with extreme impoverishment and, usually, a more general giving up on the care of the home as well as of the children. Nearly all the children were thought to be neglected (91 per cent) and three-quarters to be living in extreme poverty. Forty-two per cent of the children lived in overcrowded homes with no outdoor space to play in. Descriptions of the housing included accounts of bare rooms with little furniture and nothing for the children to play with, dirty homes with the smell of stale urine pervading the bedrooms, and dogs and cats given the run of the house. Some of the children had no bed of their own and slept on chairs or on the floor.

These conditions exposed babies who were learning to crawl and explore to constant infections or led parents to keep them in cots or on reins for much longer than was appropriate. Nurseries and schools reported children arriving smelly and hungry such that some schools had to feed and bathe the children before the school day could start.

Conditions were often especially poor when both parents had learning disabilities. In one case, environmental health contractors refused to go into the home although four young children were living there. Health visitors and family support workers described grim conditions and children whose feet were blue with cold and who were hungry, smelly and grubby. Social services attempted to help clean up. Conditions often improved while they were visiting but quickly deteriorated once the help stopped.

Parents tended to not look after themselves either and were often described as "childlike", not understanding their own or their children's needs. Sometimes even children under five did the shopping or made tea. Some were found begging for food or milk. Ten per cent of the children were admitted to hospital because of failure to thrive, infections or food poisoning.

Not all the children were neglected through this general impoverishment and demoralisation. Some (38 per cent) were actively rejected by their birth parent and treated differently from other siblings. These children were often the *only* children in the house not to have their own bed, did not eat with the rest of the family and were often locked up for long periods. They were rarely spoken to and received no stimulation. In three families all the children were treated badly while the parents lived much more comfortably. These rejected children were not only neglected but also subjected to sadistic maltreatment, including physical and psychological torture.

Physical abuse: Most of the children were slapped and hit, boys somewhat more likely than girls (75 per cent versus 58 per cent). Physical abuse was suspected in far more families than was confirmed by clear injuries. Violent arguments between parents could quickly turn into a violent attack on the child while other children lived in fear of saying or doing the wrong thing, which might provoke an assault. For 64 (49 per cent) of the children, their physical injuries involved broken bones, bite marks, cigarette burns and head injuries. There were hospital admissions for 12 per cent of children at least once due to the severity of the injuries, with babies and infants being admitted more readily than older children. In two black children's files it was of concern that NHS consultants stated they had been unable to recognise the signs of physical abuse (burns) on black skin, as training had not been given.

Sexual abuse: Sexual abuse was confirmed for 19 (15 per cent) of the children and suspected for a further 26 (20 per cent). The average age of all the sexually abused children was three years, although some were still babies. Unlike some studies, this study found no gender differences between the sexual abuse of boys and girls.

Fathers or stepfathers sexually abused eight of these children, seven children were multiply abused by father and mother and more than one other adult, two were sexually abused by their mothers, one by a friend outside the family and one by kin. In a few cases, women were still living in fear of their own fathers who continued to sexually abuse both them and their children. There were also reports of children witnessing adult sexual activity and watching pornographic videos. The seven multiply abused children were used for the sexual gratification of adults within and outside the immediate family. They were penetrated anally, had sharp instruments inserted and were made to hold down their siblings in turn for the abuse to occur.

A Schedule 1 offender was either living in or frequently visiting 32 per cent of the children's homes. Eighty per cent of these men had attached themselves to mothers who had some degree of learning difficulty. The presence of these offenders in the home was often unknown to the social worker, sometimes because mothers refused to believe their partner was capable of such behaviour and pretended that he was no longer resident. These men continued to abuse the children and often other children in the neighbourhood as well.

Rejection: Thirty-eight (38 per cent) of the children were rejected by their parents to some degree: 20 (15 per cent) completely so. Fifteen of the 20 completely rejected children were boys. These children were abandoned at bus stops, train stations, GP surgeries or dropped off at SSDs. Some children experienced this several times, entering foster care only for the mother to change her mind or be persuaded by the social worker to try again. They were nearly all physically abused and neglected. Physical injuries were noted in 90 per cent of this group.

The majority of all the children (90 per cent) had experienced at least one form of abuse. Most of these (68 per cent) had been multiply abused, with neglect combining with other types of abuse. Rejected children were also likely to have been physically abused and neglected but were unlikely to have been sexually abused. As concerns about the children grew so did attempts to improve the family's circumstances. These efforts are described in the next chapter.

Summary of the children's lives in their birth families

- The children's birth parents had multiple overlapping problems with domestic violence, mental health problems and drug/alcohol abuse as common features.
- Sixty-three per cent of the birth mothers had been in care when they were younger.
- Schedule 1 offenders were often present in households where the mother had learning difficulties.
- Seventy-nine per cent of the children had been referred to SSDs before they were 12 months old.
- Ninety per cent of the children were abused while living at home, with 68 per cent experiencing multiple forms of abuse.
- There were no gender differences in the children for whom sexual abuse had been confirmed, but a significant gender difference for children rejected by their birth parents, with boys more likely to be rejected.
- Many of the children had been looked after by adults other than their parents: 39 per cent had spent time in foster care and 34 per cent had been looked after by kin.

4 Support, decision-making and the children's development

In this chapter we deal with the support which was made available to the families when the children were living at home.

Support

Social services inputs

All the children had a social worker and the majority (74 per cent) were also being visited by a community care worker (CCW) or family support worker (FSW). The task for these workers was to help get the children up in the morning, ensure they had something to eat, provide a positive role model for parents and give advice on parenting. For 34 per cent of the children this intervention was short term but intensive – a typical pattern being two or three visits every day for 4–6 weeks. Support at this level was received by a further 17 per cent of children for periods lasting months or occasionally years. The remaining 21 per cent of children received occasional fortnightly or monthly visits. Some families (33 per cent) had specific sessions with a social worker focusing on improving parenting skills or undertaking therapeutic work. Comprehensive "orange book" assessments were undertaken on only nine per cent of families

Other inputs

Sixty per cent of children had a place at an SSD nursery or had a sponsored childminder (16 per cent). This support was intended to give the parents relief and to give the child stimulation and contact with peers. Families often turned up at SSDs asking for financial help. Regular small cash payments were made to 29 per cent of families and a further 14 per cent were given occasional payments. Transport to school (10 per cent) and short breaks (7 per cent) were also provided to some families.

The data show a considerable amount of social work activity but this often fell short of what was needed. It was seldom based on a comprehensive assessment and was usually short term. Support was not tuned to the complex problems of these families. For example, a short course for the parents in parenting skills was unlikely to have much impact on a family where there was extensive alcohol or drug misuse.

Cost of support

Social services: We estimated the costs to SSDs of providing these inputs, based on average SSD costs produced for the 2001 Children in Need census. Our estimated average cost of services using 2001 prices was £13,844 (range £120–£49,920) for each child for the entire period they were supported in their families.

Other services: It seemed to us that this figure substantially under- estimated the true cost to SSDs of the support provided, because for many services there were no data on frequency on which to base calculations of unit costs. Many of these – residential assessment centres for example – were particularly expensive and were used not only when SSDs planned this kind of intervention but also when ordered by the court.

Child protection conferences

Child protection (CP) conferences were called for 88 per cent of the children, resulting in 78 per cent being placed on the Child Protection Register. CP action plans often included increased health monitoring. Seventy-two per cent of children had increased levels of *health visitor supervision* or were monitored by a *school nurse*. Other health professionals, such as *paediatricians*, were also seeing a small number of children (7 per cent) regularly due to concerns about developmental delay or disability. As most of the children were still very young, there was little specific support from mental health services; three children were seeing a *clinical psychologist* and one was having *art therapy*. Twenty per cent of mothers also attended *family centres* provided by the voluntary sector. The centres aimed to help combat isolation, provide therapeutic help and give parenting advice.

Inter-agency working

There was little evidence that agencies co-ordinated their efforts or shared their knowledge. For example, an educational psychologist noted that one child's extensive learning and social special needs had been recognised early in development, but that there had thereafter been little co-ordinated professional work until the child was admitted to infant school. Support and services went into some of the families for many years with little evidence of improvement.

Decision-making and delay

Most of the children (88 per cent) were re-referred to SSDs after the child first became a cause for concern. The average number of re-referrals before the children entered care for a longer period was four (s.d. 4.9) but one family was re-referred 16 times. Of course, this sample is, by definition, one in which support ultimately failed. It provides no data on successful support for families with similar levels of difficulty. It is nonetheless clear from this sample that many children were "supported in their families" long after this approach seemed not to be working. How did social services finally decide that this approach could no longer be sustained? More importantly, what factors contributed to delay in deciding that the family was not going to change?

In order to look at this we defined delay operationally as a lack of planning or reassessment of the approach being used when there had been no sign of any improvements in the family circumstances after 12 months of SSD intervention. It should be noted that it is far easier to identify "delay" with hindsight and with the benefit of knowing the whole child's history.

Delay defined in this way was identified for 88 (68 per cent) of the children. Children remained at home on average for 2.7 yrs (s.d. 2.0) from the date of the first social work involvement until becoming looked after. However, the range was wide, varying from nine months to over eight years later. It is important to reiterate that, where delay was identified, children were usually living in families where they were continuing to be abused and neglected.

In order to understand what was happening, we looked to see what factors were influencing the delays in decision-making. Social work decision-making is a complex activity and this was reflected in the number of factors (four on average) that contributed to delays in decision-making.

A judgement was made about the primary reason for delay from the case file material, but this was often compounded by other factors in the case. For example, the lack of a clear plan would be exacerbated by a lack of information on which to base a plan, with staff sickness/vacancies contributing to delay.

Primary reasons for delay

Drift caused by lack of social work assessment, planning and action accounted for 53 per cent of delay in decision-making. Unallocated cases and lack of managerial oversight contributed to delay in 15 per cent of cases. Slowness to act was also associated with unfocused social work practice combined with a number of other circumstances. The quality of social work assessment was generally poor. Thirty per cent of files only contained pages of unsynthesised information. Very few files contained any kind of chronology. In the absence of good assessments, plans were unfocused and gave no clear indications of what changes were being aimed at and within what timescale. Often, a plan was just a statement that the aim of intervention was " to keep the family together". Sometimes the plan seemed only to postpone the inevitable removal of the child, particularly where mothers had severe mental health problems or had significant learning disabilities. In these cases, children (15 per cent) were often left with their mothers until the mothers could no longer provide even basic care. Mothers with severe learning disabilities could just about manage a baby with intensive support, but the toddler quickly outgrew the mother's ability to provide a safe environment.

For 18 per cent of the children, the social worker's focus was on another member of the birth family and the child's plight went unnoticed. For example, in one family all the girls were removed quickly as it was believed the boys were safe. Unfortunately, that was not the case.

Legal delays: The problems did not always lie with the social worker's practice. In 22 per cent of cases where there was delay, social workers expressed deep concerns about the family but the SSD legal services or their own managers thought there was not sufficient evidence to reach the significant harm threshold so the children remained at home. In 12 per cent of cases lengthy care proceedings contributed to delay. Guardians sometimes insisted that another assessment be made and appeared reluctant to accept social work assessments and wanted assessments repeated again or additional evidence that they specified. Judges too ordered psychiatric reports or required expert witnesses to be appointed. Legal issues were therefore the main factor in 34 per cent of the delayed cases.

Birth family actions: The social workers were often dealing with families who were hard to support, whose circumstances were complex, or who acted deviously. Thirty-five per cent pretended to comply with plans but lied to social workers about their circumstances, saying, for example, that Schedule 1 offenders were no longer living with them when, in fact, they were. Others (14 per cent) moved house when their ability as parents was questioned and it took time before they were found. A new social worker would then take over and assessments would start all over again. Social workers could also be intimidated by the high levels of violence in these families and in a few cases were physically assaulted. Many parents did not allow their children to be taken into care without a fight, which was often personally vindictive and frightening.

Entry to longer-term care

Towards the end of the phase in which the children were "supported in their families" there was a noticeable increase in concern about them. Concerned calls from neighbours increased, as did anonymous letters. Concerns also grew as nursery attendance became sporadic or stopped and parents excluded professionals or disappeared without warning. Visiting social workers noted a worsening of circumstances or saw injuries and bruises that would be clear evidence of significant harm.

Frequently, it was when children started to speak or went to school or nursery that action to remove them began. For some, concerns about odd behaviour or disclosures of abuse led to action. Others had siblings in care who began to talk about the abuse they had suffered at home. In 73 per cent of cases the main factor in the decision to take the child into care was the conclusion that the children were at increased risk of harm. A further 20 per cent of children were abandoned by their parents or relatives, while the remaining seven per cent came into care because of homelessness or the death of a parent.

Age: At the point of entry into longer-term care, seven per cent of the children were under one, 73 per cent between one and four, 18 per cent between five and nine and just 2 per cent (two children) were age ten or over. The average age was three (s.d. 2.1).

Legal status: By the time they went into longer-term care, 24 per cent of children were already on supervision orders. Eight per cent were subject to full care orders and place of safety orders (now emergency protection orders) were made on a further 47 per cent. Thirty-nine per cent were accommodated without recourse to any legal action.

The children's developmental needs as they entered longer-term care

In this section we review what was recorded on the files about the children's developmental needs as they came into longer-term care. Even at this point there was little written that reflected any systematic assessment of their needs. Much more space was taken up with accounts of social work visits. What descriptions there were of the children's development came from nursery nurses or from reports from family support or community care workers. There were no health visitor reports. Information from health visitors sometimes appeared at child protection reviews but this was limited to their comments on the children's height and weight.

Specific areas of need

The seven "looking-after children" developmental areas were used to organise what information we could discover. These data are given below. Developmental delay was coded for children over the age of two, educational, behavioural and relationship difficulties from the age of four and offending behaviours from the age of seven. Therefore, the number of children where these needs were coded ranged from 91–130 children. There were insufficient data to assess "identity" or "self-care skills".

Growth, infections and accidents: Growth delay was reported for 43 per cent of all the 130 children. More than half of these (57 per cent) had delays in two or more of the areas measured on the NHS growth charts commonly used by parents and health visitors. They and the GPs also reported that nearly a quarter of all the children (23 per cent) had had frequent infections, resulting in numerous courses of antibiotics. Twenty-three per cent of children had had "accidents" involving broken bones or burns. Chronic health problems such as asthma and eczema were noted for 11 per cent of the children.

Mobility and clumsiness: We recorded problems with mobility for children over the age of two years (n = 91). Two children were severely physically disabled but even when these were excluded, 31 per cent of the children had problems with co-ordination and gross motor skills. For example, nursery staff reported that children had very little confidence in climbing or running. The reasons for this are not known but it seems likely that the lack of stimulation from their environments played a large part, as well as the consequences of low birth weight and poor nutrition.

Hearing and speech: Referrals for hearing assessments were made for 12 per cent of the children following hearing checks (n = 117). Fifty-four per cent had some speech delay or other language difficulties reported (n = 93). More than half of these had moderate to severe language delay but only 18 per cent saw a speech therapist. Speech therapy was the health service most in demand but was not readily available because of long waiting lists. As the children entered care, only 15 per cent had no physical health problems recorded.

Social presentation: The children were often smelly and poorly dressed. Nursery and school reports mentioned infestations of head lice. Thirty-two per cent had sores (such as scabies) on their bodies. The great majority, even those over the age of four (82 per cent), were enuretic and 64 per cent were encopretic. These problems in social presentation had a serious effect on their ability to make friends at school. There were many reports of peers not wanting to sit near or play with them.

Education: Only 21 per cent of children were old enough to be at school (n = 28) but there was a great deal of concern over those that were. Difficulties in learning to read were noted for 17 of them. Fourteen had already been referred to the educational psychology service. A statement of special educational needs (SEN) had been made on five children while at nursery and a further three children's statements were nearing completion. Additional support within school – such as additional time with special needs teachers or classroom assistants – was organised for five (14 per cent) children. Exclusions for five children (18 per cent) were also beginning. Two of these children were permanently excluded, one with some tutor support, the other with no provision. The remaining three children had experienced short periods of exclusion.

Emotional and behavioural development: Behavioural difficulties were coded for children over the age of two. Ninety-one (70 per cent) of the 130 children were of this age when they entered longer-term care. Many of these children (32 per cent) had comments about their inability to play with others or alone. Some (14 per cent) were described as "live wires" – that is, attention-seeking, always on the go and having marked temper tantrums involving screaming and crying. Seventeen per cent were showing inappropriate sexualised behaviours, for example, a young boy asking other children at nursery "to suck his willy". Twenty-four per cent were described as having eating difficulties such as gorging, eating inedible objects or being very fussy.

Other children were described as fearful and cowed and were either loners mistrusting of all adults or very anxious to please and clingy. These children were described as anxious and worriers (27 per cent) and some (18 per cent) had sleep disturbances. Although not specifically coded by the researchers, a description that was sometimes used by teaching/nursery staff to describe some of the children's lack of curiosity and spontaneity was a "deadness".

Family and social relationships: Although the quality of attachment relationship between parent and child was coded from birth, problems with friendships, bullying, and conflict with siblings were not coded until the child was two (n = 91). The combinations of poor personal hygiene, delayed speech, a failure to understand the social rules of play and being "always on the go" were characteristics that inevitably led to many of these children (61 per cent) having difficulty making friends. Twenty per cent were described as bullies, 18 per cent having physically harmed another child. A further 12 per cent were being bullied themselves.

Twenty-six per cent of those with siblings had a conflictual/hostile relationship with them and, of these, 70 per cent were children who had experienced some rejection by a birth parent.

Social work comments on the quality of parent–child relationships were often lacking or seemed improbable. Parents could be described as "loving" when their actions seemed patently self-centred. For example, in one case, the social worker argued strongly that a father loved his son although he seemed to want to keep his son mostly because he believed this would keep him out of prison. He wanted his son to grow up to be a hard man like himself and consequently refused to let him cry or show emotion. The child had no bed and was often found wandering the streets at night alone when he was only three years old. He witnessed his father's drunken violent assaults and was himself encouraged to take knuckle dusters into primary school and attack other children. The father was finally arrested after a high-speed car chase with his young son in the back of the car.

Judgements on the reasons for apparently poor social work assessments of parenting are necessarily speculative because of the inadequacy of the recorded information. However, social workers often seemed to have difficulty in distinguishing between the parenting behaviour that met the parents' needs and that which met the child's. These parental needs included their own emotional dependency or the use of the children for buying drugs or providing domestic help. Social workers clearly felt sympathy for many mothers or fathers but this sometimes led to interpretation of clingy and fearful behaviours as evidence of "strong attachments".

Summary of support, decision-making and the children's development

- Most families (74 per cent) received family support services but these did not lead to sustained improvements.
- Other agencies were also involved. In 22 per cent of birth families, a parent was under the supervision of a probation officer and 23 per cent were in contact with adult mental health services.

- From the time of the first referral, the children lived at home on average for 2.7 years before becoming looked after.
- Delays were identified for 68 per cent of the children, of which 53 per cent were attributable to social work inaction and staff shortages and 34 per cent to the impact of legal delays.
- The children were aged between one and 10 as they entered care, with the average age being three.
- As the children entered care, 85 per cent had recorded health problems, with emotional and behavioural problems becoming more apparent as they began school.

5 From long-term care to the best interests decision

This chapter gives details on the children's lives from the time they entered care for more extended periods until an adoption panel made an "adoption in best interests" (AIBI) decision. As foster carers learned more about the children, the quality of recorded information became better and a more complete picture of their difficulties began to emerge. Even so, as we shall see, the children and their carers received little professional help. Rather, the carers were often left to manage the children's distress as best they could.

Planning and patterns of placements

The first placements for most of the children were with foster carers (89 per cent). Relatives looked after a further 10 per cent of children and one per cent were placed in residential care in order to keep siblings together. Social workers tried to keep brothers and sisters together whenever possible, but the lack of suitable placements and the size of some sibling groups meant that they were sometimes split. Sixty-five per cent of those with siblings were placed with at least one of their brothers or sisters.

The initial plan

Three kinds of plan were made at this point. Reunion with the birth family was envisaged for over two-fifths of the children (42 per cent). A further 31 per cent of plans involved a last chance attempt at restoration but with an expectation of permanent substitute care (twin tracking) if that failed. The remaining 27 per cent of children were expected to need long-term or permanent substitute care, although these plans were sometimes vague on timescales. For example, one plan stated '(child) . . . needs to be in care a long time . . .'. In practice, there were no attempts at returning home for three-quarters of the children even though rehabilitation had been an aspiration for most of them.

Attempts at reunification

By definition, reunification was not attempted or failed during this period, since in the end a "best interests" decision was made. Return home was attempted for 25 per cent of children: 22 children were returned home on one occasion, seven children twice, three children three times and one child four times.

Failures occurred for a number of reasons. Where reunification was the plan, parents (20 per cent) said they wanted their children home, but their commitment was not quickly put to the test. A year or more often went by before a date was set for the children's return. As the date drew near, parents changed their minds and asked that the children remain looked after. Other parents were unable to follow through on their promises to enter drug/alcohol rehabilitation centres or change their lives in such a way that the children could be returned safely.

In other cases, attempts sometimes seemed half-hearted or set in motion to show the court that rehabilitation had been tried and failed. Some children (9 per cent) returned home because the court directed that this should occur. Courts were persuaded by guardians, psychologists or psychiatrists, who argued that the birth mother should be given another chance, and ruled against the social worker's application for a care order.

Four children (3 per cent) who had not previously been sexually abused went home and were sexually abused as a consequence of changes in family circumstances. For example, one child was returned home at the same time as his father was released from prison and the father began to sexually abuse the child. Forty-two per cent of the children who were returned home were known to have been physically and/or sexually abused in the past and abuse was suspected for a further 33 per cent. Most of the children (81 per cent) where reunification was attempted re-entered care within a matter of months (mean 14 weeks), following further abuse.

Planned changes of placement

Attempts at rehabilitation, moves in kinship placements and other moves resulted in only 39 nine (30 per cent) of the children remaining in the same placement during the period from entering care to the time of the AIBI decision. Forty-four (34 per cent) of the children had "planned

45

moves" only. The average number of placements was two, with a range of one to seven. Sometimes moves were planned to enable siblings to be reunited or a move was made from the initial emergency placement to one intended to last until adoptive parents could be found. Children were also moved as a way of pre-empting a disruption when it was clear to the social worker that the foster carers either did not like the child or could not meet his or her needs.

Disruptions

In addition to planned moves, there were unplanned moves for 47 (36 per cent) of the children who between them had 67 disruptions. Seventy per cent of relative placements disrupted, with one of these children having a disrupted foster placement as well. Kin placements disrupted for three main reasons. First, relatives did not protect the child from an abusing parent because they did not believe the allegations and allowed unrestricted contact. Secondly, the birth parent was so violent that relatives became afraid for their own and the child's safety. Finally, relatives often had unrealistic expectations and could not cope with the child's needs or behaviour. There is a poignant description on one file of the social worker being telephoned and asked to remove the child immediately. As the car drew away and the child turned to wave goodbye, the door had already been shut, leaving the child confused and distraught.

In over half (52 per cent) of the instances of disruption, the foster carers asked for the child to be moved because of challenging behaviour. Some found the children hard to like and some children seemed to provoke rejection or harsh treatment. In other cases (20 per cent), the effects on the foster carers and their own children led to the breakdown. The behaviour of the birth parents (18 per cent) also affected placement stability, particularly when the parents came to the foster home. Carers were threatened with violence or contact arrangements caused the child distress. A small number of placements ended (6 per cent) because of allegations of physical abuse by the carers. Some children (4 per cent) expressed such strong dislike of the carers that the placement was ended.

Quality of placements

Foster care: Foster carers generally worked hard with the children in their care and argued strongly for their need for therapeutic help. Just over half the children (51 per cent) were in placements that were rated as being of very high quality. But not all placements were so successful; 13 per cent had descriptions of low warmth and harsh criticism towards the child. Physical abuse or inappropriate punishments by the foster carer were known to have occurred for 11 (8 per cent) children. Another three children (2 per cent) were sexually abused by other children in the placement. Most of these placements ended but seven per cent of those in which there were concerns about a lack of warmth continued because there were no other placements available.

Residential care: As children moved around the care system, so concerns about the extent of their difficulties grew. Concerns were so great for three children aged four, six and eight that it was concluded that they could no longer live with a family and that residential care was the only option as funding was not available for an independent foster placement. Another child who had returned home for two years was taken into residential care after his parents said they could not cope with his behaviour and believed that he would receive the help he needed in residential care. Concerns were expressed on the case files of all the four children in residential care. Teachers wrote to social services departments (SSD)s and complained that the children arrived at school dirty and in ill-fitting clothes. There were also broader concerns about the likelihood of further abuse. Each was by far the youngest child in their residential unit. Older teenage residents often behaved in a violent or overtly sexual way and the units seemed to be in continual crisis.

Contact with birth families

Arrangements for contact with birth parents were made in the context of frequent changes within the birth family home. New siblings were born for 30 per cent of the children and 37 per cent of mothers had at least one new partner. Schedule 1 offenders were still present in 33 per cent of the children's homes. Housing instability continued with 35 (27 per cent) of the children's families becoming homeless for a time. The longer the child remained in care the less detailed were case notes about the birth family's circumstances. However, the families with an established pattern of numerous changes of address continued to move around (range 4–10 moves) and this created difficulty for social workers trying to maintain contact.

The great majority of the children (81 per cent) had some form of contact with their birth families when they first came into care. Three-quarters of all contact took place in the foster carers' or the birth family home. Home visits by 32 per cent of the children were often made to parents whose circumstances had changed. There might be a new baby or their mother might be pregnant again or have a new partner. Sometimes contact arrangements were complex and set at unrealistic levels, which birth parents and foster carers found impossible to stick to or manage. Contact between siblings was less regulated. Foster carers often took over making these arrangements when SSDs did not do so.

Case file recording included many comments about foster carers' reports of children's distress following contact visits. Children (15 per cent) were often disappointed by parents not turning up or some (five children) arrived at their birth home only to be refused entry. Twelve per cent of the children were physically abused during unsupervised contact, returning with unexplained bite marks or burns on their bodies. Six per cent continued to be sexually abused by their father or stepfather. For a further 11 per cent of children, ongoing physical or sexual abuse was suspected but there was a lack of evidence to support social workers'/ foster carers' suspicions.

In a quarter of cases, contact was supervised in a contact centre. Our ratings of parental warmth as described in case recording found a quarter of this contact was warm. However, the content was often described as of poor quality. Parents sometimes spent the visit looking for support and parenting for themselves from the foster carer, or parents found they quickly ran out of things to talk about as their shared experiences became more distant. Other reports included accounts of parents whispering to children and making threats or of parents being drunk and assaulting social workers.

Although social workers worked hard at maintaining links with birth mothers, fathers seemed to be less considered, both when relationships were reasonable and when they were not. It may have been this lack of attention to relationships in the triad of father, mother and child that left some children vulnerable to further abuse. Siblings had the same contact arrangements, regardless of their individual needs or the family dynamics. For example, one child was scapegoated and blamed for all the family difficulties when at home. This experience was replayed during contact. In another case, a mother lavished praise and presents on the eldest sibling while the youngest one sat in a corner and was never spoken to.

Parental contact visits diminished over time. The numbers of children whose parents refused any form of contact with them grew from 10 per cent when the children first entered care to 34 per cent at the point of the AIBI decision. Most of these children had been rejected by their birth parents and/or parents found contact visits too unsettling. Contact was also stopped by SSDs in 14 per cent of cases because the parent's behaviour was unreasonable and abusive.

The cessation of abuse

For most of the children (72 per cent) sexual and physical abuse stopped once they became looked after. Abuse was much easier to prevent than parental rejection, which continued to be experienced. For some children, their disclosures of abuse led to instant and complete parental rejection. For example, one child, after disclosing abuse, received in the post, without warning, an envelope containing every card and present she had ever given her birth mother with the demand that she never contact her again.

Although physical and sexual abuse had stopped for most children, eight per cent of never physically/sexually abused children experienced new incidents of physical or sexual abuse while they were looked after.

The decision for permanency

In considering the timeliness of the decision-making and implementation of permanency plans, delay was defined as lack of care planning after a child had been looked after for more than 12 months.

Planning for children where there was no delay in permanency planning

For the majority of children (59 per cent) an early assessment made it clear that the initial hopes of reunification were not attainable and that plans for permanency had to be made. The decision that a long-term placement should be sought was usually made or confirmed at the six-month review point. There was usually little disagreement over the decision that the children could not return home but more about what the best placement would be.

Frequency of contact often determined what the plan should be. High levels of contact at the start of the placement led to the assumption that long-term fostering was the best placement. Much less attention seemed to be paid to the *quality* of contact. Birth parents too had a great deal of influence on the planning and often wanted their children to be fostered, not adopted. This influence was strongest where children were being accommodated without a legal order. There was evidence that some social workers (10 cases) disagreed with the idea of adoption and preferred foster care because they were able to ensure contact decisions were enforced. Other social workers just had not considered adoption but had assumed the child would remain in care. As contact reduced or parents made it clear they either did not want the child home or were unable to protect the child from an abuser, adoption began to be considered. The foster care panel provided a check on plans where long-term fostering was being recommended for very young children. In four cases they overruled the plan in favour of adoption. Children's own wishes to be adopted accounted for five per cent of decisions.

Decision-making and planning where there was delay

Frequency of delay: Fifty-three children (41 per cent) waited longer than a year before the making of a permanency plan. The average length of time these children were looked after before a permanency plan was in place was 2.7 years (s.d.1.9) and with a range of just over 12 months to eight years later.

Causes of delay: Delay was caused by a number of factors. Lack of active planning or acceptance of the status quo accounted for most of it (53 per cent). The need to move towards permanence appeared to become a low priority once children were in apparently stable foster care placements, so that years sometimes went by before plans moved on. Social workers' attention was sometimes focused on new siblings still in the parental home and the need to protect the child at home meant that planning for children "safe" in foster care was postponed. In a few cases (four) the birth mother had disappeared and social workers felt unable to make plans.

Legal hold-ups accounted for 34 per cent of delays. Social workers were reluctant to make any plans for adoption in the absence of a care order and applications for these proceeded slowly, with many adjourn-ments. Courts ordered further assessments of parental mental health or allowed more time for parents to present their case or guardians asked for further work to be done. In a few cases, care orders took several years before they were finally completed.

Professional disagreements (13 per cent) about whether adoption was the right choice or whether there should be more rehabilitation attempts were also evident. Usually the disagreements were between the various agencies working with the family. Although four children voiced their opposition to plans for adoption, in only one case did this result in delay.

So, 59 per cent of the children had a plan for a substitute family made within a few months of entering long-term care while the remaining 41 per cent of children waited more than a year before a plan was in place. The permanency plan had to be acted upon before the adoption panel could consider the children's placement needs and therefore delay was also examined at the next stage in the adoption process.

Delay between the plan for adoption and the date of the panel's AIBI decision

At this point, delay was defined as a period of more than 12 months between the social work decision that a substitute family was needed and the date the adoption panel met to discuss whether adoption was in the best interests of the child. Fewer children (31 per cent) experienced delay at this point in the adoption process but 14 (11 per cent) children experienced delay at both time points. The next section provides data on the second kind of delay.

The average delay between the plan for permanence and the date of the adoption panel was 1.9 years, with a range between just over 12 months to five years. Although delays were shorter and fewer children were subject to them, 11 per cent of children waited for more than two years for their papers to be put before the panel.

In the majority of cases (73 per cent) a failure to take forward the plan for adoption was the reason. A lack of urgency, staff shortages, sickness and social worker's reticence about foster carers applying to adopt all contributed to this. Legal delays and parental opposition were less evident at this stage. On the other hand, a small number of children (2 per cent) had such challenging behaviour that concerns were growing about the appropriateness of adoption without therapeutic help.

Although there was less delay, the lack of movement created insecurity among the children and gave birth parents hope that maybe they could have their children returned. Sometimes attempts were made through the courts to rescind care orders or challenge prohibited contact. This created further delay and uncertainty in the children's lives.

Long delays

Eleven (8 per cent) children waited six or more years from the time they entered care until the date the adoption panel met. Three of these were planned kin adoptions that did not go before panel because grandparents were concerned about losing SSD financial support and supervised contact. The remaining long delays were the result of poor planning. The following quote from adoption panel minutes discussing one child illustrates this:

> Extensive delay between 1982–1991 during which time no clear plan appears to have been formulated . . . mother is said to have 'little or no insight into her child's needs' but her impact on his life appears to be significant in terms of limiting the possibilities of placement for him.

By the time the children's papers were ready to go to the adoption panel, the plan for all the 130 children was that adoptive parents should be sought. Some plans covered all eventualities, for example, that a foster placement with a "view to adoption" should be sought, or that a search for adoptive and long-term foster carers should proceed simultaneously.

Those carers who were most suitable or were found soonest would then be chosen.

Children's wishes and feelings

There was very little on the files about the children's feelings as delays mounted, plans changed or parents failed to turn up for contact. Comments were sometimes recorded in reviews or foster carers and teachers expressed concerns on behalf of the child that plans were not being taken forward. One teacher reported that the child wrote in their schoolbook, 'What will happen to me?' Other children were reported accosting strangers and knocking on doors asking, 'Will you be my mummy?'

Foster carers were often incensed that the expectation of adoption had been raised with the child but that the SSD seemed no nearer finding a family several years later. There was concern that the children had not been told why this was so, and that their already poor self-image was being confirmed because they believed there was no family that wanted them.

The children at the time of the best interests decision

By the time the children's Form Es went before the panel, they were between three and 13 years of age. Most of the children (79 per cent) were subject to care orders with very few children subject to freeing orders (1.5 per cent).

The frequency of special needs

Information about the children's special needs at the time they were approved for adoption was collected from the Adoption Medical Report and their Form E. Each developmental area was coded as either having no difficulty or of being mild, moderate or severe. A rating of severe was given if the difficulty had already received a diagnosis/assessment stating that, for example, the learning difficulty was severe. In cases where there had been no assessment, severity was judged on the frequency, persistence and the extent of the problem. Again, we present these data in line with the seven dimensions of development in the Integrated Children's System.

Health: The period the children spent in care had caused considerable improvements in their health in some areas. Most of the 87 per cent who had entered care with growth delay had caught up. Only eight per cent still had moderate to severe delay in growth. On the other hand, chronic health conditions were less likely to disappear. Only two per cent of health conditions cleared up and a further 11 per cent developed problems such as asthma as they grew older. Thus 21 per cent of children still had chronic health problems.

Difficulties in co-ordination and gross motor skills were also more persistent. Problems remitted or were mild for 12 of the 21 children that had these problems as they entered care. Indistinct speech or delays in language development had become a significant problem for 23 per cent, but less than half had received any help.

Table 5.1

Frequency of reported health problems at entry to care and at the time of the best interest adoption decision*

	Entry to care	*Persisting from entry to AIBI decision*	*Not reported at entry but reported at AIBI*	*Total number at AIBI decision*
Growth delay	56 (43%)	10 (8%)	3 (2%)	13 (10%)
Frequently ill	30 (23%)	6 (4%)	4 (3%)	10 (7%)
"Accidents"	30 (23%)	2 (1.5%)	2 (1.5%)	4 (3%)
Chronic conditions	15 (11%)	13 (10%)	15 (11%)	28 (21%)
Hearing	13 (11%) n=117	4 (3%)	13 (10%)	17 (13%)
Language delay	30 (32%) n 93	11 (8.5%)	19 (14.5%)	30 (23%) n129
Mobility	21 (19%) n 112	9 (7%)	5 (4%)	14 (11%) n129
Enuresis	11 (29%) n 38	3 (3%) n 38	11 (12%)	14 (15%) n 95
Encopresis	11 (29%) n 38	3 (3.5%) n 38	9 (9.5%)	12 (13%) n 95

* where Ns are not given the number =130

Concerns about children's health led to referrals for medical assessments, which were completed for 48 per cent of the children. Twenty-three per cent of the children had regular contact with health professionals, including consultants, occupational therapists or physiotherapists.

Social presentation: Foster carers had an immediate impact on the way children were presenting in social settings. For most of the children who had been arriving at school smelly and dirty, clean clothes and bedding ensured a change. There were accounts on case files of some children expressing their sheer delight and joy at having clean, nice clothes to wear. For a few children (2 per cent) personal hygiene continued to be a problem. The case files of the children in residential care continued to have comments from schools about the poor condition of their clothes, their ill-fitting shoes and their poor personal hygiene.

Problems with enuresis were coded (n = 95) from the age of four. As the children grew older, more children had problems with enuresis. A total of 15 per cent of the children were enuretic, 13 per cent had problems with encopresis and 12 per cent had problems in both areas.

Education: Eighty-seven (67 per cent) children had started school by the time of the adoption panel. Of these, 79 per cent were in mainstream education. Sixteen children (18 per cent) were being educated in special schools or units and one child was permanently excluded with no provision. Learning difficulties were beginning to be recognised, with 17 per cent described as having mild learning difficulties and a further 11 per cent as having moderate to severe problems. Seventeen per cent of children had completed statements of special education needs and a further 14 per cent were awaiting completion.

Difficulties in learning to read were reported for 26 per cent of the children attending school. Children were also often described by teachers as lacking curiosity or having no interest in learning or being "unable to learn". More than half (54 per cent) were described by teaching staff as under-achieving, for example, one child's school reported that the child had an average IQ but was in the bottom seven per cent of all pupils.

Emotional and behavioural development: Over half the children (55 per cent) were described as having moderate to severe emotional and behavioural difficulties. Common problems included overactivity, difficulty playing, nightmares and sleep disturbances and behaving younger than their years. The number of children (15 per cent) displaying inappropriate sexual behaviour also increased as they became older. Three of these children had also sexually abused another child. Although most of the children were young, eight per cent had eating problems and a few (three) were self-harming by cutting themselves. Self-harm was not coded until the child reached seven years as we had expected these difficulties to emerge mainly in adolescence. However, we were surprised by reports (four) of very young children self-harming, with children as young as four deliberately tearing their hair out (one child had a permanent bald spot) or cutting or poisoning themselves.

Mental health assessments were undertaken on ten of the children. In addition, a further four children were part of a mental health assessment that involved members of their birth family. But only seven per cent of all the children received a sustained therapeutic intervention from a CAMHS team. This included only one of the four children in residential care. There were many more requests for assessment and interventions. Case files contained sheaves of letters in which social workers, teachers and foster carers pleaded for help. One headteacher wrote, 'Will nobody help this child? . . . It is almost too late', but the children were not seen as a priority.

At the time these children were in care, the policy of the area CAMHS clinics was to refuse to offer long-term work with children who were not in a stable placement. Not surprisingly, these were the children showing the most disturbed behaviour. Thus, although the children referred were those with the most challenging behaviour, help was refused because foster placements were disrupting.

Family and social relationships: Thirty-six per cent of the children continued to have very poor peer relationships. They did not know how to play and this often led to arguments and fights. Some (13 per cent) were seen as bullies and were known to have physically harmed another child. Forty-five per cent had moderate to severe difficulties in forming attachments with adults. These short descriptions of three children's behaviour taken from Form Es illustrate the nature and the multiplicity of some children's difficulties.

Danny has been unable to form any attachments to people, siblings or even to objects. He is unkind to animals, hurting his foster carer's dog by deliberately riding his bike over the dog's legs. At nursery he will eat dirt, bite his skin and obsessively washes his hands. He has no interest in stories or cuddles but spends his time pacing up and down. He self abuses, ripping his hair out, putting knives down his throat and deliberately foams at the mouth. In public he lets loose ear shattering screams and pulls down his pants.

Follows unknown men into toilets . . . eats until he is sick . . . sucks thumb . . . will not clean self or bottom. (child aged ten years)

Lack of interest in learning . . . craves adult attention . . . rummages in bins for cigarette ends . . . makes considerable efforts to obtain the dregs of alcohol from glasses . . . needs constant supervision.

Figure 5.1
Number of special needs when approved for adoption

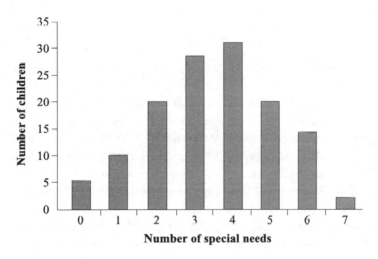

As Figure 5.1 shows, most of the children had multiple special needs (mean 3.5, s.d. 1.62). Indeed, 52 per cent had four or more and only five children had none.

Cost to social service during the "looked after" phase

Table 5.2

Cost to social services of caring for the children from the time they became looked after until the best interest decision

	Number of children	Total number of weeks	Cost per week	Total cost
Children supported in their families	30	1,862	£120	£223,440
Local authority foster care	127	13,008	£318	£4,136,544
Independent foster care	2	218	£630	£137,340
Local authority residential care	4	357	£1,646	£587,622
Independent residential care	1	23	£2,000	£46,000
All accommodation types	130	15,468	n/a	£5,130,946

Table 5.2 gives the total cost to SSDs of looking after children from the time the 130 children entered care to the time when the best interest decision was made. The data on the number of weeks children spent in each type of care were collected from case files. The cost per week of each type of care has been calculated from the Children in Need census calculations (2001) and financial data from the largest authority's "Best Value" exercise. The total cost is calculated by multiplying the total number of weeks spent in different types of accommodation by the cost per week in 2001/2.

The average cost per child using 2001 prices while looked after was £39,469. If we look at children who had different experiences from entering care to the AIBI decision, the costs look very different. It is useful, therefore, to consider the most and least costly groups of children. First, we look at the children (n = 48) for whom decisions, once they became looked after, were made and implemented quickly. For this group, a child's average length of time spent in foster care was 26 weeks before the AIBI decision, they had no rehabilitation attempts and made no use of any private sector placements. The average cost for these children was £8,904. Second, at the other extreme, the children with the longest delay (n = 11) waited for more than five years before a decision was made. Six (54 per cent) experienced attempts at reunification and two (18 per cent) spent periods in residential care. The average cost for these children was £94,551. Third, the "median" children (n = 37) waited two years before the AIBI decision. Three (8 per cent) had reunification attempts but only local authority foster care provision was used. The average cost for a "median" child was £28,903.

Summary of the children's adjustment and needs at the time of the best interests decision

- Contact between the parents and child dropped from 81 per cent to 52 per cent over the period from entering care to the best interest decision.
- Rehabilitation was planned for 73 per cent of children but only attempted for a quarter.
- The majority of children (59 per cent) did not experience any delay in the making of a permanency plan, but 41 per cent of children waited on average more than two years before a plan was in place.
- When children were being considered by the adoption panel, 92 per cent were in foster care, five per cent were living with kin and three per cent were in local authority residential care.
- Fifty-two per cent of children had multiple special needs. More than half (55 per cent) were described as having emotional and behavioural difficulties but only seven per cent of all the children had ongoing therapeutic help from a CAMHS team.

6 From the panel to the follow-up: What happened to the children?

We knew before the study started that not all the 130 children had been successfully adopted. At follow-up, 80 were living with an adoptive family (the adopted group), 34 had found some stability, mainly through long-term foster or kinship care – we refer to these children as the *permanently placed group* – but 16 children had very disrupted lives and numerous placements. These children are referred to as the *unstable care career group*.

Why were some children successfully adopted and others not? Were the children or their families different in some way before the AIBI decision was made? We looked at this at two points in their earlier lives: when the children entered longer-term care and when they were approved for adoption. The data were analysed statistically to see whether any characteristics of the children or their birth families were related to the children's later care careers. Statistically significant associations are reported at the five per cent level of significance or better.

Group differences at entry to care

The successfully adopted group were younger when they entered care than those in the other two groups, which did not differ significantly from each other. A number of variables were tested to see if there was any relationship with outcomes, including gender and family characteristics. Only maternal mental health showed some association with outcome. The mother's educational level, physical and learning disability, health conditions, leaving home as a teenager, having been in care, being a victim of child abuse, having already had a child removed/adopted and previous violent relationships did not.

The mothers' mental health was significantly poorer in the unstable care career group (63 per cent had problems) compared with the permanent group (38 per cent) or the adopted group (32 per cent). The parents of children in the unstable care career group were nearly four times more likely to have been sectioned under the Mental Health Act – 31 per cent had been sectioned, compared with nine per cent of the permanent placement and the adopted groups. It was surprising that length of involvement with social services departments (SSDs) was not associated with earlier entry to care. All three outcome groups were very similar in this respect.

The case note data were not consistent enough to show whether the involvement of mental health services was associated with delayed entry to care. There were comments on case files that suggested that in some cases the focus of services was on the mother rather than the child. In other cases, mental health professionals argued in the courts that treatment would be effective or that the parent should be given another chance, against the recommendation of the social worker. So, the children whose mothers had the severest mental health problems remained at home longer than children in the other two outcome groups.

Other significant associations

The data showed three other important associations. First, there were significant differences in the ethnicity of the children. Seven of the ten children were in the permanently placed group – 21 per cent of that group overall, compared with 13 per cent of the unstable group and only one per cent of the adopted group. Second, two aspects of abuse differentiated the groups: Schedule 1 offenders were more often found in the birth homes of the adopted children (39 per cent) than in the birth families of the unstable (23 per cent), or the permanently placed groups (18 per cent) and, although individual types of abuse were not more common in one group than another, the range of abuse was. Third, children in the unstable care career group had suffered more kinds of abuse than the other two groups. From descriptions on the case files, the unstable care career group had not only experienced more forms of abuse but it often had a sadistic quality to it. For example, one girl said that throughout her life her mother had never sent her a birthday card, but when her mother found a card the child herself had bought for a friend, she stole it and sent it to the girl.

Children's special needs: The special needs of the three groups of children were compared. Some needs, such as emotional/behavioural difficulties, were not included unless a child was aged two or over. The results are summarised in Table 6.1.

Table 6.1
Areas of need in the three placement groups

Area of need	Adopted Yes %	Group Permanent Yes %	Unstable Yes %	Df	Chi square
Physical disability	4	12	6	2	2.78
Learning difficulty	3	18	0	2	8.12*
Health condition	4	18	0	2	6.58*
Emotional/behavioural difficulties (EBD)	24	21	56	2	7.25*
Sexualised behaviour	6	0	13	2	2.89
Overactivity	11	7	19	2	1.37
Poor attachment	28	30	44	2	1.69
Development delay	30	39	31	2	0.81

*p<0.05

As can be seen, the permanently placed group had a higher recorded prevalence of physical disability, and significantly more learning difficulties and chronic health conditions than the other two groups. There was some evidence that these differences were significant for learning difficulties and health conditions. The unstable group also showed much higher levels of difficult behaviour. They were more likely to have emotional and behavioural difficulties, sexualised behaviour, overactivity and attachment difficulties, although only the difference on emotional and behavioural difficulties overall was found to be statistically significant. The absence of learning difficulties in the unstable career group may reflect poorer case file recording for them.

Summary

At the point the children entered care, there were already differences that related to their later care careers. Age at entry, ethnicity, maternal mental health, multiple abuse and number and extent of emotional and behavioural problems and special needs were significantly associated with their later outcome group. There were few differences between those who went down the adoptive or stable long-term foster care paths, although there were some features, notably ethnicity and physical and learning disabilities, that were more common among the permanently placed children. The presence of a known Schedule 1 offender was more common in the birth homes of the adopted children.

The children who were successfully adopted not only entered care at a younger age but were also subject to speedier decision-making than the other two groups. The children whose later care careers were unstable were already different at the time they entered care. They were older and more troubled and from more pervasively problematic families at the time permanency planning began.

Group differences at the time of the best interests decision

The second point at which the groups were compared was at the time the children were approved for adoption. At this point the adopted group were, on average, 4.8 years of age, the unstable group 6.7 years and the permanent group 7.1 years.

Placement history

The time between the entry to care and the AIBI decision was the most drawn out for those in the permanently placed group (mean delay 3 yrs s.d.2.6) compared to those in the unstable group (mean 2.6 yrs s.d.1.5) and those adopted (mean 2.2 yrs s.d. 1.3), but the earlier instability in the lives of the unstable group was repeated even after they became looked after. Reunification was attempted for 44 per cent of them, compared with 29 per cent of the successfully adopted group and only nine per cent of the permanent group. Not surprisingly, these different patterns were reflected in the number of placement moves the children had, although not significantly so. Eighty-four per cent of the adopted children had three or fewer placements compared with 76 per cent of the permanently placed group and 63 per cent of the unstable group. Thus, the unstable group had more moves around the case system as well as more attempts at reunification. Of course, the frequency of the latter contributed to the former.

Residential placements only occurred among the unstable group. Four of them (25 per cent) had seven residential placements from the time they entered care to the time of the adoption approval. Surprisingly, these were not the oldest children in the group. Two of the children were four years old when they went into residential care, one was six years old and the other was eight years old.

Disruptions

Disruptions were also much higher in the unstable group. Over three-fifths of them (63 per cent) experienced these, compared with 38 per cent in the permanent group and 29 per cent in the adopted group. There was some evidence that multiple disruptions were more common in the unstable care career group.[1]

Quality of substitute care

Re-abuse rates were similar in the three groups, but the carers of the unstable group were more likely to be noted as not warm (25 per cent) than the permanently placed group (9 per cent), or the adopted group (14 per cent). These differences were not statistically significant.

Children's development at the time of the best interests decision

At the time the children were being considered for adoption, some children had not received a diagnosis for medical conditions. This was partly due to the lack of multi-disciplinary assessments but also it was only as children grew older that the full extent of these difficulties became apparent. The table below indicates the extent of "known" areas of need at the time of the AIBI decision.

The psychosocial differences that were apparent as the children entered care had persisted. Learning difficulties and health conditions were most common in the permanently placed group (Table 6.2).

---

[1] on a binary split $\chi^2 = 6.80\ 5$; df = 2; p<0.03

Table 6.2
Group differences in special needs at AIBI

Area of need	Adopted Yes %	Permanent Yes %	Unstable Yes %	Exact probability (Fisher)
Physical disability	6	21	0	0.30
Learning difficulty	19	41	19	**0.04**
Health condition	16	44	31	**0.01**
EBD	55	62	75	0.08
Sexualised behaviour	14	6	38	**0.02**
Overactivity	15	18	37	0.12
Poor attachment	46	29	69	**0.03**
Peer problems	26	47	63	**0.01**
Developmental delay	19	35	19	0.37

Two composite variables were created. The first combined the children's emotional and behavioural difficulties including: overall emotional behavioural difficulties, sexualised behaviour, overactivity and attachment difficulties. The unstable group continued to show the greatest number of difficulties on this measure (mean 4.5, s.d. 1.9). The adopted group had fewer problems (mean 2.5, s.d. 2.0), a level similar to that in the permanently placed group (mean 2.5, s.d. 1.7). These differences were not statistically significant.

The second composite variable summed the number of special needs across all of the categories. By including physical and learning difficulties in the count of special needs the difference between the groups narrowed. The unstable group had on average slightly more special needs (mean 4.9, s.d. 1.7) than the permanently placed group (mean 4.2, s.d. 2.1) or the adopted group (mean 4.0 s.d.2.5) but these differences were not statistically significant.

Summary of the children's needs at the AIBI

These analyses have been concerned with looking at the experiences and adjustment of the children before and at the time of the best interests decision. The point of this has been to see to what extent the different careers or paths that the children subsequently followed might be related to these earlier factors. It should be remembered that these groups have been defined in terms of outcome – that is where they ended up. Any analysis undertaken on this basis is likely to emphasise differences and that seems to have happened here. The children who later followed unstable care careers seemed to have had a particularly terrible time before they went into longer-term care, suffered poor decision-making, were subject to many more reunification attempts and then had a much more disrupted and unsatisfactory experience in care. They were older and much more troubled by the time the best interests decision was made, by which time it appeared too late for adoption to be a successful option – at least without very substantial and professional support. This was rather weakly reflected in the Form Es, where it was clear that the intention was they should be placed alone (81 per cent), separated from siblings and in an adoptive family in which they would be the youngest or only child in the family.

On the other hand, the differences between those children who were successfully adopted and those who finally entered stable foster placements were much fewer. Generally, prior placement experiences, reunifications and disruptions were not significantly different, nor were the levels of emotional and behavioural problems. Where the samples did differ was in the much higher levels of physical and learning disability in the permanently fostered group, as well as differences in ethnicity. Table 6.3 summarises these differences.

We undertook multivariate analyses in order to gain a better understanding of the ways in which these different factors interacted and contributed to outcome. Because our sample size was modest and had limited numbers within each outcome category, we initially tested several small predictive models in binary logistic regression to identify what features appeared to distinguish the members of each outcome group ("adopted"/"permanently placed"/"unstable care career").

The analyses took account not only of the variables found to be significant in bivariate analysis but also, on the basis of our in-depth knowledge of the case material, other variables thought likely to be influential. These included delay (defined here as the number of years between entry to care and the AIBI decision) and scores for a range of

Table 6.3

Factors differentiating the permanently placed and unstable care career groups on entry to care and at time of AIBI decision

Outcome group	Factor	Entry to care	Best interests
Permanently	Age at entry to care	**	
placed	Ethnicity	***	
	Learning difficulty	*	*
	Health condition	*	*
Unstable care	Age at entry to care	**	
career	Maternal mental health	*	
	Multiple abuse	**	
	EBD	*	
	Poor attachment	*	
	Sexualised behaviour	*	
	Peer problems	**	
	Reunification attempts	*	
	Disruptions	*	

*p<0.05; **p<0.01; ***p<0.001.

problematic externalising behaviours, which together reflected the child's level of conduct disorder. The variables that emerged as significant predictors of outcome group membership were then considered together in multinomial regression. This final model included age at entry to care, ethnicity, delay, violent behaviour shown towards others or animals, and sexualised behaviour.

The analysis showed that, when comparing the "permanently placed" with the "adopted" group, the significant predictors of permanent placement were being older at entry to care,[2] being of black or black mixed parentage,[3] and experiencing delay.[4] It appeared that for these children the odds of not being adopted increased 1.7 for every extra year of age at entry to care, and 1.6 for every extra year of delay in reaching a best

---

[2] p = 0.000; odds 1.7, 95 per cent confidence interval for odds, 1.31–2.21

[3] p = 0.002; odds 36.1, 95 per cent confidence interval for odds, 3.71–350.9

[4] p = 0.001; odds 1.6, 95 per cent confidence interval for odds, 1.2–2.15

interests decision. Being of black or black mixed parentage also appeared greatly to increase the odds of not being adopted, but it is important to remember that our sample included only ten children of black or black mixed ethnicity, of whom only one was still in an adoptive placement at follow-up, seven were permanently placed and two had unstable care careers.

Comparing the "unstable care career" with the "adopted" group, the significant predictors of having an unstable care career were, again, being older at entry to care[5] and showing violent behaviour towards others or animals.[6] For children who had an unstable care career, it appeared that the odds of not being adopted increased 1.5 for every year of age at entry to care, and 3.4 for every stepped increase in the level of violence they showed at the time of the AIBI decision (on a scale from 0–3). Sexualised behaviour was not found to be a worthwhile predictor in distinguishing between children who had an unstable care career and those who were adopted. There were indications, however, both from the case material and from the use of CHAID (the Chi-Squared Automatic Interaction Detector), that the presentation of sexualised behaviour by young children (aged less than three at entry to care) significantly reduced the likelihood of being adopted.[7]

When the degree of overlap between these predictor variables was explored, there were modest correlations in the adopted group between age at entry to care and delay (r 0.20, p<0.05), and between age at entry and the child's level of sexualised behaviour (r 0.22 p<0.01). In the permanently placed group, age at entry and delay were again correlated (r 0.33 p< 0.01). It also appeared that these children's levels of violent and sexualised behaviour were correlated (r 43 p<0.01). In the unstable care career group, the presentation of violent behaviour was related neither to the child's age at entry to care nor to sexualised behaviour. It therefore appears that the children's level of violent behaviour was, independent of the other factors, a powerful predictor of outcome.

---

[5] p = 0.008; odds 1.55, 95 per cent confidence interval for odds, 1.12–2.14
[6] p = 0.003; odds 3.424, 95 per cent confidence interval for odds, 1.541–7.610
[7] p = 0.001 Chi-square = 17.1305; d.f. = 2

Summary of the earlier experiences of children following different care careers

- Children who were adopted were not only younger on entry to care but were also subject to speedier decision-making when they entered care. Both age at entry to care and the length of time between entering care and having a best interests decision were found to be significant predictors of not being adopted.
- Children in the permanently placed group were more likely to have learning difficulties and chronic health problems than children in the other two groups.
- Children who had unstable care careers were more likely than the other children to have mothers with mental health problems and were more likely to have suffered multiple forms of abuse.
- Children who had unstable care careers had more reunification attempts, more foster care placements and more disruptions, and were the only children to have residential placements before the adoption best interest decision.
- Children with unstable care careers were also more likely to be exhibiting emotional and behavioural difficulties than children in the other two groups.
- Those who, by the time of the best interests decision, were exhibiting violent behaviour were at particular risk of an unstable care career. This may well have implications for the level and type of therapeutic input they need as permanency plans are made.

SECTION III

Life in the adoptive family

7 The adopted children and their new families

In this chapter we describe the adoptive families and their experiences as they waited to be matched. We then pick up the stories of the 80 adopted children and summarise their experiences from the time they were approved for adoption to the time they were placed.

The adoptive families

Demographic characteristics

Sixty-six families adopted the 80 children. Just over a quarter were adopted by their foster carers (21 per cent) or kin (6 per cent) and the remainder (73 per cent) were adopted by families not known to the children (stranger adoptions). The characteristics of these families are shown in Table 7.1.

Nationally, foster carers adopt approximately 14 per cent of children (Ivaldi, 2000), somewhat lower than the 21 per cent of the children in this study. All except two of these were adopted into foster families where there were children already. These were usually older, but in four families there was a mix of older and younger children. Birth children were still living at home in all except three of the foster families. Eight families also had other adopted or fostered children living with them.

In contrast, only 13 of the 58 children adopted by strangers joined families where there were children already. Four rejoined siblings and the remaining 11 joined adoptive families with older children they did not know. In the majority of families, these were older birth children, but in one family there was an older adopted child. One disabled child was placed with an adoptive mother who had already adopted two other disabled children, because she had appropriate expertise.

Three of the four kin adopters adopted their nieces and one their granddaughter. In all these cases, the birth parents had been struggling with problems of drug or alcohol misuse or, in one case, with the extent of the child's disability. Two of the kin adopters (both without dependent children) had known the children quite well before adopting them, whereas the other two did not. Since they already had birth children at home, their families ended up being rather large.

Just under half of the children (46 per cent) were placed on their own in a family. Fourteen children (18 per cent) had no siblings they could have been placed with, while 23 children (29 per cent) had been separated from their siblings. The remaining 54 per cent were placed with a full or partial sibling group. Some of these siblings were not in our sample because they did not meet the sampling criteria, being under the age of three at the time of approval. Fewer than half (41 per cent) of the childless strangers adopted singletons, compared with 69 per cent of the stranger adopters who already had children and 73 per cent of the foster carer adopters. Some of these families subsequently adopted or fostered further children.

The majority of children were adopted by white married couples, but five per cent were adopted by one partner from a cohabiting couple and seven per cent by single women. The one minority ethnic adopter in the interview sample was matched with a child from the same ethnic background. The childless stranger adopters were very slightly younger and tended to have been together for the least amount of time but were more likely to have a professional occupation. Very few adopters were unemployed, but of those that were, half were kin adopters.

The adopters' stories

All of the adoptive parents were invited to interview and 54 (82 per cent) of the 66 families took part: half of the kin adopters, 40 (85 per cent) of the 47 stranger adopters and 12 (80 per cent) of the 15 foster carer adopters were interviewed.

Motivation to adopt: Two-thirds (67 per cent) of the parents adopted because of primary or secondary infertility. Secondary infertility affected 54 per cent of the stranger adopters, 33 per cent of the foster carer adopters and 25 per cent of the kin adopters. These parents had usually undergone extensive fertility treatment without success or experienced many miscarriages and lived through much heartache. Some were desperate to be the same as other families and this not only influenced their motivation to adopt but also their response to the adoption preparation course.

Table 7.1

Characteristics of the adoptive families

	Foster carer adopters (n = 15)	Kin adopters (n = 4)	Childless stranger adopters (n = 34)	Stranger adopters with children (n = 13)
Number of sample children	17 (21%)	5 (6%)	45 (56%)	13 (17%)
Children already in the family	13 with children (87%)	2 with children (50%)	0 with children (100%)	13 with children (100%)
Marital status	12 married (80%) 2 cohabiting (13%) 1 single mother (7%)	4 married (100%)	31 married (91%) 1 cohabiting (3%) 2 single mothers (6%)	11 married (85%) 2 single mothers (15%)
Relationship duration	Mean 17.5 years	Mean 17.5 years	Mean 10.5 years	Mean 14 years
Age when child placed	Mothers mean 38 years Fathers mean 42 years	Mothers mean 38 years Fathers mean 39 years	Mothers mean 37 years Fathers mean 39 years	Mothers mean 40 years Fathers mean 41 years
Ethnicity	29 white (100%)	8 white (100%)	65 white (98%) 1 ethnic minority (2%)	44 white (100%)
Socio-economic status	4 professional (27%) 10 non-professional (66%) 1 unemployed (7%)	2 professional (50%) 2 unemployed (50%)	23 professional (68%) 11 non-professional (32%)	6 professional (46%) 6 non-professional (46%) 1 unemployed (8%)
Religious participation	3 active faith (20%)	3 active faith (75%)	9 active faith (26%)	6 active faith (46%)
Adopted single child or siblings	11 singleton (73%) 4 sibling group (27%)	2 singleton (50%) 2 sibling group (50%)	14 singleton (41%) 20 sibling group (59%)	9 singleton (69%) 4 sibling group (31%)

The remaining 33 per cent of families adopted for a variety of reasons. Foster carer and kin adopters wanted to bring up children whom they already saw as part of their families, whereas the stranger adopters wanted to help a child in need. Altruistic adopters thought that their motivation to adopt had been viewed suspiciously by social workers, even though they seemed more prepared than those motivated by infertility.

We were both very experienced with young people and I had also worked with the unemployed and the "hard to help" so we weren't going into it with our eyes closed. We did it because we wanted to help young people like that, not because we couldn't have children. But people couldn't understand that, we kept having to justify it, we felt like lepers.

Assessment: All of the families underwent an adoption assessment. Most (78 per cent) received some adoption preparation or training, but second-time adopters or foster carers were not expected to attend preparation courses again. Adoptive parents voiced mixed feelings about the assessment process. Most had found it an enjoyable and enlightening experience, but some said that it had been intrusive, particularly if they had had to explore difficult feelings about their own childhood experiences or infertility.

I enjoyed it. I found out a lot about myself. How often do you sit back and write your life story? You don't tend to sit back and think 'who am I and where did I come from?'

Nevertheless, three-quarters of the adoptive parents (72 per cent) said that they had been truthful during the assessment process, although some (28 per cent) felt the need to appease social workers and say 'what they wanted to hear' even if that was not strictly how they felt. Several told us how resolving issues had held up the assessment process for weeks or months.

It was clear that they wanted stereotypical families where, as one social worker told me, 'The mummy stayed at home baking cookies'. Because we were not married and because I was working and was not planning to give that up, it was very hard for us to get taken on by social services.

In some cases, social workers and prospective adopters did not like each other and this made the assessment process difficult. Three-quarters of foster carer adopters (77 per cent) did not receive any formal adoption preparation/training and most would have preferred the time to have been spent on this instead of assessment.

Preparation: Adoption preparation courses covered the previous experiences, needs and vulnerabilities of children waiting to be adopted, the birth parents' perspectives and the reality of adoption. Social workers had tried their best to explain the challenges of adoption but sometimes without success. Many adopters admitted that they had not taken in the extent of the children's problems, preferring to think that they were exaggerating difficulties or they believed that it would be different for them.

You are so desperate to have children that you hear the good stuff they are saying, but not the bad.

Some adopters complained that the implications of terms like "learning difficulties" and "emotional behavioural problems" had not been sufficiently explained and that this could result in disappointment and unmet expectations.

"Learning disabilities" is a cop out. Our understanding was of a child who might need a little extra help at school. Our social worker made us think there was more we could do with nurture. We didn't realise that he wouldn't be able to tie up his own shoe laces.

Sixty per cent of those who attended preparation groups had negative or mixed feelings about their usefulness. The general message was that, although what had been presented was generally good, with hindsight it had not gone far enough.

They did their best to alert us to possible problems, but there were no answers, no management strategies.

Parents wanted more detailed information about the disorders the children might present and how to manage them. They also wanted to be better prepared for the emotional and relationship problems they and their own children might have to face. Birth children were somewhat neglected during the preparation process. Only one child had any further preparation on top of the Form F assessment interview.

Some of the adopters who understood that the children might have difficulties nevertheless believed that with love these difficulties would dissipate. A few had something of a rescuer mentality and thought that whatever the children had suffered, they could make it all better. With hindsight, most felt that they had very little idea of the reality of the adoptive experience, even after having attended a preparation group, and several suggested ways that this could have been improved. One was that prospective adopters could act as respite carers for adoptive families in need of a break. Another involved the development of a mentoring scheme where prospective adopters were paired with experienced ones.

Stranger adoptions

A number of aspects of preparation and placement apply primarily to stranger adoptions. These are dealt with here.

Family finding

Accounts of family-finding activities dominated the case files during the pre-adoption period for the 58 children who were subsequently placed with strangers. Just over half of them (55 per cent) were placed through local SSDs. The remaining children were promoted via voluntary agencies or in publications such as *Be My Parent* or *Focus on Fives* (a section of *Be My Parent*, now discontinued). These children were significantly older than those who were not promoted and also took significantly longer to be linked with an adoptive family. Surprisingly, those who were subsequently placed with siblings were not more likely to have been promoted than those placed singly. This may reflect the fact that a number of sibling groups were not placed together, as no adopters came forward and the children were ultimately placed separately.

Some children were very easy to place. Just over half were linked with new families within six months (56 per cent) and over three-quarters were matched within a year (85 per cent), but it took up to four years for permanent adoptive families to be found for the remaining 15 per cent of the children. Those who took longer to be placed often had to be promoted several times before placements were found.

SSDs typically considered between two and four prospective families for each child or sibling group before they approved a link. There was very little evidence on file that the children were consulted in this process. For 16 per cent of the children, social workers had no choice and only one family was considered. In these situations, rather less than perfect matches were sometimes approved.

These difficult-to-place children had more special needs than those who were placed quickly (on average 4.25 needs compared with three) and were older (average age five years four months compared with four years ten months). Only the difference in the number of special needs was statistically significant. No individual need significantly affected placement prospects, but children with moderate to severe learning difficulties were harder to place (50 per cent) than children with any other difficulty. Some children (10 per cent) also experienced delay because of poor social work practice, because they themselves were not ready for adoption, or because they experienced an adoption disruption before they went on to be successfully placed.

Preparation

Many adopters had made books about themselves, their home and their wider family and social workers and foster carers had gone through these with the children. This was extremely helpful when it came to the initial meetings, as it gave both the children and the adopters somewhere to start.

We'd done the book and she was looking at it when we arrived, she looked up at us then back at her book. Andrew had fallen instantly in love with her.

Not all of the children received such preparation, and some (10 per cent) had hardly any time to get to know the adopters, as they were moved into the placement within two or three weeks of the match. Although introductions typically took eight weeks, 20 per cent of the children waited between three and six months. Introductions were delayed or prolonged for a number of reasons, ranging from birth parents contesting the adoption to concerns about the child's happiness with the match, to the adopters delaying while issues of support were resolved. Introductions also tended to take longer for out-of-area placements. Well-planned, progressive introductions were generally the best received and meant that adopters were able to take account of the children's wishes as they decorated their rooms and prepared for their arrival.

Matching

The end of the assessment and preparation period signalled a time of intense emotion for the majority of stranger adopters. They were thrilled to have been approved and could not wait to be matched. There was much excitement and anticipation. These feelings, however, quickly turned to disappointment or despondency if they were unsuccessfully matched or if nothing seemed to be happening.

Some parents began avidly searching through publications like *Be My Parent* and, in one adopter's words, "bombarding" social workers with calls about children they were interested in. Adopters pointed out that relationships with other adopters they had met on the preparation courses could be damaged during the matching process. These experiences created a competitive environment that did little to encourage adopters to be reflective about the appropriateness of the suggested match.

It's a torture. It's a lottery. We have had it where another couple we got friendly with rang us up and said, 'We've got matched up' and we said, 'So have we' . . . same kids. So there's your friendship gone or at the least strained.

Most (68 per cent) were overjoyed when matched and felt that it was "right" from the outset. Many of those who expressed these feelings specifically mentioned how much the child looked like one or other of their family members.

I saw the girls in Be My Parent *and knew these were the ones. They looked like me and my family and it was almost as if I wanted a sign or a signal and my middle name is Emily, and they shouted at me out of the page instantly. I looked at them and thought 'I want them, I want them', and it was really exciting because I knew these were the ones and it felt right. I wanted to be a part of them instantly.*

However, a third of the stranger adopters (32 per cent) had concerns about the match and did not feel comfortable about proceeding with it.

Half of these were disappointed or concerned about the child's age. They believed that they had little choice about who was placed with them and felt that if they refused this child, then they would not be offered another.

We felt slightly disappointed because we would have liked a younger child and we were concerned because of how overweight she was. But there was pressure put on us to take Melanie and we were told that if we turned her down it would be a long time before there was another child. You're not really given a choice.

First meetings

The first meeting with the children was often remembered fondly and described movingly. Adopters often spoke of falling in love with the children.

We met them on a Saturday afternoon and the boys were called in and I can see it now, it brings tears to my eyes, they walked in shoulder to shoulder like little soldiers and they stood in the middle of the room looking down. And the foster mother said to them 'Well, what do you think then?' and their eyes looked up and they said 'Yes'.

Subsequent concerns

Once the adopters had actually met the children, their concerns increased as the information they had received took on meaning and they began to question their own abilities to cope. These concerns were not necessarily shared with their social workers.

. . . but it wasn't until we met his foster carers that we really started finding out about this child and we thought 'Are we talking about the same child here?'. They said 'We've scraped the pooh off the walls, we've redecorated, he's got no sense of danger, he doesn't listen to instructions' and we heard things about him that we'd never heard before. And you do worry because you think will this work, will it change our relationship, does it matter that we've missed the first seven years of his life? But as long as the positives outweigh the negatives, you go along with it.

The plan for continued contact with the birth family was the single issue that most concerned adopters at this stage, with half (48 per cent) of those where continuing contact was planned expressing worries.

We were wary about it all at that time, because a lot of people we knew were just a photo and letter at Christmas but we had the highest level of contact, so we were quite concerned really. I felt that she (birth mother) was quite a threat to me.

The extent of children's emotional/behavioural difficulties (32 per cent), sexualised behaviour (24 per cent) and learning difficulties (16 per cent) also worried them. Sometimes the adoption medical adviser or another professional spoke to adopters about the child's past experiences, current behaviours and possible future outcomes. The opportunity to have a consultation was described as helpful. But 22 per cent of adopters had important reservations over and above the reasonable anxieties felt by most adoptive parents at this stage. Relationships in these adoptions were noticeably strained from the outset. This suggests that persistent misgivings like these should not be ignored.

Information

Adopters wanted a lot of information, but found it difficult to get.

We wanted to speak to the psychologist he had been seeing and that was seen as a strange thing to do and it was very hard even to get a school report. I actually wanted to speak to the head but nobody would let me. It was as if we should just go along with the social work assessment and not form our own opinions. There didn't seem to be any account taken of the fact that we were suitably qualified and experienced to have been able to make sense of the information ourselves.

Over half (58 per cent) thought that there had been big gaps in the information they had received about the child and a further 10 per cent thought it was insufficiently detailed. The most frequently mentioned omissions included information about the children's early experiences, previous behavioural problems and medical conditions. Occasionally, adopters were not even clear about very basic details like why the child had come into care.

I'm still not clear why he was taken away from his mother really and he has a scar on his leg which was apparently caused by his eczema, but it goes all the way around his leg so I'm not really sure what caused it and you want to know these things because they will ask you.

Some adopters had received additional information only verbally but wanted it in writing so that they could refer to it later. With hindsight though, many adopters acknowledged that they had not really understood the full implications of the information they had received. This is not surprising since information was often given during the busy introductory period when they were trying to build a relationship and prepare for the child's arrival.

Over half (54 per cent) felt that further training from appropriately qualified professions would have been helpful at that time or shortly after the child had joined them. Adoption preparation had used case studies and seemed abstract. Adopters wanted specific help in understanding the meaning of their own child's history and experiences.

We needed to be more aware of the impact of her kind of background on a three-and-a-half year old girl. I knew quite a lot about the history, but nobody explained to me the implications of that. It's a classic catch 22 situation, you don't know what you don't know until it happens.

Meetings with foster carers gave adopters the opportunity to gain a more realistic picture of the child and in some cases allowed relationships to develop over a longer period.

We've got a brilliant relationship with the foster carer and she was extremely supportive of us adopting Darlene and prepared her really well to meet us. We see her on average about once every three months and she's been away with us for weekends. Really, Darlene looks at her like a grandmother, you know, an adopted grandmother. There is a very strong relationship between the three of us, not just Darlene.

Moving in
The adopters' predominant feelings were ones of excitement and anticipation. Ninety per cent of adoptive mothers and 95 per cent of adoptive fathers were thrilled that the placement was going ahead. Some adopters had remained enthusiastic and unconcerned throughout the

matching and introductory period and had just wanted the children to move in as soon as possible.

You are so blinkered. You think it's going to work. You think you are going to pour your love into these children and they are going to love you back without any problems at all.

Moving-in day was frequently a very emotional time for both the children and their new families and many adopters recalled it poignantly.

When I think of them I always think of when they were walking up the garden path the first day they came to live with us. He had a pair of black daps on and no socks and shorts that were dirty and she had on these black patent shoes and these grey socks, filthy dirty socks, and this blue check dress with this awful cardigan and they were their best clothes, they were their only *clothes. That's the image that always comes into my head, when they were walking down the path with their black carrier bags the day they came to live with us.*

In the majority of cases, good planning enabled the move to occur smoothly. However, in a few cases where foster carers were antagonistic either to the adoption plan or to the adoptive parents, the move was fraught. The role of foster carers was perceived by adopters as crucial in getting the placement off to a good start.

We didn't have a very easy time with Amanda's foster carers. They'd been told they could adopt her, but then the team leader had decided that she should be adopted out of county so that fell through. The foster mother cried throughout the whole interview that we had with them, it made us feel as though we were doing something wrong and the fort-night during which we got to know Amanda was very stressful. Then, on the day that she was to move in with us, we were advised just to go to her foster home and take her, because of how upset the foster mother would be, and that was awful because we felt as though we were snatching her. We just went in, took her and left. It was really horrible. It was very difficult for Amanda because of the emotional tie she had with the foster mother. I certainly think that she resented the fact that we took her away from the foster carer.

Foster carer adoptions

Foster carers chose to adopt because the child was already part of their family and relationships were strong. When the idea of adoption was raised, it seemed natural for them to pursue it. But most broached the idea with the child's social worker themselves, with a mixed response. Over half of the social workers (54 per cent) were supportive of the idea from the outset but the remainder either had mixed feelings about it (23 per cent) or were perceived as being opposed to it (23 per cent), often because it would mean losing a fostering placement. Occasionally, however, the social worker's persuasion had been the main impetus for the foster carers to proceed because no other adopters came forward. We were also aware of one case (not interviewed) where the family had wanted to adopt the younger of two siblings placed with them, but were told that the two came as a package or not at all and so reluctantly also adopted the older child.

> *His parents rang and asked if they could come to see us. They basically begged us to adopt him because they knew they couldn't have him back and they wanted us to have him. The pressure was awful because it wasn't really what I wanted . . . and I wasn't sure if I could cope, but we'd had him so long I didn't know if we could live with ourselves saying goodbye to him.*

Nevertheless, 86 per cent of the foster mothers and 92 per cent of foster fathers, were happy that the adoption was going ahead. Most felt at the time that they were making an informed decision, based on a good knowledge of the child and his or her history. Surprisingly though, with hindsight, 43 per cent of foster carer adopters felt that there were significant omissions in the information they had about the child and a further 28 per cent felt that it had been insufficiently detailed.

The adopted children

How representative is our sample?

It is useful briefly to check how our sample of children compare with those adopted nationally. These data are given in Table 7.2 and compare our sample with data from roughly the same period. There are some differences in these data, although it seems likely that these arise mostly because our sample excludes those with best interests decisions under the age of three.

The proportion of boys and girls is comparable. Boys are slightly underrepresented in both. Boys form 52 per cent of our complete sample and 53 per cent of children in care nationally. Minority ethnic children were underrepresented in our adopted sample. There were ten minority ethnic children in the full sample (8 per cent) but only half of these were matched with adopters. Two disrupted during introductions, one before the adoption order and one afterwards. Thus, only one of the adopted minority ethnic children was still in their adoptive placement at follow-up.

Table 7.2
Characteristics of the adopted children

	Sample children (n = 80)	*National data (Department of Health, 2002)*
Gender	52% boys	53% boys
Minority ethnic children	1%	10%*
Time in care before Adoption order	Mean 4 years 9 months	Mean 2 years 10 months
Time from best interests to matching	Mean 6 months	Mean 7 months
Age at placement **	Mean 4 years 3 months	Mean 3 years 2 months
From matching to placement	Mean 1 month	Mean 1 month
Age adopted	Mean 7 years 5 months	Mean 4 years 5 months
Foster carer adoptions	21%	16%

*Ivaldi, 2000
** Mean age at adoptive placement (for foster carers date of matching) was five years six months.

There are differences in the children's ages at the different stages of the adoption process. On average, the children in our sample were looked after longer, were only just over a year older at placement than the current national norm, but three years older on average by the time they were adopted. This partly reflects the older age of the children at approval, but also reflects recent changes in adoption practice.

Characteristics of the adopted children by placement type

There were marked, although not statistically significant, differences in the characteristics of the children adopted by foster carers, kin or strangers as shown in Table 7.3. Stranger adopters were more likely to adopt boys (59 per cent) than girls (41 per cent) but the reverse was true for kin adopters (who in this study only adopted girls) and foster carer adopters. These results echo recent Department of Health findings (2002), which show that foster carers adopt more girls (55 per cent) than boys.

Department of Health statistics also showed that children adopted by their foster carers were older than children adopted by strangers (average age for a foster carer adoption six years five months, for other adoptions four years). These findings were not repeated in this study of non-infant adoptions, but the five children adopted by kin were older than the other children. Two of these children also had fewer special needs.

Interestingly, children who had suffered multiple forms of abuse and who had more special needs were more likely to be placed for adoption with stranger adopters who already had children than with childless stranger adopters or foster carer adopters. This may be because practitioners, at that time, tended to place more difficult children with experienced parents. Unfortunately, we were not able to ascertain the children's views about the placement process or final placement outcome.

The children from approval to placement

At the same time that the adopters were being trained and assessed, many of the children knew that they were soon going to have a new "forever family" and were waiting to meet them. In this section we look at the experiences of these children from the time they were approved for adoption until they moved to their new homes, typically a period of around six months (range between four weeks and just over four years).

For the majority of the 80 children, this period was a time of relative stability, with only nine children (11 per cent) experiencing further

Table 7.3

Characteristics of the adopted children by placement type

	Children adopted by foster carers (n = 17)	Children adopted by kin (n = 5)	Children adopted by strangers without children (n = 45)	Children adopted by strangers with children (n = 13)
Gender	8 boys (47%) 9 girls (53%)	5 girls (100%)	25 boys (56%) 20 girls (44%)	9 boys (69%) 4 girls (31%)
Time in care prior to adoption order	Mean 5 years 5 months	Mean 6 years 3 months	Mean 4 years 4 months	Mean 4 years 11 months
Age at adoptive placement*	Mean 5 years 0 months	Mean 7 years 4 months	Mean 5 years 3 months	Mean 6 years 4 months
Age adopted	Mean 7 years 5 months	Mean 9 years 1 months	Mean 7 years 1 months	Mean 7 years 11 months
Extent of abuse	Mean 1.9	Mean 1.8	Mean 1.7	Mean 2.1
Number of special needs	Mean 3.4	Mean 2.6	Mean 3.2	Mean 4.0

* For foster carer adopters this is the same as the matching date.

placement moves. Six of these were disrupted foster placements, mostly because their carers were finding their behaviour difficult to manage, but three children were subject to planned moves. These three children were part of a sibling group who were unsuccessfully promoted for adoption together. The foster carers adopted one child and the others were moved to different placements.

There was evidence in case files to suggest that nine children (11 per cent) had been abused by foster carers during this time. Six were rejected or emotionally abused and three were over-chastised or physically abused. Some of the children only disclosed this once safely in their adoptive homes.

> *We didn't like the foster carers they were with and we later found out that they had mistreated the children. One day David had wet his trousers and so I said to him, 'Go on then, jump in the shower' and a while later I found him standing in the shower fully clothed, heart-broken. He said, 'Are you going to go and make me stand outside now?' Apparently that's what his foster carers had made him do if he wet his pants – get in the shower fully clothed and then stand outside until his clothes were dry* (adopter cries). *They were treated worse there than by their own parents.*

Contact

The 80 children had been in care on average two years three months by the time of the best-interests decision (range four months to seven years). Two children experienced the drug- or alcohol-related deaths of their parents between the AIBI and placement. Both of these children were referred to CAMHS and received therapy to help them grieve for the loss of their parents, but no such interventions were provided for the children whose losses were not so obvious.

Approximately a third were still having direct contact with their parents. Contact had often dwindled because of SSD planning or because parents had failed to turn up for visits, been imprisoned or disappeared from the area. Even where contact was ongoing, the frequency usually reduced once the adoption decision had been made. Often all direct contact ceased either shortly before or shortly after the children moved into their adoptive homes. There were a few descriptions on file of emotional "goodbye" meetings but the detailed content of the majority of these important final meetings went unrecorded. Sometimes the sense on file was that the termination of difficult and distressing contact had come as a relief to the social workers, children or their foster carers.

Summary: the adopted children and their families

1 The characteristics of the adoptive placements

- The 80 children were adopted into 66 families. Half (46 per cent) were placed on their own and a third separate from their siblings (36 per cent). Just over a quarter were adopted by foster carers or kin (21 per cent and 6 per cent respectively) and the remainder by strangers.
- Children adopted by foster carers were usually adopted alone (73 per cent) into non-professional families (73 per cent) where there were already children (88 per cent). They were more likely to be girls (53 per cent compared with 41 per cent for stranger adoptions).
- Stranger adopters were not a homogenous group. Around a quarter already had children (28 per cent). Older children with complex abuse histories and more special needs were generally placed singly into these families.
- Childless stranger adopters tended to be slightly younger, to be professionals (68 per cent), to have been together for less time and to adopt sibling groups of younger children with fewer special needs (59 per cent).

2 The adopters' experiences prior to placement

- Around 90 per cent of the childless stranger adopters and half of the stranger adopters who already had children were motivated to adopt by primary or secondary infertility.
- All of the stranger adopters but only a quarter (23 per cent) of the foster carer adopters attended adoption preparation groups. With hindsight, 60 per cent thought that, although good, these had been inadequate. Birth children received little preparation.
- When matched, 60 per cent of stranger adopters felt the child was "right" from the outset. The remainder were disappointed, often because of the child's age. A competitive and pressured environment

sometimes influenced adopters' decisions to proceed with the placement.

- Contact plans caused adopters the most concern, followed by the children's emotional behavioural difficulties, sexualised behaviour and learning difficulties. Fifty-four per cent would have valued professional advice on the implications of these issues. Most did not receive this and subsequently felt inadequately informed (58 per cent).
- Some said that the introductory period was very short and did not really give them time to take in lots of information about the children, build relationships with them and prepare for their arrival.
- The predominant emotion before the children moved in was excitement, but 28 per cent of adopters admitted they were apprehensive. The support of foster carers was very important for the children's successful transition from foster care to adoption.

3 The children's experiences prior to placement

- The children had been in care on average two years three months when approved for adoption. A third had face-to-face contact with birth parents.
- Over half of the children (55 per cent) were linked through local SSDs without promotion. These children were younger, had suffered fewer forms of abuse and had fewer special needs. Those with learning difficulties were especially hard to place.
- SSDs typically considered between two and four prospective families and agreed a link within six months. Over three-quarters of the children were matched within a year.
- Some children were subject to delay because of poor social work practice, because they themselves were not ready for adoption or because they experienced a disruption during the introductions before they went on to be successfully placed.

8 Life in the adoptive family in the first year

In this chapter we look at what happened when the children moved in and the changes the adoptive parents experienced in their lives and circumstances in the first year of placement. Twenty-four of the fathers and 53 mothers were interviewed. Adopters were asked to recall in detail what happened during the first year, to summarise the intervening years and to recount family life and the children's development in the 12 months before the interview. The follow-up data are given in the next chapter.

The adopters' experiences in the first year

The first days and weeks after the children moved in were a rollercoaster of events and emotions. Adopters, especially those who were childless, were thrilled that 'it was finally happening' and derived great pleasure from just having the children in their homes and introducing them to new experiences.

> *They were a joy to be around, very happy, bright, cheerful. It was just great seeing the smiles on their faces and seeing them extremely happy and settled . . .*

However, adopters also remembered being extremely tired as the reality of parenting hit them, especially those adopting sibling groups. Very few adopters (six) had a "honeymoon" period as children were challenging from very early on and adopters often felt ill-prepared and out of their depth. Conduct problems, attachment difficulties and sexualised behaviours caused the most concern.

> *She would scream and scream and throw herself down on the floor and she'd keep that up for ages, sometimes several hours, when she was inconsolable. It was incredibly difficult.*

> *Kelly was frightening for me* (dad)*, she kissed me with tongues, she used to do things in the bath.*

However, in spite of difficulties, the majority of mothers (63 per cent) and fathers (73 per cent) felt they were becoming close to the child and that relationships were developing.

Case summary: The pressures on new adopters

Mary and Tom were desperate to adopt. Mary saw her two girls Jenny and Kate in *Be My Parent* and fell in love with them at first sight. Her social worker found out about the children and recommended that Mary 'did not touch them with a barge pole'. She told Mary that there were easier children out there. Mary was determined, however, to have the two girls. The worse their story got the more she felt she could make it all better and the more she committed to them and so the girls moved in. Very quickly all was not well. The girls exhibited sexualised behaviour and unpredictable outbursts from day one. Mary described days when she dreaded getting up because she feared she could not make it through another day. She stopped going out and frequently burst into tears. Both Tom and the social worker were extremely concerned about her and eventually encouraged her to go to see her GP who prescribed Prozac.

Impact on work, lifestyle, income and expenditure

Coming to terms with being an adoptive parent was rarely the only adjustment adopters had to make. There were major impacts on their lifestyles as well.

Work: Adopters thought that the social workers wanted them to give up work or reduce their hours, in order to give their time and energy to the children. Consequently, 48 per cent of the adoptive mothers and 10 per cent of adoptive fathers did so. This was most common among childless female stranger adopters, 70 per cent of whom stopped work compared with only 29 per cent of those who already had children.[1] Although these

---

[1] $\chi^2 = 8.6$, $df = 1$, $p<0.05$

mothers adopted somewhat younger children, three-quarters were old enough to have started school.

Table 8.1
Impact on work and lifestyle

	Stopped work or reduced hours		Much-reduced leisure activities	
	Female adopters	*Male adopters*	*Female adopters*	*Male adopters*
Childless adopters (n = 28)	70%	11%	79%	58%
Adopters with children (n = 26)	29%	9%	46%	48%

Lifestyle: Leisure activities were also affected. Seventy-nine per cent of these women stopped most or all of their activities to be with the children.

> *Lifestyle, I didn't have one! There wasn't time to have a bath and shave my legs let alone do anything else. I had to give up the veggie plot in the garden . . . and nights out and little handbags – they were gone.*

Many of those who already had children also found that activities were squeezed out after the adoption, but not as often as the childless stranger adopters.[2] Partners generally had fewer lifestyle changes. Only 11 per cent of the childless male adopters and nine per cent of those with children altered their work patterns. The childless male adopters also dropped fewer of their leisure activities than their partners, but still over half reported that these had been considerably curtailed. Interestingly, this differential impact was not the case for those who already had children, where a similar proportion of mothers and the fathers gave up activities to help with the childcare.

> *Joanne was so much more demanding than our own daughter so my husband did get involved and he enjoyed it. I think he realised what he'd missed out on . . . We did more things as a family, it was nice.*

---

[2] $\chi^2 = 6.07$, $df = 1$, $p < 0.05$

On the other hand, many adopters recounted new pleasures like going to the zoo or the beach. Not surprisingly, those without children were more likely to describe these than their counterparts with children – 64 per cent and 23 per cent respectively for female adopters[3] and 58 per cent and 36 per cent respectively for male adopters.[4] It was also noticeable that fathers who helped with the children described enjoying their role. At the other extreme, there were three children to whom neither parent described being close in the first year.

Income: Families (65 per cent) who changed their work patterns generally experienced a decrease in their income, even after any allowances they received. In addition, many were faced with substantial expenditure. Only a quarter of adopters (24 per cent) managed to maintain their prior standard of living, and this was only possible for a third of them because of an allowance. Nearly half of the families (45 per cent) struggled financially or had to be more careful about money. A fifth (21 per cent) had built up an overdraft, got into debt or gone without essential items. Three-quarters of these (77 per cent) had been in receipt of an adoption or fostering allowance. Other families relied heavily on their savings.

Relatively quickly after having him we had virtually no savings and within two years any savings we'd had were completely gone. We haven't got anything to fall back on any more and that isn't a very nice feeling.

Some relied on the generosity of others in order to make ends meet.

We were really struggling . . . We would have got into debt but we were part of a church that was very generous. Someone took over paying our heating bills so that we could have it on 24 hours a day (as adopted child was very ill). *I don't know how we would have heated the house otherwise. Other people helped pay the tax on the car.*

Foster carer adopters were more likely than stranger adopters to struggle financially (69 per cent compared with 40 per cent), although this difference was not statistically significant.

---

[3] $\chi^2 = 15.78$, $df = 1$, $p < 0.001$
[4] $\chi^2 = 8.35$, $df = 1$, $p < 0.01$

Expenditure: The great majority (80 per cent) of families experienced a substantial increase in expenditure because of the adoption. They were often surprised by the cost of equipping the children with the things they needed. Adopters complained that children came with few clothes. In some cases, previous foster carers had held on to the children's clothes or toys for their next foster children.

> *They had nothing when they came, not even a pair of pyjamas. We had to kit them out completely really.*

Adopters often also talked about their desire to give generously to the children to compensate for their difficult early experiences or to 'get them up to the same level' as other children.

> *Randall was very behind in his play and development so I can remember going to the Early Learning Centre to buy lots of things to help him with that. I remember spending £150 one day just like that.*

Parents spent on average £732 in the first year on furniture, clothes, toys, equipment and other "set-up" essentials, regardless of whether they already had children. Almost half spent £1,000 or more on these items. This made quite a big hole in savings and contributed to financial strains from the outset. In addition, for 67 per cent of adopters, the children's special needs meant expenditure on activities, equipment or services. Some had to make extensive adaptations to their homes or buy bigger cars simply to accommodate the children.

> *Then once we'd had the building work done it was very costly re-decorating. We had to re-carpet the hall and the bedroom, altogether it was about £2,000. We also had to upgrade the car to get her wheelchair in it, but we got no financial support for that because Suzie couldn't have a mobility allowance until she was five. So that cost us about £4,000.*

A few (seven families), seeing that their children were not coping in main-stream schools, bought private educational services. More discovered there were long waiting lists for services such as speech therapy so they dug deep to purchase these privately. Altogether, one in eight adopters purchased private services for their children during the first year of placement. There were many more (41 per cent) who were not able to afford these and worried that their child's development might have suffered as a consequence.

There was an 18-month waiting list for speech therapy, but to go privately was £50 an hour.

Adopters spent up to £8,400 on special needs equipment, activities or services during the first year of the adoptive placement. Foster carer adopters spent noticeably less on average than stranger adopters (£190 compared with £554) and, not surprisingly, childless stranger adopters spent more than their counterparts with children (£632 and £332 respectively). All had spent around the same amount on further specific purchases to enhance their children's development (on average £848).

For many adopters the expenditure did not stop there. Some children were destructive or started stealing and parents found themselves footing the bill for damaged or stolen goods. Other children wet or soiled themselves so regularly that the costs of nappies and bedding rapidly escalated. Contact could also be costly, especially where separated siblings lived in different parts of the country.

They are all split up, they are all over 100 miles away, but the onus is always on us to make the arrangements and do all the travelling because foster carers are paid for what they do and they won't do it any more.

Paying nursery fees or childminder fees could also be expensive.

We'd been told by social services that she had to go to nursery, but the only place we could get was private and so we ended up spending £55 a week on private nursery fees . . . I would rather have had her at home with me.

Thus, on top of routine expenditure on food and clothes and toys, most adopters incurred numerous additional costs totalling on average £1,500. One family spent almost £10,000 and one in ten spent over £3,000. A quarter of adopters would have liked help with these expenses. These costs have not been adjusted to today's prices and so reflect approximate costs on average seven years ago. They are also very probably underestimates, as adopters had difficulty remembering expenditure accurately.

Figure 8.1
Average first year stranger adopter expenditure using 1997 prices

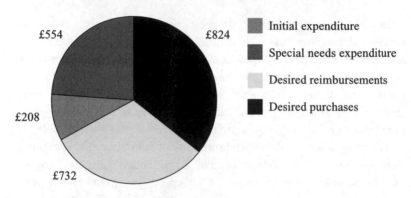

Impact on family life and relationships

As adopters' time and energies became focused on the child, family life and other relationships were affected.

Impact on the couple's relationship: Many of the 49 couples interviewed described their relationships as very strong when the adoption began, especially where they had already withstood the impact of infertility. Lifestyle changes and the demands of adoptive parenting, however, often proved stressful and 45 per cent experienced moderate or major tensions in their relationships during the early part of the placement. Couples described having no time or energy left for each other or arguing over how to handle situations.

We had frequent arguments about our different styles. I thought he was leaving everything to me, he thought I was being over controlling, whereas we hadn't had those tensions over our own child who was a very manageable child.

One couple separated shortly after the child was placed.

I was totally absorbed with Martin and couldn't even see that it was affecting other people at the time. Every bit of energy, every bit of emotion I had was going into building up my relationship with Martin. That meant that Cliff and I lost a lot in our relationship. We didn't have any time for each other because most conversations, everything we did just revolved around Martin.

Difficulties were more common among the childless stranger adopters (54 per cent), but several stranger adopters with children (36 per cent) and foster carer adopters (33 per cent) also reported tensions. Moderate tensions might be expected given the demands of "special needs" adoption, but one in five couples thought they had experienced major problems, for example, because the child got on well with one parent but not the other or had greater learning difficulties than had been expected. Conversely, almost a third of all couples (33 per cent) felt that their relationship had been strong to start with and remained so during the first year of the placement, and nearly a quarter felt that the adoptive experience had brought them closer together.

Foster carer adopters were the least likely to feel that their relationship had been enhanced by adopting (25 per cent) but were also the least likely to report that it had become strained. Stranger adopters who already had children (45 per cent) were the most likely to report that their relationship had strengthened after the adoption. These were the families where the fathers had become more involved in family activities.

Impact on children already in the household: Almost half (43 per cent) of the interviewed families already had either birth, fostered or adopted children in the household. These children were reported by their parents to have reacted to the adoption in a variety of ways. Some (17 per cent) were thrilled that they had finally got the brother or sister they had always wanted and became close straight away.

When she first came he was really excited, he was telling all his friends, 'It's my new sister, it's my new sister!'.

Other children (22 per cent) either disliked their new adopted sibling (especially if they had learning difficulties or conduct problems) or felt pushed out. Three children were also very unhappy that their birth sibling was joining them in their own adoptive family.

Caroline was furious. It seemed like her bubble had burst. She had had two adoring parents and suddenly there was an intruder who got some attention.

Not surprisingly, the children in stranger adoptions were more likely to be distressed than those in foster adoptions (47 per cent versus 17 per cent). Only a third were reported by adopters to be completely happy compared with half of the children of foster adopters.

The response of the children was often critical to the success of the placement. Some adoptive parents spoke highly of their children's endeavours to welcome their new sibling.

Early on there was an incident at school when Anthony got involved and defended Simon. I picked him up about it. But he said, 'Simon's my brother,' and that's the way it's been.

None of the adopters, however, suggested that their children's reactions prompted them to question at the start their decision to proceed with the adoption.

Impact on wider family: Seventy-four per cent of extended family members were supportive of the plans to adopt. Some (16 per cent), however, changed their minds when confronted with a difficult or disruptive child and others (47 per cent) had mixed feelings about the legalising of the adoption.

It is very difficult to take a child into your family who has behavioural or emotional problems because they can be starkly different to other children and that can be difficult for people to understand. My mother-in-law certainly found Megan difficult and took offence at her really. She couldn't tolerate her behaviour, especially because a lot of it was aimed at Joe and he was her son.

Grandparents were protective of their own children (i.e. the adopters) and could take a considerable amount of time to come to terms with the fact that adopted children had difficulties. Aunts and uncles were sometimes perturbed that their children had been earmarked as playmates. Interestingly, the kin of foster carer adopters (28 per cent) were more likely to respond negatively to the adoption than stranger adopters' wider family

(12 per cent), which seemed to be because they already knew the children and were concerned about what the adopters were taking on.

My mother and brother were really anti us adopting Gareth . . . (He) was not invited to my mother's 80th birthday, all the rest of the kids were, but not him. But I had a really supportive aunt and she just said, 'we'll take him,' so we all went. My brother and his wife just walked out, but time heals and my brother and I have mended our relationship now.

Half of the adoptive families' extended families did go on to develop very good relationships with the children during the first year and were often essential sources of support for the adopters.

Impact on friends and neighbours: Some friends could be very supportive and encouraging while others appeared rejecting. The friendships of foster carer adopters were the most robust, with only eight per cent adversely affected by the adoption, compared with 20 per cent for the stranger adopters. Friendships could suffer because adopters were consumed with their new childcare activities or because friends were dismayed by the children's behaviour.

Other friendships, especially those with neighbours, strengthened or blossomed. This had more impact on the stranger adopters, many of whom felt that they fitted in much better with their friends and neighbours once they too had children.

We suddenly discovered that we'd got neighbours! Before, we had lived here for ten years and knew hardly any of our neighbours because they'd all got kids, then we knew nearly all of them!

Parent–child relationships: During the first year, adopters strove to establish relationships with the children, to encourage their development and to understand their behaviour. This was often not easy. Learning difficulties, conduct problems, rejection of the adopters and phoniness were the most often cited obstacles. Adoptive mothers reported that they, rather than their partners, had found it significantly harder to develop a relationship with older children.[5]

---

[5] $F(1, 63) = 11.17$, $p < .001$

You are emotionally all up in the air because the feelings are not what you expected them to be. I was absolutely staggered at how angry I felt a lot of the time. I didn't really know what it was about, but there was a lot of anger and a lot of frustration. I found it very hard to love Tamsin and I was angry with myself because of it and angry with my friends who said that you can feel that way about your own children. I could care for her, but I don't think I actually liked her a great deal and I don't think she liked me a great deal in the beginning either. As an intelligent person I don't know why it didn't dawn on me before, that you can't expect to say to a child that this is going to be your forever family and expect them just to be able to give back all the love that you are giving to them.

Importantly, the majority of adopters (74 per cent) felt they had grown closer to the children over the year, and described really enjoying their company. Indeed, 45 per cent said that by the end of the year they felt as close as they could possibly be.

There was one noteworthy exception to this generally positive picture (Table 8.2). Fewer mothers who already had their own children felt attached to the children than those without children.[6] They were less likely to enjoy the child's company and less likely to feel that the children were close to them by the end of the year than their partners or the childless stranger adopters.

Table 8.2
Mother's accounts of closeness in the parent–child relationship

At end of first year:	Stranger adopters with children n = 9		Childless stranger adopters n = 31	
	Mothers	*Fathers*	*Mothers*	*Fathers*
Parent close to child	46%	73%	81%	80%
Parent enjoys child's company	54%	55%	81%	77%
Child close to parent	38%	64%	76%	77%

[6] $\chi^2 = 7.36$, $df = 1$, $p < 0.05$

These differences, as described by the mothers and fathers who were interviewed, were evident in the extent of conflict and confiding between the parents and the children (Table 8.3). Children placed into established families were more likely to have conflicted parent–child relationships and less likely to confide in their parents or to disclose their prior abuse than those placed into childless families. However, none of the differences was statistically significant.

Table 8.3

Mother's accounts of conflict and confiding in the parent–child relationship

At end of first year:	*Stranger adopters with children n = 9*	*Childless stranger adopters n = 31*
Child confides in parents	8%	32%
Child discloses to parents	25%	35%
Conflict between parents and child	77%	46%

Not surprisingly, foster carer adopters tended to feel closest to the children at the start of the adoptive placement (86 per cent of mothers and 83 per cent of fathers) and to maintain these levels of closeness throughout the year. They also largely felt that the children felt positively towards them (64 per cent of mothers and 67 per cent of fathers). On the whole, they enjoyed the children's company (71 per cent of mothers and 75 per cent of fathers), although some of the novelty had worn off by the end of the first year. They described the least conflict in their relationships with the children (36 per cent) but the most confiding (46 per cent) and disclosure (42 per cent).

Children may have felt more able to disclose their previous traumatic experiences to these adopters because they had lived with them for longer and established trust or because the trained foster carer adopters were comfortable with hearing what they had to say. Some stranger adopters, on the other hand, found it very hard to listen to the abuse the children had suffered.

There was a stage when Steven started coming out with some stuff that very much affected me. He started talking about his abuse and that was very difficult. When social services tell you about it before they come to you it's in the abstract and you think 'oh that's awful', but when it's your son and they start talking to you it's painful, very painful.

Others were confused that, despite their traumatic early experiences, some of the children (20 per cent) had significant loyalties to one or other of their birth parents. Adoptive parents could feel threatened by the child's continuing affection for the birth mother. For some adoptive fathers, conflict with birth fathers over the patriarchal role was very evident.

She (child) *accepted that mum was unreliable and that was the way she was, it was dad that was the problem. Daddy was wonderful, we were just dirt.*

At the end of the first year, adoptive fathers were significantly less likely to feel close to children who had face-to-face contact with birth mothers.[7] This remained significant even after adjusting for the effect of age at placement on adoptive mothers' closeness to the child.[8]

Birth family contact in the first year

Face-to-face contact

Twenty children (31 per cent) had face-to-face contact with one or both of their birth parents in the first year, half unsupervised by SSDs. Fourteen per cent had face-to-face contact with only their birth mother, 12 per cent with both birth parents and five per cent with their birth father only. A much larger number (90 per cent) had face-to-face contact with birth siblings, most (75 per cent) supervised just by the adopters. A third of the children (34 per cent) also had direct contact with their grandparents or another birth relative, again mostly (75 per cent) unsupervised.

Contact was most common for children in established families (54 per cent), less likely for foster carer adoptions (36 per cent), and least for those with childless adopters (22 per cent). Though striking, these differences were not statistically significant and were not echoed in sibling or

---

[7] $\chi^2 = 17.065, df=9, p<0.048$
[8] $\chi^2 = 5.9, df = 1, p < 0.05.$

birth relative contact. Children placed in established families were older and it may have been that contact patterns were more firmly established or there may have been more support for contact from these families.

At the start, some adopters thought that they had been led to believe that contact arrangements were non-negotiable. It was only after discussions with other adopters or with solicitors they discovered that they could alter arrangements. Others thought that birth parents were trying to buy affection or provide evidence of their parenting capacity for the courts by bringing extravagant presents to contact visits.

He would go to dad with a list in his pocket of things we wouldn't let him have and his dad would buy it. It would cause a lot of problems. Social services just said that dad could spend what he liked. He could spend £50 if he liked and we had to accept it, as he was the parent. Never mind the effect it was having on us.

Only two adoptive families reported that the children became very distressed during contact visits. However, not all visits were supervised.

The birth father asked Martin where he lived and said he'd go looking for him in every school and after that it was awful. We had to make different arrangements for picking him up from school because we didn't want him to be alone in the playground and I had to take him everywhere – even just down the road. After that, contact was supervised until it stopped altogether.

Most adopters (60 per cent) were supportive of contact, with adoptive mothers more so than adoptive fathers (59 per cent v 36 per cent).

With mum he would come back very happy and show us things he'd got, it would be very positive.

It was the build up to and after-effects of contact that bothered adopters most. Adopters reported that 45 per cent of the children were more "wound up" and anxious in the weeks preceding contact with birth parents.

I'm totally for contact, but it is quite exhausting because there is a lot to do, all the arranging and then dealing with the aftermath in his emotions and then worrying about the emblem on his school jumper and all sorts of things that make it quite complicated.

This would show itself in more wet beds, bad dreams and generally more difficult behaviour. There were also knock-on effects in the weeks after contact, with some families (30 per cent) reporting that the children took several weeks to settle down again.

> *Roger frequently got into trouble at school after a contact, it unsettled him. We began to prepare ourselves for difficulties afterwards and in the end we moved it to the school holidays.*

Only 10 per cent of adopters were happy with the guidance and support they received from their social workers. Indeed, the vast majority (90 per cent) had received no guidance at all. During the first year many made contact arrangements more manageable for themselves by changing the timing and frequency of visits. By the end of the first year, most (75 per cent) of the face-to-face contact with birth parents had occurred only once or twice. Three children were still seeing their birth parent(s) three or four times a year and two children continued to see their mothers fortnightly.

Sibling contact was, on the whole, well received both by the adopters (67 per cent) and the children, who were thought to have largely enjoyed it.

> *When he saw him they'd just have a great time playing, they were like two peas in a pod, it was lovely to see.*

However, 22 per cent of children were reported as showing distress as a consequence of contact with siblings. Adopters thought this was because children were upset at being separated from siblings or because knowing that a sibling remained in foster care could cause feelings of guilt and sorrow.

> *He'd always be very quiet and withdrawn for a couple of days after the contact because of the disappointment of not being with his brother.*

Adopters (90 per cent) generally believed that the children should maintain links with their birth siblings, but some found that doing this could, in reality, be quite an undertaking, especially if children lived a long way apart or if their parents or carers were not supportive of contact.

I just don't know what the problem with that woman (sibling's adoptive mother) is. To not even let Caroline send letters and cards. Robert has a real longing for Caroline. Why not let her write letters?

Adopters were also largely positive (76 per cent) about contact with other birth relatives.

They (the grandparents) are very nice people. They obviously cared a lot about Carrie and always gave us a nice lunch and we reciprocated.

However, 44 per cent of children were described as being distressed before and after these visits. Adopters thought this might be due to unhappiness about separation or reminders of the past. For three children, there were concerns that grandparents were exposing the children to abusive situations.

He saw his gran about once every three weeks, she used to come and take him out, but she was meant to take him to the park or somewhere, but we found out that she was taking him to a house so the social worker stopped that.

Letterbox contact in the first year

Just over half of the children (56 per cent) had letterbox contact with one or more members of their birth family. Some children were distressed by the content of letters they received.

His mother sent him a letter and a sweet shop as a present and the social worker just came around and gave it to him. I was quite cross about that because it was quite disturbing as it said stuff like his mum wanted him back. He was just getting settled . . . But he just said 'Rubbish, rubbish, my mummy loved me, rubbish' and 'I don't want to go back'.

Other children became upset if they didn't receive an expected card or letter, especially from their birth parents.

Birthdays are still a very painful time for him. It's painful if he does get something from them and painful if they don't send anything . . . I don't see the point, it's like keeping a wound open all the time, isn't it?

Indeed, very few adopters spoke positively about letterbox contact with birth parents in the first year, although this indirect contact with siblings was generally welcome. Adopters could resent the intrusion into their new family life and several commented that the children were often reluctant to write letters. Most (67 per cent) complained that they had received very little guidance about how to handle letterbox contact and said that deciding what might be identifying information when the letters were sent out or what wasn't appropriate in messages that came in could also be stressful.

Challenges and rewards: The great majority of adopters found the first year of the adoption very testing. This was especially true for the stranger adopters, 88 per cent of whom described it as moderately to extremely challenging, regardless of whether or not they already had children. Surprisingly, 61 per cent of foster carer adopters also felt this way even though the children were not new to their families.[9] For some, the adoptive task had proved much more stressful than they had anticipated and 40 per cent of both foster carer and stranger adopters described experiencing a period of anxiety or depression.[10]

For some, this occurred quite soon after the child was placed with them. For others, it developed when the child's behaviour showed no improvement. Some adopters consulted their GP and were prescribed medication (19 per cent of stranger adopters and 16 per cent of foster carer adopters) but several did not seek help because they did not want to admit they were struggling.

> *I only ever told social services about the serious things that Jade did, I wouldn't have told them how I was feeling or that my marriage was precarious.*

Female stranger adopters (49 per cent) were somewhat more likely to feel depressed and anxious than their partners (30 per cent), regardless of whether or not they already had children. Surprisingly, more male foster

---

[9] $\chi^2 = 4.51$, $df = 1$, $p < 0.05$

[10] Almost a fifth of the adopters had also experienced another significant event such as a bereavement or redundancy during the first year of the adoptive placement but these adopters were not more likely to have experienced feelings of anxiety or depression.

adopters (50 per cent) felt depressed or anxious than did their wives (31 per cent). These parents were dealing with particularly difficult children with ADHD or other conduct problems. Despite all these struggles, 60 per cent of the foster carer adopters and 74 per cent of the stranger adopters reported that the first year of the adoptive experience was rewarding.

It was brilliant being a family. Almost immediately there were rewards and they got more as time went on. There has to be, otherwise you wouldn't cope.

Summary of impacts and adopters' experiences in the first year

- Adopters experienced a rollercoaster of emotions from pleasure to exhaustion to anguish at the children's challenging behaviour. Only seven per cent did not experience difficulties. Most new parents, however, still felt close to the children.
- The adoption had a wide-ranging impact on the work patterns, leisure activities and relationships of adopters. Seventy-nine per cent of child-less female adopters stopped their leisure activities and 70 per cent left work. Women who already had children, and partners, also made adjustments but to a lesser extent.
- Changing work patterns and increasing expenditure had an impact on the income of many families. Almost half (44 per cent) found the year financially challenging and a fifth got into debt.
- Just over half (54 per cent) of the adopters experienced moderate to major relationship problems over the year. These arose particularly when adopters were parenting children with attachment or learning difficulties. The marital relationship of childless stranger adopters was the most vulnerable to difficulties.
- Almost half (47 per cent) of the birth children in adoptive families also found the first year difficult, compared with 17 per cent of the children of foster carer adopters, especially when the adopted child had learning or behavioural difficulties. Little improvement was noted in the majority of these relationships over time.
- Most kin were initially supportive of the adoption (74 per cent) but

support halved when difficulties began to emerge. Kin of foster carer adopters were the most negative, while their friendships were the most robust.

- Most adopters felt close to the children at the end of the year, but mothers from established adoptive families with older children, with more special needs and higher levels of birth family contact, were the exception to this. They also described less confiding and more conflicted relationships with the children.
- A third of the children were having face-to-face contact with one or both birth parents during the year and 90 per cent with birth siblings. Adopters were more supportive of sibling contact than with birth parents.
- Few adopters had had any guidance on how to manage contact. Adoptive fathers were significantly less likely to feel close to children who were having direct contact with their birth mother.
- The year was described as very challenging by 88 per cent of stranger adopters and 61 per cent of foster carer adopters. Levels of anxiety and depression were quite high but, for most, the rewards outweighed the challenges. Fifteen per cent of parents described rewards without challenges. They tended to have adopted younger girls with fewer special needs.

9 Life in the adoptive family at the time of the follow-up

By the time of the follow-up in 2001/2 the children were between eight and 18 years of age (mean 13.5 years) and had been adopted for between two and ten years (mean seven years).

Crises and disruptions

In the years since placement, most (75 per cent) of the families had experienced some form of "crisis", often triggered by an event such as the child's exclusion from school or criminal activities. Not all of these crises threatened the stability of the placement but some did. These placements only survived through the perseverance of the adopters or by timely post-adoption support. Three placements disrupted just before or just after the follow-up interviews after three and ten years of placement when one of the children was eight and the others 14 and 17. Two young people were moved into supported accommodation and one into foster care. The adopters found their experiences extremely distressing.

> *The sense of failure and sense of guilt is amazing. To be told that you've got her to 16 and that she's not pregnant and has got her GCSEs doesn't really help.*

> *We didn't set out to be cruel, but in the end we said 'take him away'.*

There were no plans for the children to return to them and plans for continuing contact seemed vague. One family did not even know where the child had been placed.

There were also a few adoptions that had not broken down, but where the adopters were hanging on until the children came of age and could leave home.

> *We feel that we can't trust her in the house anymore. I've given up my part-time job so that I can be in and if she's around we find ourselves putting everything out of sight. This isn't our home any more while*

she's in it, which is why we've asked her to leave when she's 18. To be honest we can't wait until she's 18.

Impacts

Work and income: Adoption continued to affect the work patterns of some adopters, even after several years. A third of mothers (33 per cent) and a tenth of fathers (12 per cent), equally across the three groups, reported that they had been unable to return to work or had had to adapt their work patterns to continue to care for the child. For some foster carer adopters, this meant that they had had to give up fostering. Sometimes the child's ongoing medical or emotional needs made this necessary, but sometimes it was a consequence of school suspensions or exclusions.

Several families had forgone the second income they had anticipated once the children were older. Only 30 per cent were in receipt of an adoption allowance, even though over half (55 per cent) still had substantial additional expenditure. Forty-four per cent of the families were struggling financially or having to be careful about money. This was particularly true of the foster carer adopters (61 per cent of whom expressed concerns about money, compared with 38 per cent of stranger adopters). Many adopters had exhausted all of their savings and a quarter (26 per cent), equally across the three groups, had got into debt or had to go without essentials because of their financial circumstances. Some felt angry that they had to deal with financial worries on top of everything else and would have appreciated additional financial support.

Adoption expenditure: The range of additional expenses was striking.

There has just been a catalogue of things . . . She grew very rapidly in all directions so I needed to get new shoes and new clothes every couple of months. I brought a private tutor in for her at £15 an hour for a couple of years because she was very behind in everything and unable to learn. Then there were things, like bikes, that I bought her because they were good for her co-ordination and concentration. Then as she's got older . . . she has stolen money from me and my family, she has run up enormous phone bills every month, she has damaged a very expensive table with repair costs to the tune of £600, her carpet and bedding are wrecked and the list just goes on. It's been phenomenal.

Expenditure on private health and education services remained high, with almost a fifth of adopters purchasing private schooling, educational assessments, home tutors or music, art or play therapy in the year. These services had cost up to £11,500. As children got older their needs became more costly. This was in part because they wanted to be like their friends and have all the latest in designer fashions but many adopters also found themselves paying out large amounts of money because of their child's behaviour. Several young people had stolen from their families, from friends or shops, and adopters typically picked up the bill. Others were destructive and presented adopters with costly payments for damage.

> *He would just demolish everything, toys, beds, furniture, carpets, windows, curtain tracks. I was just a permanent repairman really and as soon as you got him something or fixed something it was broken again and so you had to go and get it again. It must have cost thousands, at least £5,000 I'd have thought, and that was just the basics.*

Surprisingly, several families were still paying large amounts because of their children's continuing problems with wetting or soiling. There was a host of other reasons as well.

> *He goes through four things of soap each week for his hands and he won't use a towel, he has to have paper towels. He also has to eat pre-packaged meals, he won't eat anything that is not wrapped up. It might sound like we are just pandering to him, but if we didn't do it he wouldn't eat at all. And all of that is quite expensive. I spend about £8 a week on soap for him and more on paper towels and about 20 odd pounds on ready meals that I wouldn't otherwise buy. I know it sounds silly, but it does all just add up.*

Half of the foster care adopters (50 per cent) and stranger adopters (56 per cent) said that they had spent up to £12,500 in the last year over and above what they considered to be normal child care expenses. The average amount for foster and stranger adopters was £2,217. Almost a quarter of these families felt that SSDs should have helped with this and a third had additional items or services that they would have liked to purchase if finances had not been restricted. Computers, to encourage educational attainment, were often high on the wish list, as were private tutors and therapists.

The couples' relationships: By the follow-up, one couple had separated and 43 per cent of adopters reported moderate or major tensions between themselves. One couple had separated. Often the strain was the result of years of unrelenting difficulties, but in some cases it was recent, precipitated by crises as the children entered adolescence.

Case study: Emma and Simon's story

Andrew made it clear from the beginning of the placement that he did not want Emma, his adoptive mother, to get close to him, while his relationship with Simon was quite solid from the start. This caused a great deal of strain in the marriage and even eight years later Andrew still had not shown any attachment to Emma. She had found this very difficult. Occasionally, if he wanted something, he would be nice to her but would then revert back to his usual behaviour. Simon did spend time with Andrew and enjoyed his company and this often left Emma feeling extremely isolated. She said that she rings the Samaritans when she needs to talk to someone who is not biased.

The majority (76 per cent) of the adopters who reported strain had also reported being been depressed or anxious. Both maternal and paternal depression were significantly correlated with problems in their relationships.[1] Unlike the first year when childless stranger adopters were the most likely to experience tensions, such difficulties were by now experienced equally across the three groups.

Conversely, over one-quarter of couples (28 per cent) felt that the adoptive experience had brought them closer together. Foster carer adopters were the least likely to feel adoption had enhanced their relationship (17 per cent compared with 35 per cent of the childless stranger adopters and 36 per cent of the stranger adopters with children), echoing the findings from the first year.

---

[1] Pearson correlation coefficient .37, $p<.01$ for mothers and Pearson correlation coefficient .46, $p<.001$ for fathers

Sibling relationships: Adopters had hoped that birth, already adopted or foster children would form good relationships with the adopted child. Adopters reported this was the case for 33 per cent of the children of stranger adopters and 14 per cent of the children of foster carer adopters. However, adopters also reported conflicts in sibling relationships; 40 per cent of the children of stranger adopters and 14 per cent of the children of foster carer adopters.

> *In the end she resented the fact he would go in her room when she were asleep and go through her drawers. When you can't even know that when you are asleep your room is safe, nothing was sacrosanct.*

Two-thirds of these "disliked" adopted children had learning difficulties. Birth children sometimes took on responsibilities for the adopted child and became concerned that they would always need to care for them.

> *Initially Jasmine was the spokesperson, if Samantha wanted to ask us something she didn't have the courage to ask us direct so she did it through Jasmine. Samantha would confide through Jasmine her worries. It was a big responsibility for a five-year-old. But over the years Jasmine has got less tolerant, not to do with Samantha being adopted, but because of the learning difficulties. She is more of an embarrassment with her friends. Jasmine has also asked whether she will have to look after Samantha when we die. This shocked us as she is still very young.*

The rest of the birth children either had mixed feelings about the adoption (43 per cent of the children of foster carer adopters and 22 per cent of the children of stranger adopters) or the parents thought that it had had no obvious impact (29 per cent of the children of foster carer adopters and 5 per cent of the children of stranger adopters).

Relationships with the wider family: The families of childless stranger adopters had grown to be more likely to view the adoption positively (39 per cent compared with 23 per cent of the kin of foster carer adopters and 15 per cent of the kin of established families). Relatives were often important supports for the adopters.

> *Our families were initially both quite critical, they thought we were*

being harder on Ben than on Josh, but now they've seen the behaviour
for themselves and have come to understand our difficulties and so
they are quite supportive and full of admiration for us. They just sing
our praises and say how lucky the boys are now.

As the children entered adolescence and more problem behaviours
emerged, kin were more likely to be adversely than favourably affected.
Many had mixed feelings about the adoption (42 per cent) and a sizeable
proportion (30 per cent) struggled to accept the child. They tended to
resent the impact the adoption had had on the adopters. Grandparents,
particularly, could find the situation difficult.

My mother hates Sonia. If she could take her out and sink her in the
nearest ocean she would and that's because of all the hurt she's caused
me. My whole family dislike Sonia intensely.

Problems between the couple were significantly associated with kin
negativity.[2] Where there were birth or placed children already in the
household, kin negativity was also significantly associated with sibling
conflict.[3]

Relationships with friends and neighbours: Many adopters made new
friendships since adopting (23 per cent of the foster adopters and 32 per
cent of the stranger adopters). Several adopters said that other adopters
they had met at support groups had become important sources of advice
and help.

The relationships of the adopters with friends and neighbours, especially those of foster adopters, were sometimes adversely affected. For
almost a quarter (23 per cent), some relationships had deteriorated and
adopters thought this was due to the child's conduct problems.[4]

One time he was babysitting the neighbour's child, he was very good
with him and because they weren't going to be back until late, they said
for him to stay overnight. They said all the usual things 'help yourself
to drinks' and all that, so he did! He had got into alcohol that year and

---

[2] $\chi^2 = 5.01$, $df = 1$, $p < 0.05$
[3] $\chi^2 = 6.95$, $df = 1$, $p < 0.05$
[4] $\chi^2 = 11.02$, $df = 1$, $p < 0.01$

he had most of the beers in their fridge! But it gets worse. He'd also had a few cigarettes out on the patio and then couldn't close the patio doors properly, but had promptly forgotten about it. The next day he remembered he'd left the door open and realised that they would be out, so he went over our back fence, into their house, took the rest of the beers and left the door open. We couldn't believe it. Everyone was very upset about the whole thing and it has completely destroyed our relationship with them.

Parent–child relationships: Given the difficult experiences many adopters had described, it was surprising that at follow-up the majority of adopters described feeling close to the children and enjoying their company (Table 9.1). There was no relationship between the child's age at interview and maternal or paternal feelings of closeness to the child, enjoyment of the child's company or child's closeness to parent, neither were there any differences between the three groups on any of these variables.

Table 9.1
Mothers' accounts of closeness in the parent–child relationship at follow-up

At follow-up:	Foster carer adopters n = 15		Childless stranger adopters n = 34		Stranger adopters with children n = 13	
	Mothers	Fathers	Mothers	Fathers	Mothers	Fathers
Parent close to child	86%	75%	65%	79%	62%	64%
Parent enjoys company	57%	67%	54%	68%	69%	73%
Child close to parent	71%	67%	70%	76%	92%	82%

Parent–child relationships thus appeared to have evened out since the first year, with group differences no longer evident. Foster carer adopters continued to feel close to the child but enjoyed the children's company less than they had in the first year. Stranger adoptive mothers with birth children showed a marked increase in feelings of closeness to the child and enjoyment of their company. They also saw the child as closer to them (an increase from 38 per cent to 92 per cent). However, mothers who had been childless showed a reduction in closeness. This suggests that the initial feelings of exhilaration had moderated over time. Only nine per cent of children were now thought to have loyalties or attachments to their birth family that were hindering their relationships with their adopters. Most adopters felt strongly about the children despite any difficulties they had experienced. Many could not imagine life without them.

I love him to bits now, I can't imagine him not being here now.

But, although adopters expressed love for their children, relationship difficulties persisted. Several acknowledged that there was still some distance to go and that they needed to persevere.

I feel close to him, but the heartache is that he isn't really close to anybody, he is just living in his own bleak world. He doesn't resist affection so much now, but he'll still only let you in so far, he's still not very trusting. And he's still not given of himself yet, he's ready to receive but not give.

Factors significantly hindering parental closeness to the child were the child's attachment problems[5] and defiance[6] and, for fathers, the child's conduct problems.[7]

The number of children who confided in their parents had increased across all three groups, especially among stranger adopters with children of their own. The adopters who reported increased closeness were also experiencing less conflict. Several said how much more their adopted children confided in them compared with children of the same age. They felt that this was because they had tried to establish an atmosphere of openness and honesty from the beginning. Disclosure of previous abuse diminished as children felt less need to talk about their past.

---

[5] Attachment mothers $\chi^2 = 12.06$, $df = 1$, $p < 0.001$ and fathers $\chi^2 = 5.37$, $df = 1$, $p < 0.05$
[6] Defiance mothers $\chi^2 = 12.09$, $df = 1$, $p < 0.001$ and fathers $\chi^2 = 4.7$, $df = 1$, $p < 0.05$
[7] Fathers only $\chi^2 = 12.5$, $df = 1$, $p < 0.01$

Table 9.2
Conflict and confiding in the parent–child relationship at follow-up

At follow-up:	Foster carer adopters n = 15	Childless stranger adopters n = 34	Stranger adopters with children n = 13
Child confides in parents	54%	62%	54%
Child discloses to parents	38%	38%	23%
Parent–child conflict	64%	61%	54%

She was always pretty open, she'd tell us about what had happened, it was like she wanted to get it off her chest . . . but over the years she mentions things more rarely.

Increasing conflict tended to reflect the age of the children, their desire for independence and, in some cases, their increasing conduct problems. In some families conflicts were frequent and aggressive and extremely distressing for the adopters. Two adopters had been physically assaulted. *He has attacked me with a knife on more than one occasion, the violence and hatred that comes from him is frightening.*

Adopter accounts of the parent–child relationship were largely echoed in the findings from the parent–child communication questionnaires. These revealed high levels of parent communication across all three groups and moderate levels of child communication (see Table 9.3 below). They also confirmed adopter accounts of child confiding (with children adopted by childless strangers appearing more open than those adopted by foster carers or into established families). This difference was not statistically significant.

It was clear that warmth and the development of a relationship between parents and children made the adoptive experience rewarding and motivated them to persevere through the struggles.

Table 9.3
Parent–child communication at follow-up

At follow-up:	Foster carer adopters n = 15	Childless stranger adopters n = 34	Stranger adopters with children n = 13
Parent communication (Range 1–5)	4.15 (SD .56)	4.11 (SD .56)	4.06 (SD .89)
Child communication (Range 1–5)	2.87 (SD .86)	3.43 (SD .88)	3.04 (SD 1.07)

Birth family contact at follow-up

There had been a great deal of change in the patterns of contact since the first year. By the time of the follow-up, the children or the adopters had ended contact that was difficult or distressing.

> . . . (Father's) *wife had just had a new baby and I knew Alfie wouldn't want to go to their home. It was throwing it in his face and he wouldn't go. When I tried to arrange the next contact he said, 'I can't be bothered. I don't want to see him any more.'*

Face-to-face contact

Contact with birth parents: Eleven children (17 per cent) had had face-to-face contact with either or both of their birth parents in the year. Seven children had seen their birth mother and three of these were also in contact with their birth father. A further four had face-to-face contact with their birth father only. Seven of these 11 children had had regular face-to-face contact with their birth parents over the years. Adopters also reported new contact for four children who wanted to see or were curious about their birth parents. These meetings could be emotional but adopters thought that, on the whole, they had been a positive experience for the children.

> *Last year he started doing very odd things at school, throwing himself at cars . . . but he wouldn't say what was wrong and the teachers were very concerned. I didn't know what to do . . . and so I phoned his social worker . . . his social worker did some more life story work with*

him . . . and then one day after it, he said to me that he'd like to meet his mum. I'd always said I'd let him, so his social worker came and did lots of background work with him before it. He was quite excited about it, he'd been counting the days to it. He wasn't anxious or frightened, he'd been very well prepared . . . And his parents were very good and we had quite a pleasant afternoon really and it was actually really good for him. He's been completely OK since. All the problems at school stopped and he's quite happy in himself now. He said he just needed to know what they were like. He wasn't disappointed in them at all.

It was not possible to know how many of these new contacts were likely to continue. Contact that had continued over the years was seen by the adopters to be beneficial for the children. This was not to say that the visits were always easy or that the children did not show distress, but that there was a purpose and quality that had ensured contact continued.

Contact with siblings: In contrast to the few children still having face-to-face contact with birth parents, 55 per cent of the children who had siblings had had face-to-face contact with them in the previous year. Adopters generally saw this as positive or routine. Although fewer children were still having face-to-face contact with their siblings than in the first year of placement, contact had usually not formally ceased. It had just "not happened"; once the children became teenagers their lives became very busy and they were reported as preferring contact by email or mobile phones. This was the case for more of the children adopted by strangers (50 per cent) than those adopted by foster carers (33 per cent) but this difference was not statistically significant. Again, adopters reported that, although contact had its difficulties, children (91 per cent) were generally positive about seeing their brothers and sisters.

We see them now most weeks, more during the summer holidays. They argue and fight now like all other siblings do. It's a perfect relationship.

Ten children (16 per cent) were also still having good-quality contact with other birth relatives. There were no significant differences between the adopter groups in patterns of all face-to-face contact.

Letterbox contact at follow-up

Over the years, two-thirds of the children adopted by strangers and all of the children adopted by foster carers maintained letterbox contact with their birth family. For a handful, letterbox contact was a continued reminder of a painful past. For others, the passing of time had lessened the emotional impact and it had become routine.

> *Quite recently I* (adopter) *met his father's wife and we both talked about how we could help the father and son to have a better relationship. Then I wrote his father a letter, which was very truthful, saying how he was fundamental to Alan, but how angry Alan had been and asking if he wanted to write back. It took him a while, but he wrote back saying how he'd tried his best, but couldn't work it out with his mum and couldn't manage Alan on his own and that helped Alan very much because it was obvious he cared.*

Adopters' accounts of challenges and rewards

At the follow-up, half of the families still thought that the challenges they faced were considerable or extreme (compared with 63 per cent in the first year) and a further 20 per cent described them as moderate (the same number as in the first year). Interestingly though, in a reversal of the first year findings, it was the foster carer adopters who had found the year prior to follow up the most difficult.[8] On the other hand, the rewards of adoption were still an important part of the experience. Sixty-six per cent of adopters (65 per cent of mothers and 63 per cent of fathers) described the rewards, stranger adopters (68 per cent) more frequently than foster carer adopters (54 per cent), although the difference was not statistically significant. Given the many difficulties in the adoptive experience, it is important to point out that over a quarter of adopters (28 per cent) described successful, happy placements with very few struggles and a great deal of reward.

It was most common, however, for adopters to describe joys and rewards alongside difficult experiences (62 per cent). For them, the

---

[8] 85 per cent of foster carer adopters described the year as moderately to extremely challenging compared with 66 per cent of stranger adopters.

rewards were key to their determination to persevere in the face of disappointments or difficulties.

The whole thing is the reward. Taking on children who've had a desperate time and seeing them grow and flourish. It's a great reward and seeing the end result will be a reward, when they're into adulthood. We were dead chuffed when their social worker came back to see them after the adoption and said 'they're whole'. We were really pleased when she said that, we were really taken by that.

Only seven per cent of mothers and 12 per cent of fathers could not think of any rewards (in contrast to the first year when it was 32 per cent and 26 per cent respectively) reflecting the increased closeness in the majority of relationships. Those who could not recall rewards tended to be parenting children with marked attachment difficulties, conduct problems or learning difficulties, and had often experienced difficulties in many spheres of their lives.

It is so difficult, I can't really remember any rewards. It feels as though we have the weight of the world on our shoulders all of the time.

More of the parents who found it difficult to identify rewards, particularly the fathers, had experienced a period of anxiety or depression (80 per cent) than parents who described rewards (54 per cent). A quarter were prescribed antidepressants, sometimes after many months or years of difficulty.

My husband was advised by the doctor to give him up because he was on Prozac after a nervous breakdown and the doctor thought Kelvin was too much like hard work. But we said 'no' because he's part of the family.

In all, 20 per cent of adopters were prescribed medication, with a further 36 per cent stating they had not consulted their GP but had experienced periods of depression or anxiety. Women were more likely to report these symptoms than men (67 per cent compared with 45 per cent) and were twice as likely as men to consult their GP or be prescribed antidepressants (26 per cent compared with 12 per cent).

Adopters' reflections

It was clear that much of the emotional and financial cost of adoption was borne by the adoptive families. What kept them going through times of difficulty? The parents' accounts showed that their loyalty to and love for the children and the fulfilment they had found in the adoption made the difference.

There were many times in the first couple of months when I could have picked the phone up and said 'I'm sorry, I can't cope with this', but now I couldn't imagine being without him, I'm so very glad we persevered.

He has kept me sticking at it. He is a trier. He's got so many good points and I've seen him develop over the years. He's worth sticking with. And he's always given 200 per cent. He's a lovely lad.

The adoptive families in 2001/2

- Adoption still affected the work patterns of a third of mothers. Many families had forgone an anticipated second income and a quarter were in debt.
- Problems in couples' relationships were experienced equally across the three groups (43 per cent) and were associated with children's attachment or conduct problems. Seventy-six per cent of adopters with such relationship troubles had experienced a depressive episode.
- Kin relations were adversely affected by sibling or couple negativity, whereas for friendships, tensions were associated with the child's conduct problems.
- High levels of closeness were reported by most adopters (60–85 per cent) regardless of group, as well as higher levels of confiding. A lack of closeness was associated with attachment problems or defiance. There had been significant improvements in the parent–child relationship among stranger adopters with children.
- Most of the previous face-to-face birth parent contact had ended but some new contact had occurred at the children's request. Sibling face-to-face contact had also declined or lapsed.
- More foster carer adopters (85 per cent) than stranger adopters (66 per cent) had found the last year challenging. Most, however, still also experienced rewards (54 per cent of foster carer adopters and 68 per

cent of stranger adopters). Those that did not appeared to be at risk of mental health problems.

- Almost a third of families (28 per cent), many of whom had adopted only one child, described settled placements with few struggles and much reward but a further third of families, especially those facing attachment or conduct difficulties, had problems in many areas of their lives. The remainder reported rewards as well as challenges and difficulties.

10 **Supporting adoptive placements**

In this chapter, we explore support before and after the adoption order, adopters' feelings about seeking help and about the help they got. We had data from social services' records on this for all the children pre-order and from the adopters on 64 children after the order.

Support from social services

All of the families of the 64 children had support from at least one social worker during the first year and had visits from their family placement worker (FPW) and the child's social worker (CSW). Families were visited on average 21 times (range 4–42 times), often with more intensive visiting at the beginning of the placement. The majority of adopters felt the visiting frequency had been about right, but a fifth remembered being visited fewer than five times.

> *I can remember saying to a neighbour that we could have killed Sally and hidden her under the patio and nobody would know.*

Twenty-seven families (42 per cent) had one change of social worker (25 per cent CSW and 17 per cent FPW), and one change of both. Adopters' feelings about this varied with their view of the social worker's competence and the quality of their relationship, but most were saddened by it to some extent (81 per cent CSW and 72 per cent FPW).

Adopters' attitudes to seeking help from SSDs

Adopters were asked what they felt about asking SSDs for help. In the first year, 17 per cent were pleased to use services and had felt strongly encouraged by their social worker to do so, but the majority were not expecting ongoing support. Forty-seven per cent thought that SSDs only offered financial help, but not all would have used services even if they had known about them. The families of 18 children (28 per cent) said so and a further 14 (22 per cent) wanted to be free of SSD involvement.

> *I was always told I could contact social services if I needed to, but to*

be honest I wanted to get rid of social services because I'd been involved with them for so long. I just wanted us to get on and be a family.

Fourteen per cent felt there was a stigma attached to asking for help and would have only contacted SSDs as a last resort.

You're very conscious of putting on a good front and initially don't want to ask for help because it would seem like a bit of a failure, an admission that you're not coping, like you're admitting defeat and you desperately want to be coping.

Over the years, attitudes to seeking help changed. More of the adopters (30 per cent) wanted services but these were either not available or adopters did not know of their existence. By the follow-up, the stigma associated with asking for help was rarely mentioned. Only eight per cent said that they had felt actively discouraged from seeking help.

Confidence in the social worker's professional abilities

The majority of adopters felt that they had developed good enough relationships with their social workers by the end of the first year. Only a quarter had a poor relationship with their CSW and a tenth with their FPW. Interestingly, foster carer adopters (43 per cent) were more likely to have poor relationships with the CSW than stranger adopters (18 per cent), even though stranger adopters were somewhat more dissatisfied with the social work service they had received, although not significantly so.

FPWs were generally better thought of than CSWs, with many adopters full of praise for them.

Our support worker was one in a million, she was fantastic, and we had the same support worker from beginning to end.

Adopters were less complimentary about the quality of advice given by social workers or the help offered in crises. Over half (57 per cent CSW and 51 per cent FPW) said they had been dissatisfied with these. Many felt that their social workers had just been good listeners but did not give them the targeted behaviour management advice they wanted. Some found the visits intrusive or felt they were being scrutinised rather than supported. Others complained that sufficient work had not been done with the children and that they had had to do this themselves. Life story or some other form of direct work was done by social workers with 31 per cent of children during the first year of the placement.

We were 100 per cent dissatisfied with our support worker. In every area I can honestly say she was useless. She was always ill or cancelling appointments, she was totally unreliable and hopeless. I'm sorry to have to say it really, but we were just totally let down by it.

Adopters also wanted a quicker response and complained that social workers (CSW 43 per cent and FPW 41 per cent) were often unavailable. Half (50 per cent) said that they had been unhappy with the speed at which tasks had been accomplished, such as organising the adoption hearing or the provision of an adoption allowance, and a third (33 per cent) had wanted more help contacting schools or other agencies.

I sorted the school out on my own, but you do really need help with it because you don't know anything about it. You don't know what your entitlement is in terms of a placement and getting support for your child.

Support from SSDs at follow-up: After the adoption orders were granted, all social work visiting ceased very quickly for the majority of adoptive families. This left some adopters feeling as though they had been abandoned.

Her social worker said, 'I've been told I've got to finish with you. I don't envy what you're doing. I think you're very brave. Goodbye.'

By the time of the follow-up, 18 children's families (28 per cent) were still receiving social work support: FPWs were supporting 11 families and CSWs ten families. Three families received visits from both workers. Although a small number were receiving support, there were many others who would have liked it (see following case summary).

Case summary: Requesting help

Tania, aged eight, was placed out of county with Sara and Martin. Although exhibiting sexualised behaviour, attachment difficulties, peer problems and a nervous tic, Tania was not offered therapeutic help nor were Sara and Martin prepared with services in place. Tania had problems bonding with Martin and was hostile and aggressive towards him from day one. After six years, the situation had not improved and the marital relationship was also strained. At puberty, Tania started smoking, skipping school and being extremely defiant. Sara and Martin approached Tania's placing authority for help but were told to contact the authority that had approved them. When they did this they discovered that the authority would not help as they had moved. At follow-up, their third call to their local SSD had also failed to elicit any response and all of the family relationships were extremely strained.

Social workers visited those still getting support every eight to ten weeks on average, much less frequently than in the first year. Half of these families thought that they should be visited more often.

It seems like everyone has washed their hands of you. I felt I had been conned . . . After I mentioned the word "breakdown", I got a few more phone calls and visits but I felt like 'Why do I have to be at this point before anyone will take any notice of me?'

Children adopted by their foster carers were more likely than children adopted by strangers to be supported by a CSW at follow-up,[1] perhaps because foster carer adopters were better at arguing for support or because they were more visible to SSDs if they had continued to foster. There were no differences between the groups on support from FSWs.

Families were still receiving support for a number of reasons. Seven families were in a crisis that was severe enough to be threatening the

---

[1] 36 per cent of foster carer adopters compared with 10 per cent of stranger adopters $\chi^2 = 5.49$, $df = 1$, $p < 0.05$

placement, others (three) were experiencing more difficulties as the children entered adolescence. Some families still had contact with SSDs because of ongoing birth parent contact (four) or the child (three) had physical or mental health needs for which support had been agreed. One family was visited because they had adopted for the second time and the child was still a looked after child. The adoptive families therefore had differing expectations about what they wanted from post-adoption support.

Very few of the 11 families who wanted help because of the young people's behaviour were positive about the services they received. Seven were dissatisfied with the quality of advice and the responsiveness of services. They questioned the ability of SSDs to help them manage very challenging behaviour and had poor relationships with their workers. The remaining four families had a mixed view of the support they had received.

Everything is just slow, slow, stop when it comes to social services.

One day I rang up duty social services and said, 'He is having a huge tantrum, I can't cope with this child. You've got to help or I'm going to do something to him.' They said, 'Can you ring me back next Tuesday?' I thought, 'Oh, I'll kill him by next Tuesday' . . .

Table 10.1
Adopter satisfaction with social worker support

	First year (% satisfied with service received)		Last year (% satisfied with service received)	
Aspect of social work service:	*CSW (n = 61)*	*FPW (n = 59)*	*CSW (n = 10)*	*FPW (n = 11)*
Visiting frequency	62%	75%	50%	64%
Support and reassurance	56%	66%	40%	55%
Behaviour and parenting advice	43%	49%	30%	45%
Availability and responsiveness	57%	59%	40%	64%
Help contacting other agencies	34%	59%	40%	73%
Relationship quality	75%	90%	70%	82%
Speed completing tasks	49%		39%	

Relationships between the adopters and workers were far more positive where families were receiving support because of the child's physical health or disability, or because of supervised contact. These families generally felt that they had received good support and advice.

Although a quarter (22 per cent) of adopters had not wanted any further contact with SSDs during the first year and a third (31 per cent) during the year prior to follow-up, only nine per cent of adopters had felt this way over the whole period of the placement. We do not, of course, know what view the adopters who were not interviewed would have taken (n = 32). Table 10.1 summarises adopter satisfaction with the social work service they received during the first year and the last year of the placement.

Financial support

All the adopters were aware of the existence of adoption/fostering allowances, but some were disappointed at their low level or that means testing excluded them from receiving an allowance.

Money wise we were broke, because social services said I couldn't work and I accepted that like a fool. It's your life in their hands.

Adoption/fostering allowance: Sixty-eight per cent of families received an allowance (51 per cent a fostering allowance and 17 per cent an adoption allowance) in the first year. Some were initially surprised that they were eligible or felt slightly uncomfortable about it. Once expenditure began to mount up, however, many felt that it had become indispensable.

For some, particularly foster carers, the provision of an adoption allowance had been a crucial factor in their decision to adopt. Almost 10 per cent of these placements were delayed while issues around continuing financial support were resolved. For many, their fears that they would be worse off when they adopted were realised. Under half of foster carer adopters (43 per cent) were still in receipt of an adoption allowance at follow-up.

Looking back now I wish we'd long-term fostered her instead of adopting her because they don't give you nothing financially and as she's getting older we could have done with it.

The total number of families receiving an allowance had dropped from 68 per cent to 30 per cent at follow-up. Several adopters felt that this had had a detrimental effect on the range of experiences they could give their children and felt very strongly that more could have been done to make their lives easier.

> *We didn't qualify for an adoption allowance . . . Adopters get nothing, absolutely nothing . . . What harm would it have done to give us a free swimming card. It's not the money, it's the principle. Why can't adopters get some recognition for what they are doing?*

Those in receipt of an allowance at the follow-up were getting between £23 and £110 per week with £66 per week the average amount. Provision varied with time and across authorities but some received very meagre allowances.

> *We got £3 a week adoption allowance. I called that my funny money . . . when you think that he's bitten all the bunk beds and kicked a hole in the bedroom wall and ripped I don't know how many sheets and pulled the wallpaper down and that I have to do washing every day because his bedding is always wet and we had to get a tumble dryer because in winter we couldn't dry anything . . . then it doesn't really go very far at all.*

Adopters frequently felt that SSDs did not take these kinds of financial pressures into account when calculating eligibility for allowances.

Set-up grants: The majority of stranger adopters (80 per cent) had spent considerable amounts (between £200 and £3,000) purchasing essentials necessary for their child to join the family (see Chapter 8). Thirty-nine per cent of families got help with these initial costs. The average grant was £222, although grants ranged between £35 and £607. A recurring complaint was that the set-up grants had not gone far enough. Adopters had spent on average £732 on set-up costs, £500 more than the average set-up grant. For several, this meant there were financial strains from the outset. Only 28 per cent of families received a set-up grant and an adoption or fostering allowance prior to the adoption order.

> *The fostering allowance was still coming to us and without that it would have been quite difficult really because they needed so much stuff. Money was just going very quickly.*

Other financial support: A third (34 per cent) of families received other financial support from SSDs before the making of the adoption order. This was typically clothing grants or mileage reimbursements to foster carer adopters which, along with birthday and Christmas allowances, often continued until the adoption order. Other families received reimbursements for loss or damage caused by the child, childminding fees or solicitor's fees (in the case of a contested adoption). Payments ranged from £15 to £1,070, but half were under £100.

By the time of the follow-up, it was a very different story. Only five families (8 per cent) had received other financial support (of between £90 and £2,400) from SSDs during the year. Three of these payments were to finance various types of therapy. These additional payments were last-ditch attempts to keep placements intact. Two of these placements subsequently broke down.

Childminding and respite care

During the first year, some adopters were too exhausted or immersed in their new role to go out socially, but, as the children were still looked after, those that wanted to could find getting social services approved babysitters a hurdle.

Going out was difficult. We didn't go out for 18 months because getting babysitters was difficult, as they had to be approved by social services. It would have been helpful if social services could have provided someone who was police-checked to babysit.

In some cases, the children's behaviour was so difficult that repeat babysitter bookings were refused. This made it difficult for some parents to attend adoption support groups or spend time together as a couple. Many adopters would have welcomed access to an approved childminding service, but only four families (4 per cent) received help with this during the first year. With an absence of "breaks", many adopters admitted that tensions were liable to rise. Several had been desperate for a break during the early months of the placement but had felt unhappy that the children would perceive it as a rejection. Consequently, only six adopters (6 per cent) received respite care during the first year of the placement, three trying to salvage placements in difficulty (although one did subsequently break down) and three foster carer adopters with existing short break arrangements.

By the follow-up, a third (33 per cent) would have liked short break care but had not received it. A few felt very strongly about this.

I would love respite care. It seems unfair that if you long-term foster children you get it, but when you adopt them you can't have it. David is an ADHD child and is quite intense, way over the top half of the time, and you do need it. Just a weekend off every now and again.

Five families (8 per cent) had received short break care in the year prior to the follow-up interview. All except one of these families had come close to breakdown at some stage, two had been subject to child protection investigations and three had a child with ADHD. Thus, SSDs appeared only to provide short break care as a last resort. Getting breaks in other ways could also be tricky. Family holidays could be difficult and a few recounted tales of being asked to leave campsites because of the children's behaviour.

Babysitting: Many adopters recounted how they had quickly used up the babysitting goodwill of their family and friends, especially if their children had difficult behaviour. Some still did not feel that they could leave the children with anybody and a handful had not been out alone as a couple *at all* since the children were adopted. Adopters in this situation could become very isolated.

It's hard just to get babysitters. It needs to be someone who knows that he could fly off the handle and lash out and, to be honest, there's not many people that I would put in that situation. My nephew and his girlfriend babysat once and in the end they had to phone us up. He'd thrown everything everywhere and scratched things, they couldn't cope and we had to go home.

Half (50 per cent) of adoptive families wanted access to a childminding/babysitting service but none had received such support during the 12 months prior to the follow-up interview.

Additional help

Most adopters did not want support from additional workers during the early stages of the placement because they felt it not to be appropriate. However, many did not know about the possibility of additional help and a few, especially those adopting sibling groups or children with a disability, would have valued help with their domestic chores to enable them to focus on the children.

I asked for domestic help, because suddenly you've got all this washing and all the rest of it. Definitely for the first six months this would have been helpful, so you can concentrate on the children. But they just said 'We're not doing your washing for you'.

In the first year of the placement, a family support worker or a social worker from the disabled children's team was supporting five families. At follow-up, six families (9 per cent) were being supported in this way, after vigorous campaigning by two adoptive families.

Parenting skills: Only one family attended a specific parenting skills course. The adopters, not the child, had been the source of much professional concern in this unusual case and had been required to attend 12 hours of parenting skills training at an SSD family centre.

Summary of adoption support

Table 10.2 below summarises the adoption support received by the families in both the first year and the last year of the placement. It can be seen that after the adoption order only a minority of families received any further support from SSDs. Over half (54 per cent) of the adoptive families received no support at all and a further 13 per cent of families received only an adoption allowance. Twenty-one families (33 per cent) had received a post-adoption service from social workers in the year prior to follow-up but this was usually short term and consisted of only a few sessions. Social workers were providing more intensive support (visiting monthly) to three families.

Adopters had suggestions for improving support services and these are detailed in Appendix B.

Table 10.2
Adoption support received from SSDs

	First year support received (n = 96)	Last year support received (n = 64)
Social worker support	100%	28%
Life story work/direct work	31%*	2%
Initial set-up grants	39%	–
Adoption or fostering allowances	68%	30%
Other financial support	34%	6%
Respite care	6%	8%
Childminding/babysitting	4%	0%
Additional worker support	5%	9%
Parenting skills training	1%	0%
Voluntary agency support module	4%	0%

* n = 64.

Facilitating contact with birth families

This study did not look at all aspects of intended as well as actual contact. Data were only collected on contact that occurred. It was clear from the case files that a great deal of social work time was spent trying to arrange contract, not all of which occurred.

Supervised contact: During the first year, two-fifths (39 per cent) of the 64 children had supervised face-to-face contact with a member of their birth family. A third of these 67 contact visits (30 with birth parents, 26 with birth siblings and 11 with birth relatives) took place at an SSD contact venue. All were supervised by a social worker (in two cases two social workers) or a community care worker. Some of these contacts were final goodbyes or one-off opportunities for the adoptive and birth parents to meet. Other visits continued according to an established plan that had sometimes been stipulated by the court.

By the time of the follow-up, much of the contact had been terminated or was no longer supervised. Only eight children (12 per cent) had supervised face-to-face contact with a member of their birth family; one child with a birth mother, one with a birth father, one with maternal grandparents and three with siblings in foster care. The other two contacts were supervised as the birth parents had a new partner. A sixth of these 24 contacts were held at an SSD contact venue. The strongest message from the interviews, however, was that adopters frequently felt disregarded when it came to contact. Only 10 per cent of adopters were satisfied with the quality of guidance they received in relation to managing it.

Five families received travel expenses related to contact during the first year. By the follow-up year this had reduced to three families.

Letterbox contact: During the first year with their new families, 56 per cent of the children were exchanging information with their birth parents, siblings or kin. By the year prior to the follow-up, this had reduced to 39 per cent. The frequency had also declined slightly (from two letters on average per year to 1.2). In order to understand the resource implications of providing this service, using 2001/2 prices we gathered data about the letterbox systems operated by our participating local authorities and estimated a unit cost per item (£38) for our largest local authority.

There was varying practice in relation to letterbox contact. Staff in some authorities only read letters sent by adopters to ensure they did not contain any identifying information. This task was seen as a clerical one with little social work input. They did not screen the letters sent by birth parents, believing that it was the adopters' responsibility to decide whether a letter from a birth parent was suitable. These authorities emphasised the importance of strengthening and not undermining the adoptive parents' role. Other authorities had a different view and carefully checked every item from *all* parties sending mail. This took significant amounts of social work time. These authorities believed they had a responsibility to help keep the children safe and were aware that birth parents sometimes tried to extend agreements or place pressure on children to reveal where they were. This group of authorities had growing concerns about the emotive content of some letters and the possibility of "grooming" behaviours by known paedophiles. Some adoption managers were also increasingly worried that letterbox was being seen by child care social workers as a risk-free activity and was being offered to most birth parents without any assessment of the likely benefit to the child.

Health, CAMHS, education and police service provision

Figure 10.1 shows the percentage of children seen by health (specialist services), CAMHS, education or police professionals during both the pre-order and post-order periods of the placement.

Pre-order (when the children were aged three to 12), 43 per cent of children had been referred to an education professional, 40 per cent to a health specialist and 26 per cent to a CAMHS professional. By the time of the follow-up (when the children were aged eight to 19), 67 per cent had received additional education input, 59 per cent had been seen by a health specialist, 55 per cent had been referred to CAMHS and 30 per cent had been involved with the police or a Youth Offending Team.

Figure 10.1
Health, CAMHS, education and police service provision

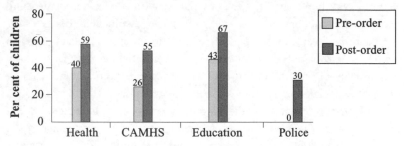

Pre-order, 64 per cent of children had been involved with at least one agency, rising to 84 per cent post-adoption order. Of course, not all of the children got services from all of them. Many children, however, *had* received services from more than one agency. Prior to the adoption order 11 per cent of children had received services from health, CAMHS and education and 22 per cent from two of these agencies. Two-fifths of the children (19 per cent) had been involved with health, CAMHS, education and police services, a further quarter (25 per cent) had received services from three of these agencies and a fifth (20 per cent) from two. Even given the extent of the children's special needs, this level of service use was surprising, as adopters complained during the interviews that they had difficulty securing services for their children.

Health

Details about children's contacts with paediatricians, clinical medical officers, physiotherapists, occupational therapists, hearing specialists, speech therapists and consultants were recorded. Two-fifths (40 per cent) of the children had seen one or more of these professionals pre-order and three-fifths (59 per cent) post-order.

Pre-order, the children's health needs were diverse, but what was surprising was how little of this health provision was for physically disabled children (6 per cent). Most of it was for assessment or treatment connected with the children's emerging difficulties and tended to be a consequence of schools' or adopters' concerns about ill-health or developmental delay. Hearing specialists and speech therapists were most frequently seen, with 19 per cent and 16 per cent of children respectively visiting them.

The children seeing paediatricians or clinical medical officers (15 per cent) tended to have complex combinations of difficulties, for example, learning difficulties alongside health conditions such as ADHD or epilepsy. Consequently, several of these children had also been referred to other health specialists for assessment or monitoring of their health conditions pre-adoption.

She had a lot of tests when she was about three that didn't find anything . . . but she's just been diagnosed with Asperger's syndrome.

In total, 11 per cent of children saw consultants, five per cent occupational therapists and one per cent physiotherapists. The children tended to see consultants for monitoring of ongoing complaints such as heart or skin conditions and to see occupational therapists or physiotherapists for problems with motor development.

Adopters often found the children's health conditions quite difficult to deal with, especially when the prognosis was uncertain or when they had been unprepared for the difficulties they encountered.

The worst thing was his epilepsy, he was fitting up to 11 times a day sometimes. Usually he'd fit before school and then sometimes at school as his medication was wearing off. I used to have to go down to the school a couple of times a day to look after him and then he'd usually fit again in the evening . . . so it was 24-hour care, you couldn't leave him, full stop.

In these circumstances, several adopters said that they would have welcomed the opportunity to request a full health assessment, especially the small number where health conditions were not identified for many years.

After the making of the adoption order, health service provision for children with recognised physical disabilities, such as sight or hearing loss or a diagnosed syndrome, had almost doubled (11 per cent) as more disabilities were diagnosed. The number of children seeing hearing specialists and speech therapists continued to be high, with 30 per cent and 23 per cent of children respectively visiting these professionals. This may reflect late assessment of developmental delay or long waiting lists.

We've always thought there might be a problem but you think 'Do I fuss, do I not fuss?' At one stage we looked into getting him a private assessment but it cost too much. With these things I think it should have all been looked into earlier on, for the child's sake, not ours.

A third (36 per cent) of children had seen a paediatrician or the adoption medical adviser since the adoption order was granted. This was sometimes in connection with continuing concerns such as problems with co-ordination or gait, but frequently it was because of emotional or behavioural issues or concerns about the possibility of ADHD or an autistic spectrum disorder. All except two of these children had also been referred to another health specialist.

Basically we knew we had a big problem on our hands from the start. He would continually self-harm, he would pull out his toenails if he was upset and would crack and crack his head on the pavement. He was a very vicious and violent child and even aged three he attacked me once, had me down on the floor and pulled my hair out. I asked for help right from the beginning, but we were just told he was a lively child . . . It was another two years before he was diagnosed with ADHD and we actually got some help.

Altogether 25 per cent of children had seen medical or psychiatric consultants, five per cent occupational therapists and five per cent physiotherapists. Some saw consultants for common health conditions, but some for enuresis or bowel dysfunction when problems with wetting or soiling persisted.

What we have been worried about is her problem with bed-wetting. That has been an ongoing worry for a number of years. Partly we worry from a social point of view, because it makes it difficult for her to stay with friends. We sought help in the end . . . we went to the enuresis clinic, but that never solved anything. They gave us an alarm, which did work for about a month, and then it started again. In the end the doctor put her on tablets and that sorted it out. But the problem with that is that it treats the symptoms and not the cause.

Adopters frequently voiced their frustrations about not knowing to whom to turn about their children's problems. Many would have welcomed easier access to health and mental health professionals.

Certain services you might need should be set up as a package with each child. That would include the names of people you could turn to and where to go for help, so you could use it if you want to, but you don't have to.

Figure 10.2

Health service provision pre- and post-adoption order

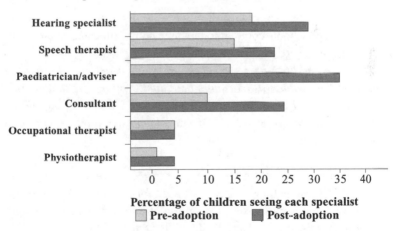

Percentage of children seeing each specialist
Pre-adoption   Post-adoption

Education

All of the children had started school before the adoption order was granted. Additional educational support from a special needs teacher or classroom assistant or referrals to an educational psychologist was recorded. Forty-three per cent of children had received one or more of these services pre-order and 67 per cent post-order.

Pre-order, 29 per cent had received additional educational support from a special needs teacher or classroom assistant, 26 per cent had been referred to an educational psychologist, 17 per cent had been issued with a statement of special educational needs and 14 per cent attended a special school or a special unit within a mainstream school. Additionally, five children received support from either an educational social worker or a school nurse or counsellor on account of their emotional or behavioural problems.

Despite these seemingly high levels of service provision, many adopters complained that they had to really struggle to get this support or that they had not been able to get additional classroom support or a statement despite their best attempts.

I was up against it, the school didn't think there was anything wrong with Caroline . . . the teachers haven't had any training on children in care.

Some protested that, even with the provision of services, there was no improvement or schools complained that the points allocated as the result of the statement were too low to meet the child's needs.

He couldn't add two plus two and he was eight years old. He couldn't count to ten, but he was learning about the Egyptians. We thought this kid needs help. He was getting substantial help, he was getting speech therapy, physiotherapy and a learning support assistant . . . but there was no progress.

The prevailing view was that education services were withheld unless there was very compelling evidence of need for provision. Adopters did not welcome this fight for services on top of everything else they were dealing with, as Alice and David's story illustrates.

Case summary: Alice and David's story

Jonathan was placed with Alice and David when he was eight. He was extremely disruptive and disturbed and seemed lost in his own world. He was expelled from the local school because of his difficult behaviour. He was then diagnosed as having dyslexia and ADHD. Alice and David decided to pay for Jonathan to attend a local dyslexia centre, which he did until he was too old to attend and had to start at the local secondary school. Despite evidence from the educational psychologist, the adoption medical adviser and his last teacher, Jonathon was not given an educational statement and the school was therefore unable to secure services for him. He continued to have educational, behavioural and emotional problems and was suspended from school several times. He eventually left school without taking any GCSEs.

By the time of the follow-up, 50 per cent of children had seen an educational psychologist, 44 per cent had received support from either a special needs teacher or a classroom assistant, 25 per cent had been issued with a statement of SEN and 20 per cent attended a special school or a special unit within a mainstream school (seven and six children respectively). In addition, nine of these children had received support from either an educational social worker or a school nurse or counsellor on account of their emotional or behavioural problems.

These high levels of education service provision in part reflect the fact that 48 per cent of the children in our sample had learning difficulties. Again though, what came across most strongly from the interviews with adoptive parents was how many adopters had struggled alone to get this support and how many had found the system confusing and unresponsive.

There was clearly a need for services beyond those that had been provided. While 50 per cent of children had seen an educational psychologist and presumably been assessed, for half this had not resulted in a statement of SEN. Without that, adequate services were generally not forthcoming.

Figure 10.3

Education service provision pre- and post-adoption order

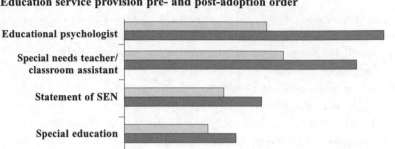

Percentage of children receiving each provision

Pre-order   Post-order

CAMHS provision

A quarter (26 per cent) of children were referred to CAMHS pre-adoption order and over half (55 per cent) post-order. Pre-order, these referrals were occasionally for psychiatric assessments ordered by the court to aid decision-making about contact, but more usually were referrals about the child's behaviour. Over half of the children referred pre-adoption had learning difficulties. Others displayed sexualised behaviour or severe internalising or externalising problems. A fifth were later diagnosed with ADHD.

Some of the referrals to CAMHS were because of problems that emerged after the child moved to his or her adoptive placement, such as rejecting or particularly difficult behaviour towards the adopters. In some cases this support was timely and essential.

The first two days were fine, but when different people turned up that really freaked him out. He was a very angry, very scared, very distressed child, hiding behind the sofa and refusing to come out. People were trying to coax him out and that just made it worse. I wanted to shout at all of them 'just get out, get out'. Poor kid, it was very distressing to see . . . there were a lot of problems and we just didn't know if we were dealing with them alright. We were just hoping we were doing the right thing, we didn't know. When we did contact SSD it was fine and we were able to see a clinical psychologist very quickly and we saw him weekly from then. If that wasn't available, I think the placement would have been in real jeopardy, we would have had real difficulties.

There were mixed views on the quality and helpfulness of CAMHS services. Some felt that they just got "tea and sympathy" when they were looking for solutions: 'They just said "carry on with what you are doing".' Others felt criticised: 'The only thing we got was Ritalin and criticism.'

Pre-order, these contacts with CAMHS were usually only short term. Only 16 per cent of the children received "long-term" support from a mental health professional. Some of this support was routine monitoring of Ritalin or other prescribed drugs. Very few children got ongoing therapeutic help. By the follow-up year, 31 per cent of children were getting "long-term" input, but again parents described having to fight to get therapeutic help for their child or felt discouraged and disappointed by their experience of CAMHS.

We did go to the CAMHS clinic but they were useless. She used to ask us questions and I said, 'We're coming to you for answers'. They didn't help. The GP referred Emma to the psychiatric department. They eventually decided to refer her to the psychotherapy department without seeing her and they told me, and I quote, 'Yes, we get lots of similar referrals, but we find that once they have met the birth mother then it all goes away. If we interfere we merely muddy the water.' This was after a 20-minute consultation.

Some families did find CAMHS extremely helpful and saw improvements in their child.

The doctor (CAMHS) . . . did some one-to-one work with him that had a REALLY positive effect. He can now talk and consider things and his behaviour at home and at school is really improving. We just feel that if only we'd had the right advice five or six years ago it would have all been so much easier.

It appeared that families found CAMHS most helpful when children had got *ongoing* therapeutic support, usually from a clinical psychologist or therapist. It was not generally the case that therapeutic interventions had been unhelpful, rather that many adopters had found it difficult to secure this kind of sustained support.

There were also a small number of children who had never received any kind of mental health assessment or intervention, despite the adopters feeling that this was necessary.

Police/youth justice

None of the children had any involvement with the police or youth justice services pre-order, but 30 per cent had been involved with the criminal justice system at follow-up due to offending behaviours. All except one of these children were aged 13 or over. Shoplifting or stealing from individuals was the most common reason, but other reasons included damage to property, fraud, breaking and entering, drug use at school or the child going missing. Two children had also been referred to a Youth Offending Team, both for serious theft.

A small number of adopters had asked the police to talk to their child, but for the majority of adopters police involvement was very upsetting and traumatic.

> *It's really caused so much hurt and heartache. We've had to pay one neighbour back because she recognised one of the bikes as hers, he'd just gone into her garden and pinched it. We feel like the bad family in the street because of him. And then we've had the police on our doorstep because he'd been stealing CDs in town . . . We feel very upset about him at the moment, we don't feel close to him at all.*

The police were also involved with a small number of families where the child had been the victim of assault or serious bullying.

Summary of support from other agencies

Most children had received some level of service provision from health specialists, CAMHS, education services and the police. Many adopters, however, had found the services difficult to access and would have valued guidance and assistance with this. Knowing what services were available under what circumstances would have been very helpful, but even when adopters did manage to access services, they often felt that the services were "too little, too late". While there were usually assessments of children's difficulties, agencies often failed to provide effective support or interventions, or these came too late.

Adopters felt that assessments needed to be done more quickly and that they then needed to be followed by appropriate support or intervention. It appeared that while agencies did acknowledge adopted children's problems, long waiting lists, various forms of gate-keeping or very high thresholds excluded many adopted children from adequate service provision.

Summary: supporting adoptive placements

SSD service provision

- All of the adoptive families had at least one social worker during the first year of the placement. Inadequate emotional support, slow task completion and poor advice were the most common causes of discontent.
- Adopters typically spent around £700 on initial set-up expenses but only 39 per cent of families received on average £222 towards these.
- Ten per cent of placements were delayed while financial support issues were resolved. Sixty-eight per cent of adopters received either an adoption or fostering allowance during the first year of placement. Even so, many adopters struggled because of the children's special needs.
- Fifty-four per cent of adopters received no ongoing support from SSDs once the adoption order was granted. A further 13 per cent of families received an adoption allowance only. Only nine per cent had not wanted any further support over the whole period of the adoptive placement, but 41 per cent did not know that services were available post-adoption.
- Families often had to be in crisis before services were offered. Social workers visited much less frequently than in the first year of the placement and adopters were often dissatisfied with the social work service they received. Of the 33 per cent of families who received post-

adoption services, none received a *comprehensive* post-adoption support package.

- Adopters most wanted SSDs to provide: financial support, childminding help, respite care, behaviour management advice, an adoption helpline or ongoing point of contact and therapeutic services for the child.
- After the adoption, SSDs were helping with birth family contact more often than with any other kind of support. Family placement workers were concerned that letterbox was being viewed by CSWs as a risk-free activity.

Health, education, CAMHS and police/youth justice service provision

- The majority of children in the sample had received services from one or more of these agencies pre- and post-adoption (64 per cent and 84 per cent respectively).
- Post-adoption, 67 per cent of children had received additional educational input, 59 per cent had been seen by a health specialist, 55 per cent had been seen by a CAMHS professional and 30 per cent had been involved with the police or a Youth Offending Team.
- There was considerable overlap of service use. Post-adoption, almost one in five children (19 per cent) had been involved with health, CAMHS, education and police services; a quarter had received services from three of these agencies and a fifth from two.
- Developmental delay, emotional/behavioural problems and ADHD constituted most of the difficulties treated by health professionals, not illness or disability.
- Over half of the children had been referred to CAMHS. Adopters often said that they were only given reassurance when what they wanted was behaviour management advice and therapeutic interventions.
- Half of the children had seen an educational psychologist, but only a quarter had a statement of special educational needs.
- By the follow-up, almost a third of the children had been involved with the police, most for minor offences. These were the older children in the sample.
- Many adopters had found services difficult to access and would have valued guidance and assistance with this.

- Adopters thought that the services they did get were generally "too little, too late". Assessments too often failed to lead to effective help and failed to meet the needs of many adopted children and their families.

SECTION IV

Outcomes

11 The costs of adoption

With the recent policy emphasis on increasing the number of children adopted out of care and improving the quality of adoption support services, the need to know more about the costs of placing children for adoption and providing post-adoption support has become extremely pressing. This study was the first of its kind to attempt to estimate the cost to social services departments (SSDs) of placing for adoption and supporting in adoptive placements a complete sample of adopted children. In this chapter, three separate unit costs calculations are described:

- an **"adoption process"** unit cost – the cost to SSDs of placing a looked after child for adoption;
- a **"post-placement"** unit cost per week – the cost to SSDs of maintaining a looked after child in an adoptive placement before the making of an adoption order;
- a **"post-adoption"** unit cost per week – the cost to SSDs of providing adoption support services to adoptive families post adoption order.

These three adoptive placement unit costs were calculated following the recommended methodology in Beecham (2000) and are described in Appendix A. Unless stated otherwise, all staff costs in this section are taken from *The Unit Costs of Health and Social Care 2001* (Netten *et al*, 2001). For the sake of brevity, this publication is referred to simply as *Unit Costs*. Details of the staff costs used in the individual estimates are given in the summary tables at the end of each sub-section. Where appropriate, expenditures have been inflated, so that all costs are given in 2001/2 values.

The data used to calculate the "adoption process" and "post-placement" unit costs were collected from SSD case files for the 96 children, aged five years seven months on average at placement, for whom adoptive homes were found. The data for the "post-adoption" unit cost was collected at interview from the adopters of 64 of the 80 children who were still in their adoptive placements at the time of the follow-up. Good information about adoption support service provision was also available on file for the five children whose adoptive placements disrupted post adoption order. These five cases were also included in the "post-adoption" sample in order to derive a representative unit cost, including both intact and later-disrupted placements. The "post-adoption" unit cost is therefore based on a sample of 69 children. They had been adopted for between two and ten years, the average length of time being seven years since the adoption order.

Adoption process unit cost

An "adoption process" unit cost was calculated. This is the mean cost to SSDs of placing a looked after child for adoption.

Identifying the activities, the unit of measurement and costs

The adoption process activities are listed here in roughly the order in which they occurred throughout the adoption process. A unit of measurement has been identified for each activity and cost estimates included.

Child's social worker: The child's social worker (CSW) was responsible for preparing both the child and the birth family for the adoption. Activities were focused in three main areas: a) writing reports, b) preparing the child and birth family, and c) attending planning meetings. The unit of measurement identified for this activity was hours of social worker time. From discussions with social workers and team managers, the following estimates of the time taken to complete these activities were assembled:

Approval activities (51 hours)
20 hours researching and writing the child's Form E (background and history)
2 hours arranging and attending the adoption medical
25 hours tracing birth family, discussing adoption, gaining consent, collecting history
4 hours attending adoption panel (pre-discussion and best interest meetings)

Matching activities (39 hours)
25 hours on matching activities

12 hours meeting suitable prospective adopters
2 hours attending adoption panel (matching meeting)

Preparatory activities (57 hours)
10 hours discussing the adoption with the foster carers
15 hours preparation of the child
5 hours planning the introductions and the move
12 hours supervising the introductions
15 hours clarifying the adoption process and contact plans with the birth family

Court activities (15 hours)
10 hours writing the Schedule II report for the court
5 hours attending court and the adoption party after adoption order is granted

All of these estimates included time to organise, travel and record each activity as appropriate and totalled approximately 162 hours of social worker time per placement. The cost of this staff input was estimated from *Unit Costs* (2001) at £25 per hour of client-related activity and totalled £4,050 per placement.

From case file data, we also found that approximately £20 per child was spent on a new birth certificate and other materials in connection with the adoption. This cost was not included in the final unit cost calculation, as it was assumed that it was already covered in the "management and administrative overheads" element of the *Unit Costs* methodology.

Adoption medical adviser: The NHS employed the adoption medical adviser. As this was not a cost to SSDs, it was excluded from the unit cost estimation.

Adoption panel: Twenty-six adoption panels were held each year in our largest local authority (LA). The adoption planning manager, an administrator, the social workers bringing cases, and a number of unpaid independent experts attended panel meetings. Salary costs for the adoption planning manager, administrator and social workers are included separately so are not double counted here.

Adoption planning manager and assistant: The adoption planning manager provided specialist adoption support for all aspects of the adoption process. The cost of this manager was assumed not to be included in the "management and administrative overheads" element of the *Unit Costs* methodology as she was not the direct line manager of any social work teams. The adoption planning manager spent approximately eight hours per child on work connected with the adoption placement process, including checking and reading the child's Form E, meeting with workers and attending adoption panel meetings. Her assistant spent approximately three hours per child supporting these activities. In addition, the adoption planning manager spent approximately four hours and her assistant approximately three hours on similar activities regarding the adopters. Using actual salary data and the standard *Unit Costs* format for calculating on-costs and overheads, jointly these staff cost £426 per placement to undertake these activities.

Legal expenses: Sixteen of the 96 children in our sample were freed for adoption before their adoptions could proceed. Practice in our largest LA was to have joint care and freeing order hearings, whereas practice at the time our sample children were approved for adoption was to apply for a care order followed, sometimes several years later, by a freeing order if necessary. Only the freeing order was strictly an adoption cost and so a proportion of present-day legal costs were included to cover this.

To ascertain the freeing order cost, 12 sets of court proceedings from 2001, concluding with freeing orders, were examined. Sixteen children were involved in these proceedings. The total cost to the SSD of these proceedings was £105,095, with £6,568 being the average cost per child. The cheapest case was £2,679 and the most expensive £12,344. For seven of the 12 cases (or nine of the 16 children), it was possible to separate out the costs of the care order from the costs of the freeing order. The percentage cost of the freeing orders in these seven cases ranged from 10 per cent to 70 per cent, with 35 per cent the average amount. Using the average cost per child of £6,568, this would mean that the freeing order component of such legal proceedings would have cost approximately £2,299 per child. However, legal experts estimated that, with care and freeing orders now made concurrently, the percentage cost of the freeing order would be approximately 20 per cent lower, which would give a figure of £1,314 per child. Using this figure, the present-day legal costs for the 16 children in our sample who were freed for adoption would total £21,024. In addition, where there were complex legal situations, the foster or adoptive parents sometimes received independent legal advice, which was occasionally reimbursed by SSDs. Five adopters in our sample received these reimbursements totalling £2,439. With inflation this is £2,890 at 2001/2 prices.

Family placement worker: Our largest LA had a family placement team that dealt exclusively with the training and recruitment of adopters and foster carers. This team kept diaries over a three-month period and supplied us with the following information detailing the time approximately taken for adopters to be recruited, assessed and approved. Unfortunately, diaries were not kept for the time taken on matching and preparatory activities and so these figures are social worker and team manager estimates.

Approval activities (96 hours)
5 hours responding to enquiries, checking forms and facilitating information evening
15 hours per household running adoption training courses
60 hours to complete the adopter assessment
14 hours writing Form F
2 hours attending adoption panel (best interest meeting)

Matching activities (29 hours)
25 hours on matching activities
2 hours meeting with the child's social worker
2 hours attending adoption panel (matching meeting)

Preparatory activities (19 hours)
5 hours planning introductions and the move
14 hours on other adopter preparation

These time estimates again included an element for making arrangements, travelling and recording and totalled approximately 144 hours of family placement worker time per placement. The cost of this staff input was estimated using measures from *Unit Costs* at £25 per hour of client-related activity and totalled £3,600 per placement.

In addition, other financial costs incurred during this process were:
£12 per household for speaker costs for the adoption training course;
£40 per household for training materials;
£10 approximately per household for mileage for attendance at training courses.

This totalled approximately £62 per household for training expenses. These costs were not included in the final calculations as they were assumed to already be included in the "management and administrative overheads" element of the *Unit Costs* methodology.

Team manager: Because of the structure of our largest LA, three different team managers were involved in supervising all the adoption process social work activities, a children and families team manager, a recruitment family placement team manager and a permanency family placement team manager. From discussions with team managers, the following estimates of the time taken on these activities were assembled:

Recruitment family placement team manager (3 hours)
3 hours supervising placement worker during adopter assessment and checking Form F.

Permanency family placement team manager (8 hours)
3 hours supervising placement worker during matching
2 hours reading prospective child Form E and chairing matching meeting
3 hours chairing planning meeting for introductions and meeting relevant people

Children and families team manager (29 hours)
2 hours supervising social worker around time of adoption decision
2 hours supervising social worker around time of reviews
3 hours assisting with development of Form E
1 hour supervising social worker around going to panel

1 hour supervising social worker around going to court

3 hours reading prospective adopter F forms and discussion of prospective adopters

10 hours discussions, for example, around contact and work with birth parents

2 hours attending introductions planning meeting

3 hours general supervision updates

2 hours reading and checking Schedule II for court

This gave a total of approximately 40 hours of team manager time per placement. The cost of this staff input was estimated from *Unit Costs* at £31 per hour of client-related activity and totalled £1,240 per placement.

Consultations: BAAF or another agency was consulted in connection with four children from our sample. Assuming a two-hour meeting, at 2001/2 prices these consultations would cost £170 each. Thus, the total spent on consultations for our sample would be £680.

Consortium membership: In the year ending 31 March 2002 our LA spent £3,202 on consortium membership for a regional matching service with some joint training on matching and placement issues. During the same period, 11 children from the LA were successfully matched through the consortium, including five sibling groups of two. This represented 32 per cent of all children matched, by our LA that year. The consortium membership fee was therefore divided by the number of children matched, to give a cost of £291 per successful consortium match. This cost was included for 31 (32 per cent) children in our sample, and totalled £9,021.

Promotions: Only a very small number of the most "hard-to-place" children are now promoted in publications. Twenty-six (27 per cent) of our sample children were promoted via *Be My Parent*, Adoption UK, local newspapers or publications aiming to reach specific audiences. Some of these children were featured more than once. As our sample consisted of older and more "difficult-to-place" children, we have included in the cost estimates the prices in 2002 for promoting these 26 children. To promote children in *Be My Parent* cost £215 per issue. A quarter-page advert in *Adoption Today*, the Adoption UK publication, cost £204.

Advertising in a local newspaper or specialist magazine was also assumed to cost £204 per advert, as no other figures were available. One child had also had a promotional video made by BAAF costing £133. Using these figures, the total expenditure on promotion for our 26 sample children was £6,517.

Inter-agency fees: Sixteen (17 per cent) of our children were either placed out-of-area (5) or via a voluntary agency (11) and were therefore subject to inter-agency placement fees. In 2002, the rates for these fees were £10,539 for out-of-area placements and £14,931 for voluntary agency placements. For placement of sibling groups, there were reductions (one-and-a-half times the fee for two children, two times the fee for three or more children). Four of the children in our sample were part of a sibling pair placed through a voluntary agency and the fee for these children was adjusted accordingly. In addition, for one child in our sample only a partial interagency fee of £360 was paid as the prospective adoptive family later pulled out. Therefore, the total spent on inter-agency fees for our sample children, at 2001/2 prices, was £202,365.

Adopters' expenses for introductions: Twenty-nine adopters from our sample had been reimbursed for expenses relating to introductions. These totalled £4,319. After adjusting for inflation, the total cost for introductions was £5,117.

Foster carer expenses for introductions: Ten foster carers had been reimbursed for expenses relating to introductions. These expenses totalled £1,390 or £1,647 with inflationary increases added on.

Initial set-up grants: Thirty-seven adopters (39 per cent) received financial support from SSDs in the form of initial set-up grants. These varied between £35 and £607, with an average of £222. The total cost for our sample was £8,680, or £10,283 allowing for inflation.

Finance: Finance officers determined eligibility for adoption allowances. In our sample, 41 families were means tested in this way, taking approximately two hours of a finance officer's time per means test. Using actual salary data and the standard *Unit Costs* format for calculating on-costs and overheads, it cost £61 to means test a family.

Table 11. 1

Information sources and costs for individual elements of the adoption process

Service component	Source of information	Total costs (n = 96)
a) Staff costs		*£897,216*
Child's social worker	Client-related activity (*Unit Costs*)	£388,800
Family placement worker	Client-related activity (*Unit Costs*)	£345,600
Team managers	Client-related activity (*Unit Costs*)	£119,040
Adoption planning manager	Derived unit cost using salary data	£40,896
Adoption clerk	Derived unit cost using salary data	£2,880
b) Family-finding costs		*£218,583*
BAAF/Agency consultations	Information from BAAF	£680
Consortium membership	Information from LA	£9,021
Promotional costs	Information from BAAF/Adoption UK	£6,517
Inter-agency fees	Information from BAAF	£202,365
c) Payments to carers		*£19,937*
Adopter expenses	Actual payments plus inflation	£5,117
Foster carer expenses	Actual payments plus inflation	£1,647
Set-up grants	Actual payments plus inflation	£10,283
Adopter legal expenses	Actual payments plus inflation	£2,890
d) Other costs		*£23,520*
Legal costs	Information from LA	£21,024
Finance costs	Information from LA	£2,496

Adoption clerk: The adoption clerk managed the archiving of all new adoption files, checked that they were in order and updated the card and computer systems for each adoption. She estimated this took two hours per adoption. Using salary data of £15 per hour and the standard *Unit Costs* format, this worked out at £2,880 for the sample.

Management and support services: The *Unit Costs* methodology includes an element for all "management and administrative overheads" necessary to sustain the service delivery settings, i.e. the children's and families teams and the family placement teams. It was assumed that all

Table 11.2
Unit cost of the adoption process

Service component	Total input (hrs)	Cost per unit[1]	No. in receipt of service	Minimum cost per child[2]	Maximum cost per child[3]	Average cost per child
a) Staff costs				**£9,346**	**£9,346**	**£9,346**
Child's social worker	162	£25	96	£4,050	£4,050	£4,050
Family placement worker	144	£25	96	£3,600	£3,600	£3,600
Team managers	40	£31	96	£1,240	£1,240	£1,240
Adoption planning manager	18[4]	£28[5]	96	£426	£426	£426
Adoption clerk	2	£15	96	£30	£30	£30
b) Family-finding costs				**£0**	**£16,219**	**£2,277**
BAAF/Agency consultations	2	£85	4	£0	£170	£7
Consortium membership	–	–	31	£0	£291	£94
Promotional costs	–	–	26	£0	£827	£68
Inter-agency fees						
c) Payments to carers				**£0**	**£2,353**	**£207**
Adopter expenses	–	–	29	£0	£696	£53
Foster carer expenses	–	–	10	£0	£230	£17
Set-up grants	–	–	37	£0	£607	£107
Adopter legal expenses	–	–	41	£0	£820	£30
d) Other costs				**£0**	**£1,375**	**£245**
Legal costs	–	–	16	£0	£1,314	£219
Finance costs	–	–	5	£0	£61	£26
Total				**£9,346**	**£29,293**	**£12,075**

[1] Social worker and team manager costs are weighted costs per hour of client-related activity.
[2] For staff costs, average costs are shown due to the way the costs were estimated.
[3] For staff costs, average costs are shown due to the way the costs were estimated.
[4] Twelve hours of adoption planning manager plus six hours of administrative time.
[5] £15 per hour for administrative assistant.

functions such as payroll, personnel and IT were included in this cost, but that additional or specific adoption services were not. No further cost has therefore been included for these functions. Table 11.1 summarises the information sources and total costs discussed above for each element of the adoption process for the sample of 96 children placed for adoption.

Calculating the unit cost

To give the unit cost per child of the adoption process, the average cost per child of each of the individual service components was calculated from Table 11.1 and these individual costs were aggregated to give the average total cost of placing a child for adoption. Table 11.2 shows these calculations with minimum and maximum costs for each input. The information in columns one to four has been described in words in the preceding section. Column one gives the service component. Column two shows the number of hours of each service component dedicated to the adoption process. Column three gives, where applicable, the cost per unit of each service component. Column four shows the number of children in the sample of 96 who have received these services. Columns five and six show the minimum and maximum possible costs of services received by these children. Where some children did not receive the service, the minimum cost is given as zero. For services that all children received, these minimum and maximum costs are the same as the average costs. The final column gives the average cost per child. Each of these columns is summed and the total given on the bottom line of the table. For example, the figure £29,293 is the cost of the adoption process assuming that a child was in receipt of all possible services.

Based on data for a complete sample of 96 children adopted during the 1990s, the adoption process unit cost per child is therefore £12,075. As all cost estimations were adjusted to reflect 2001/2 prices this unit cost represents the average cost to SSDs of placing a looked after child for adoption in 2001/2. Costs would, of course, vary depending on the complexity of the case, the amount of staff time taken to find an appropriate placement, the need for promotional activities or payment of an inter-agency fee. This is reflected in the range of costs given, from £9,346 to £29,293.

This is the first cost estimation exercise to investigate the costs of placing a complete sample of children for adoption based on actual case file data. Thus, the estimates of family-finding costs and payments to carers are precise and reliable but, due to the way the data were collected, further research is needed to verify the accuracy and generalisability of the estimates of staff time devoted to these activities. Of course, more or less staff time would have an impact on the total unit cost. We suspect that the estimates given by social workers are more likely to be underestimates than overestimates. Consequently, the adoption process unit cost may be an underestimate. The methodology employed and the data used have, however, been clearly set out and any of the components can be adjusted to reflect more accurate data if it were to become available.

Nevertheless, the figure of £12,075 does warrant comment. Staff costs made up just over three-quarters of the adoption process unit cost (77 per cent), family-finding costs just under a fifth (19 per cent) and grants/reimbursements to carers and legal/finance costs only two per cent each. It is important to note, however, that the social worker and team manager unit costs used were weighted unit costs, specifying the cost per hour of client-related activity, rather than the cost per working hour. Although it was appropriate to use these more accurate weighted unit costs (Beecham, 2000), they do alter the final unit cost and this needs to be borne in mind if comparing with other cost estimation exercises.

It is interesting that the lion's share of this cost comes out of the children and families budget and in the case of our largest LA, the adoption planning manager's budget, and that only about a third of the cost is borne by the family placement team. Clearly, this has considerable cost implications if children are placed out of area or via a voluntary agency. For example, the LA incurs an inter-agency fee of between £10,960 and almost £19,000 for a child placed via a voluntary agency in London. Although our unit cost has included an element for inter-agency fees, it is easy to see how much they inflate the cost of placing a child for adoption and why many authorities restrict the use of inter-agency placements. This problem needs to be addressed if financial constraints are not to continue to restrict placement choice. BAAF has recommended that the government make ring-fenced funds available for inter-agency placement to allow hard-pressed authorities to seek families as widely as possible and to enable voluntary agencies to recruit more families in the knowledge that the costs of recruiting and supporting these families would be assured.

These calculations could be readily amended to reflect different local authority or voluntary agency data or, if information were available, a more representative national picture. Equally, if practice changes, for example if more adopters are paid initial set-up grants or more children placed in inter-agency placements, the calculations could be amended to reflect these changes. This cost information will enable councils with social services responsibility (CSSRs) to be better able to anticipate the costs they may incur in order to meet current adoption targets and be able to budget more effectively for changes in adoption practice.

Post-placement unit cost

The post-placement adoption support service components are described below and a "post-placement" unit cost per week calculated. This is the cost to SSDs of maintaining a "looked after" child in an adoptive placement pre-adoption order. The costs to voluntary agencies may look very different depending on the level of service they provide.

Identifying the activities, the unit of measurement and costs

Prior to the granting of the adoption order, the child was still officially "looked after"; the adoptive family frequently received a boarding-out allowance or other financial support, and the child and family received social work support and services similar to those received by foster children and families. In addition, SSDs continued to facilitate contact with the child's birth family. The post-placement adoption support activities and a cost estimate for each activity are listed below.

Social worker visits: As reliable data were not available from case files, details of the frequency of social work support were collected from the interviews with adoptive families. All of the families had been supported by at least one social worker during the first year of the adoptive placement. A total of 547 CSW and 484 family placement worker (FPW) visits were made during this year. As data were only available for 64 children (exactly two-thirds of the sample), these figures were increased proportionately to give a cost estimate for the whole sample of 96. This gave a total of 820 CSW and 726 FPW visits. Each social work visit was assumed to take an hour. The cost of these 1,546 social work visits was estimated using a derived unit cost of £95 per hour (based on the *Unit Costs* adult social worker cost per hour of face-to-face contact and increased proportionately to reflect the higher wages of children's social workers). The figure of £95 per hour was used as it includes an element of time for the planning of and travel to visits, recording and additional tasks after visits. This gave a total cost estimate for the sample of £146,870 per year.

Adoption/fostering allowances: The adoptive families of 65 of the 96 children were receiving either an adoption or fostering allowance from SSDs (68 per cent) during the first year of the adoptive placement. At the time the children were placed, it was common for a fostering allowance to be paid before the adoption order was granted. We therefore applied our largest LA's 2001/2 fostering allowance for a 5–7-year-old child to this data, as average age at placement for our sample was five years seven months. In 2002 this was £85.60 per week, which over a year for the 65 families amounted to £289,328. In addition, Christmas, birthday and holiday allowances would be paid. The rates for these were approximately £70, £70 and £140 respectively and totalled £16,800 for our sample.

Other financial support: The families of 31 children (32 per cent) received payments of between £15 and £1,070 during the first year of the placement. This was typically in the form of clothing grants, especially where the child was to be adopted by his or her foster carers. These payments totalled £7,353 or £9,028 including an element for inflation.

Reimbursed travel expenses: During the first year of placement two adopters (2 per cent) were reimbursed travel expenses. These reimbursements totalled £642 or £682 with inflation.

Respite care and childminding: Six families (6 per cent) received in total 31 weeks of respite care before the adoption order. These weeks were assigned a unit cost of £247 each, as developed for a 2002 "Best Value" exercise. Thus, at 2001/2 prices a total of £7,657 would have been spent on respite care on our sample over the year. Four families (4 per cent) received 322 hours of childminding support in the year. This was estimated to cost a nominal rate of £5 per hour and totalled £1,610.

Additional worker support: A community care worker, disabilities worker or sessional worker supported five families (5 per cent) during the first year of placement. This took 414 hours of community care worker time, 98 hours of a sessional worker time and four hours of a disabilities worker time over the year. The *Unit Costs* of £12.26 per hour of face-to-face contact was taken for the community care worker. This gave a cost of £5,076 for the year. Disabilities workers are qualified social workers, so again the unit cost of £95 per hour of face-to-face contact was used for these calculations. For the unqualified sessional workers, a figure of £10 per hour of face-to-face contact was taken from information provided by our largest LA. This gave an expenditure of £380 and £980 respectively for the disabilities worker and sessional workers.

Skills sessions: One family (1 per cent) attended a 12-hour parenting skills course. The course was run by a family placement worker and was estimated to cost £300 (12 hours at the £25 per hour of client-related activity rate, assuming little additional time was necessary).

Child protection conferences: Seven children (5 per cent) were the subjects of 13 child protection conferences during the year. A small sub-study was conducted to estimate a unit cost for child protection conferences. This study estimated the child protection conference cost to social services to be £783. Using this figure, the total cost of the conferences for our study children was £10,179.

Other adoption support: Four families (4 per cent) also received other adoption support in the form of post-adoption modules from voluntary agencies. These were included at the 2001/2 price of £2,488 and cost a total of £9,952.

Letterbox contact: Thirty-six of 64 children (56 per cent) were having letterbox contact with their birth families during the first year of placement. They received between one and ten items over the year, giving a total of 130 items. Two authorities provided the necessary information on letterbox activity so that a unit cost could be developed. The unit cost per item was £38, giving a total of £4,940 for the year. Half of this figure again was added on to give an estimate of the cost of letterbox contact for the full sample of 96 and totalled £7,410.

Supervised face-to-face contact: Twenty (31 per cent) of the 64 children whose adoptive parents were interviewed had supervised contact with a member of their birth family during the first year of placement. Thirty contact visits were with birth parents, 26 with birth siblings and 11 with birth relatives. Of these, 20 took place at an SSD contact venue. Costs were incurred through social worker time plus the cost of the use of a room at a family centre. All contact visits were assumed to be two hours long, although this may be an overestimate in some cases. The derived unit cost of £95 per hour of face-to-face social worker time was used for these calculations, because of the booking, recording and other support activities that would take place outside the visit itself. A room rental figure of £25 per half day as quoted by a local family centre was used. This gave a total of £12,730 for social worker time and an additional £500 for the contact centre rental. Thus, the total cost to SSDs of facilitating contact over the year for these 64 children was £13,230. Half this figure again was added on to give an estimate of the cost of supervised contact for the full sample of 96 and totalled £19,845.

Travel expenses for contact: During the first year of placement, eight (8 per cent) adopters of the 96 children were reimbursed for travel expenses related to contact. These reimbursements totalled £1,074. Four birth parents were also reimbursed their bus or taxi fares for contact totalling £206. Thus, the total spent on expenses for contact was £1,280. Inflated to 2001/2 prices this was £1,494.

Adoption support group: Two social workers in our largest local authority ran an adoption support group that all adopters were welcome to attend. Workers estimated this involved 34 hours of face-to-face contact for each of them per year (ten × three-hour meetings and two all-day events). In addition, the social workers planned the meetings, arranged the summer and Christmas events each year and managed the administration of the group. The cost of these 68 face-to-face hours per year was estimated using £95 per hour of face-to-face contact, and gave £6,460 per year. Twenty-one (33 per cent) of the 64 adoptive families who were interviewed said they attended the adoption support group during the first year of placement. This is approximately the number that currently attends the group and so the full £6,460 was included as a cost estimate of providing the service for these families and multiplied up to give an estimate of £9,690 to provide this service for the full sample of 96.

Team managers: Team managers regularly supervised social workers. They estimated that they spent approximately four hours per year discussing with each social worker a newly placed child and family in receipt of post-placement support services. In addition, supervised contact arrangements and letterbox arrangements might require further discussions, which were estimated to take on average a further two hours per year for supervised contact and one hour per year for letterbox. This gave a total of 840 hours of team manager time, the cost of which was estimated using the *Unit Costs* £31 per hour of client-related activity and gave a total of £26,040 for the year.

Adoption planning manager and assistant: The adoption planning manager managed all post-adoption related matters, including handling queries about adoption allowances, post-adoption support and letterbox contact. It was estimated that this manager would spend an average of approximately five hours over the year on these activities in relation to a new adoptive family and her assistant three hours. Using a combination of team manager and assistant salary data and the standard *Unit Costs* format for calculating on-costs and overheads, this would cost £17,760 for the full sample of 96 children.

Finance officers: Finance officers conduct the initial means test to see if a family is eligible for an adoption allowance and annually review continuing eligibility. Finance officers estimated this took two hours of their time. We assumed that all of the families in receipt of an adoption or fostering allowance would either have had an annual review or would have been means tested for eligibility and therefore applied this cost for 65 of our families. Using actual salary data and the standard *Unit Costs* format for calculating on-costs and overheads, it would have cost £1,690 to undertake these activities in the first year.

Other: The local authority paid £312.50 to Adoption UK and £10,639 per year subscription to a local voluntary adoption support group, who provided an independent adoption helpline and counselling for adopters, adoptees and birth family members. These subscriptions came out of the adoption planning manager's budget and have not been included in the unit cost calculation as they were assumed to be part of the "management and administrative overheads" already included. The same goes for the more general management and support service costs. Table 11.3 lists these details.

Calculating the unit cost

To calculate the unit cost of post-placement adoption support, the average cost per child of each of the inputs was calculated and these costs summed to give the average cost to SSDs per year. Table 11.4 shows these calculations with, where possible, the minimum and maximum costs for each element.

The calculations for the post-placement unit cost per child per week were based on case file and interview data for a sample of 96 children adopted during the 1990s. We estimate that this unit cost is £6,070 per year or £117 per week, with a range of between £21 and £260 per week using 2001/2 prices. These figures seem surprisingly low given that the unit cost of in-house foster care in our largest LA was £318 a week.

The unit cost may be low for a number of reasons. Firstly, adoptive placements have not been supported to the same extent as foster care placements. For example, only 68 per cent of adoptive families were in receipt of an allowance, whereas all foster care placements would be. Secondly, the adoptive placement allowances were all calculated at the 5–7-year-old rate, whereas foster care placements would span the whole age range, with carers receiving considerably more for older children. Thirdly, we estimated the number of social worker visits. This estimate was based on adopters' recall of the number of social work visits they received, often more than five years ago. It may be that time had diminished their memory and that they did, in fact, receive more visits than they recall. In addition, this method of calculating staff costs has not noted the exact time taken for all the other social work activities that may have taken place to support the placements, for example, phone calls to adopters and liaison with the school. We have, however, employed a very heavily weighted cost of £95 per hour to cover these activities. This allows for approximately another three hours of activity connected to each visit, but this may still be insufficient. Lastly, the approaches to unit cost estimation were different.

Table 11.3

Information sources and costs for individual elements of post-placement adoption support

Service components	Source of information	Costs per annum (n = 64)
a) Social work visits		**£146,870**
	Derived from *Unit Costs*	£146,870
b) Financial support		**£315,838**
Allowances	Information from LA	£306,128
Miscellaneous payments	Actual payments plus inflation	£9,710
c) Other service provision		**£36,134**
Respite care	LA "Best Value" in-house fostering unit cost	£9,858
Childminding	Information from LA	£1,610
Additional workers	From *Unit Costs* (face-to-face) & LA	£6,436
Skills sessions	From *Unit Costs* (client-related activity)	£300
CP conferences	From sub-study	£10,179
Post-adoption modules	Information from BAAF	£9,952
d) Birth family contact		**£38,335**
Letterbox contact	Derived from LA information	£7,410
Supervised contact	Derived from *Unit Costs*	£19,845
Contact travel expenses	Actual payments plus inflation	£1,494
e) Other costs		**£55,180**
Support group	Information from LA	£9,690
Team managers	From *Unit Costs* (client-related activity)	£26,040
Planning manager	Information on salary from LA & *Unit Costs* method of calculation	£17,760
Finance officer	Information on salary from LA & *Unit Costs* method of calculation	£1,690

Table 11.4
Unit cost of post-placement adoption support

Service component	Total input per year (hrs)	Cost per unit	No. who received service	Minimum cost per child per year	Maximum spent on a child in the year[1]	Average cost per child per year
a) Staff costs						**£2,003**
Child's social worker	820hrs[2]	£95	91[2]	£0	£3,800	£811
Family placement worker	726hrs[2]	£95	88[2]	£0	£4,275	£718
Team managers	840hrs	£31	96	£124	£341	£271
Adoption manager	768hrs[3]	£28[4]	96	£185	£185	£185
Finance officer	130hrs	£13	65	£0	£26	£18
b) Financial support						**£3,290**
Adoption allowances	£306,128	–	65	£0	£4,731	£3,189
Other payments	£9,710	–	33	£0	£1,070	£101
c) Other service provision						**£477**
Respite care	31wks	£247	6	£0	£4,446	£80
Childminding	322hrs	£5	4	£0	£1,400	£16
Additional workers	516hrs	£12[5]	5	£0	£2,972	£67
Skills ressions	12hrs	£25	1	£0	£300	£3
CP conferences	13hrs	£783	7	£0	£3,132	£106
Post-adoption modules	4hrs	£248	4	£0	£2,488	£104
Support group	–	8[6]	32	£0	£302	£101
d) Birth family contact					**£0**	**£300**
Letterbox contact	195 items	£38	50	£0	£380	£77
Supervised contact	100 visits	£190[7]	37	£0	£4,940	£207
Contact travel expenses	£1,494	–	12	£0	£355	£16
Total						**£6,070**

[1] One child would not receive all these services. A total amount is not therefore applicable.
[2] Estimates for the full sample of 96 are based on data for 64 children whose adopters were interviewed.
[3] 480 hours of adoption planning manager and 288 hours of administrative support.
[4] £15 for administrative assistant.
[5] £12.26 per hour community care worker, £95 per hour family link worker, £10 per hour sessional worker.
[6] See text for an explanation of this support.
[7] Two hours of social work time at £95 per hour (excluding contact centre cost).

In our study we employed a bottom-up approach, detailing and costing all services received, whereas the local authority Best Value review employed a top-down approach, allocating the costs of all resources between all placements.

There is also the possibility that the low unit cost may in fact reflect the fact that the adoptive families were under-supported, an opinion that many of our adopters would hold. This possibility is reinforced by the results of a previous costing exercise where the Children in Need census data for our largest LA were examined. The costs of supporting looked after children in adoptive placements were extricated from the rest of the looked after children costs and were £63 per week.

Allowances and other financial support comprised over half (54 per cent) of the unit cost, staff costs totalled 33 per cent, other service provision eight per cent and costs associated with birth family contact five per cent. These figures do disguise the full costs of contact. A proportion of the team manager time was spent reviewing contact arrangements and thus contact does require more than five per cent of the overall resource use. It is important to underline as well that the social worker unit cost used was heavily weighted and specified the cost per hour of face-to-face contact, rather than the cost per working hour. This more accurate weighted unit cost was the most appropriate one to use (Beecham, 2000), but does give higher staff costs and this should be borne in mind if making comparisons with other cost estimation exercises that have not employed weighted costs.

Post-adoption unit cost

The post-adoption support service components are described below and a unit cost per week for post-adoption support calculated. This represents the cost in 2001/2 to SSDs of providing post-adoption support services for a previously looked after child. At the time this study was undertaken, most adoptive families were not supported by SSDs after the making of the adoption order. The SSD resource use detailed here is slightly different from that found in Chapter 8, as it is based on a sample of 69 adoptive placements, five of which had disrupted, whereas Chapter 8 only details the resource use for the

64 adoptive placements that were still intact at the time of the follow-up interviews.

Identifying the activities, the unit of measurement and costs

Social worker visits: The frequency of social work visits from the FPW and CSW in the 12 months prior to follow-up was collected. Twenty-three of the 69 families (33 per cent) had been visited by a social worker during the year; a total of 96 FPW and 109 CSW visits. Each social work visit was assumed to take an hour. Face-to-face contact at £95 per hour was used to estimate the cost of these 205 social work hours, giving £19,475 for the year.

Adoption allowances: Adopters of 25 (36 per cent) of the 69 children were in receipt of adoption allowances of between £23 and £110 per week with £64 per week (£3,343 per year) being the average amount per adopter. Therefore, the total cost of the adoption allowance for the 25 adopters was £83,564 for the year.

Other financial support: Five families (7 per cent) had received payments of between £90 and £2,400 from SSDs in the year prior to interview. These payments totalled £3,460.

Respite care: Seven families (10 per cent) received respite care for a total of 36 weeks over the year. These weeks were assigned a unit cost of £318 each (our largest LA's Best Value unit cost for in-house foster care) which gave a total of £11,448 spent on respite care over the year.

Additional worker support: Nine families (13 per cent) received support from a community care worker (552 hours), sessional worker (113 hours) or disabilities worker (four hours) post-adoption. The *Unit Cost* of £12.26 per hour of face-to-face contact was used to estimate the community care worker costs and gave an expenditure of £6,400 for the year. Disabilities workers are qualified social workers, so the £95 per hour of face-to-face contact cost was used for these calculations. For the unqualified sessional workers a figure of £10 per hour of face-to-face contact was provided by the local authority employing these workers. This gave an expenditure of £380 and £1,130 respectively for the family link worker and sessional workers.

Therapeutic and skills sessions: Two (3 per cent) families in crisis received 21 hours of therapeutic support, paid for by SSDs, from a family therapist or clinical psychologist. The *Unit Cost* of £36 per clinical psychologist chargeable hour was used for this which gave £756 for the year. In addition, three (4 per cent) families received practical support in the form of 40 hours of parenting skills sessions. In each case, these were provided jointly by the social worker and team manager. A unit cost per hour was therefore developed by averaging across the *Unit Cost* social worker cost per face-to-face hour (£95) and the social work team leader cost per hour of client-related activity (£31). This figure was used for the team leader as it was not assumed that he/she would also be involved with recording the outcome of the sessions/arranging the next sessions and so on. The derived cost was calculated at £63 per hour, which gave a total of £2,520 over the year.

Social work assessments: Two (3 per cent) families in crisis were subject to comprehensive (core) social work assessments as a consequence of abuse allegations during the year. Social workers estimated that these would have taken a day a week of social worker time for six weeks, i.e. a total of 42 hours each. This was costed using the *Unit Cost* of £25 per hour of client-related activity, giving a total cost of £1,050 per assessment or £2,100 for the year.

Child protection conferences: Four (6 per cent) children were the subjects of nine child protection conferences during the year. The cost of the nine conferences for our study children was £7,047 for the year.

Other post-adoption support: Three (4 per cent) families also received 28 hours of other post-adoption social work support. Two hours were reviews of respite care arrangements and the remainder were specific social work interventions for a placement in crisis provided by another team. The derived £95 per hour of face-to-face contact cost was used for these calculations and gave an annual expenditure of £2,660.

Letterbox contact: Twenty-five of the 69 (36 per cent) children were having letterbox contact with their birth families at the time of the follow-up. They received between one and six items over the year, giving a total of 83 items. The unit cost per item was £38 giving a total of £3,154 for the year.

Supervised face-to-face contact: At the time of the follow-up, a total of 24 contact visits had been supervised by a social worker over the year. The cost to SSDs of facilitating this contact was the amount of social worker time for 20 of the contact visits and the social worker time plus the cost of the use of a room at a family centre for the other four visits. All contact visits were assumed to be two hours long. The derived unit cost of £95 per hour of face-to-face contact was used for these calculations, along with a room rental figure of £25 per half-day as quoted to us by a local family centre. This gave a total of £3,800 for the non-contact centre visits and £860 for the contact centre visits (£100 room rental and £760 social worker time). Thus, the total cost to SSDs of facilitating contact over the year was £4,660.

Travel expenses for contact: Three (4 per cent) adopters were reimbursed for travel expenses related to contact during the year prior to the follow-up. These reimbursements totalled £480. Three birth parents were also reimbursed their bus fares for contact, totalling approximately £20.

Adoption support group: Data about, and cost estimates for, this activity were provided by our largest LA. Eleven adoptive families (16 per cent) attended an adoption support group in the year prior to the interviews. This was approximately half of the attendees at our largest LA's support group and therefore half the costs of this group (£3,320) have been included as the best estimate of the cost for this activity. (The derivation of this cost is described in the previous section on post-placement.)

Team managers: Team managers provide regular supervision. From discussions with team managers, we estimated that a social worker spent approximately two hours per year in discussions with each child and family in receipt of post-adoption support services. In addition, supervised contact arrangements and letterbox arrangements might require further discussions, which were estimated to take on average a further two hours per year for supervised contact and one hour per year for letterbox. The costs of this time were included even if the family had not received any social work visits. This gave a total of 93 hours of team manager time, which was costed using the *Unit Cost* of £31 per hour of client-related activity to give £2,883 for the year.

Adoption planning manager and assistant: It was estimated that this manager would spend an average of two hours and her assistant one hour over the year on post-adoption support activities, such as letterbox or queries about allowances. Using appropriate salary data and the standard *Unit Cost* format for calculating on-costs and overheads, this would cost £4,899 for the sample for the year.

Finance officers: Finance officers annually review adoptive families' eligibility for an adoption allowance, which takes approximately two hours of an officer's time. This would have been the case for 25 of our sample families. Using actual salary data and the standard *Unit Cost* format, £650 per year was needed to undertake these activities.

Other: The local authority paid £10,639 per year subscription to a local voluntary adoption support group, who provided an independent adoption helpline and counselling for adopters, adoptees and birth family members, and £312.50 to Adoption UK. These subscriptions came out of the adoption planning manager's budget and have not been included in the unit cost calculation as they were assumed to be part of the "management and administrative overheads" already included. The same goes for the more general management and support service costs. Table 11.5 shows the sources of information and the costs per year for each element of the post-adoption support service.

Calculating the unit cost

Table 11.6 uses the total costs in Table 11.5 to calculate the average cost per child of each of the individual service components, and to aggregate them to give the average total cost of supporting a child post-adoption. As in the tables in the previous sections, the first four columns describe the service components, their costs and the numbers of children receiving these services. The final three columns show the possible minimum and maximum costs for each input per child, and the average cost per child. Total costs are given on the bottom row of the table.

The unit cost per child per week of post-adoption support is based on a sample of 69 children adopted from four south-west local authorities. Data were collected in 2001/2. At that time, the unit cost was £2,334 per year or £45 per child per week. This unit cost shows that SSD expenditure

177

Table 11.5

Sources of information and costs per year of post-adoption support

Service components	Source of information	Costs per annum (n = 69)
a) Social work visits		**£19,475**
	Derived from *Unit Costs*	£19,475
b) Financial support		**£87,024**
Adoption allowances	Actual payments	£83,564
Miscellaneous payments	Actual payments	£3,460
c) Other service provision		**£31,885**
Respite care	LA Best Value in-house fostering	£8,892
Additional workers	From *Unit Costs*	£7,910
Therapeutic sessions	From *Unit Costs*	£756
Skills sessions	Derived from *Unit Costs*	£2,520
Social work assessments	Derived from *Unit Costs*	£2,100
CP conferences	Own cost from sub-study	£7,047
Other post-adoption	Derived from *Unit Costs*	£2,660
d) Birth family contact		**£8,314**
Letterbox contact	Derived from LA information	£3,154
Supervised contact	Derived from *Unit Costs*	£4,660
Contact travel expenses	Actual payments	£500
e) Other costs		**£11,752**
Support group	Information from LA	£3,320
Team managers	From *Unit Costs*	£2,883
Adoption manager	Information from LA	£4,899
Finance officer	Information on salary from LA	£650

on adoptive placements reduced by two-thirds once the adoption order was granted. It is likely that this unit cost is the most accurate as adopters were recalling services they had received in the last year. Allowances and other financial support comprised 55 per cent of the unit cost, staff costs comprised 18 per cent (notably less than the post-placement figure of 33 per cent), other service provision 22 per cent and costs associated with birth family contact were five per cent of the total.

Table 11.6
Unit cost of post-adoption support

Service component	Total input per year (hrs)	Cost per unit	No. who received service	Minimum cost per child per year	Maximum spent on a child in the year[1]	Average cost per child per year
a) Staff costs				**£71**		**£404**
Child's social worker	96hrs	£95	13	£0	£1,900	£132
Family placement worker	109hrs	£95	13	£0	£2,280	£150
Team managers	93hrs	£31	45[2]	£0	£155	£42
Adoption manager	207hrs[3]	£28[4]	69	£71	£71	£71
Finance officer	50hrs	£13	25	£0	£26	£9
b) Financial support				**£0**		**£1,261**
Adoption allowances	£83,564	–	25	£0	£5,720	£1,211
Other payments	£3,460	–	5	£0	£2,400	£50
c) Other service provision				**£0**		**£548**
Respite care	36wks	£247	7	£0	£1,976	£166
Additional workers	639hrs	£12[5]	9	£0	£3,825	£115
Therapeutic support	21hrs	£36	2	£0	£540	£11
Skills sessions	40hrs	£63[6]	3	£0	£1,134	£37
Social work assessments	84hrs	£25	2	£0	£1,050	£30
CP conferences	9	£783	4	£0	£2,349	£102
Other post-adoption support hrs	28hrs	£95	3	£0	£2,470	£39
Support group	–	–[7]	11	£0	£302	£48
d) Birth family contact				**£0**		**£121**
Letterbox contact	83 items	£38	25	£0	£228	£46
Supervised contact	24 visits	£190[8]	10	£0	£860	£68
Contact travel expenses	£500	–	6	£0	£205	£7
Total				**£0**		**£2,334**

[1] One child would not receive all these services. Totals therefore not applicable.
[2] See text for explanation.
[3] 138 hours of adoption planning manager and 69 hours of administrative support.
[4] £15 for administrative assistant.
[5] £12.26 per hour community care worker, £95 per hour family link worker, £10 per hour sessional worker.
[6] See text for an explanation.
[7] See text for an explanation.
[8] Two hours of social work time at £95 per hour (excluding contact centre cost).

179

Figure 11.1
Patterns of post-adoption support

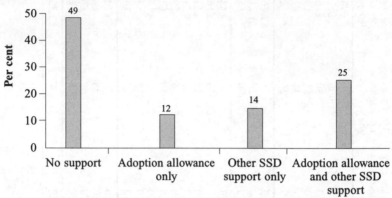

It would appear then that, for our largest LA, maintaining a child in an adoptive placement post-adoption represented a saving of approximately £284 per child per week compared with continuing to support the child in LA foster care. If placed in independent foster care, adoption would provide an even greater saving. With the present trend to increase the number of adoptions and increase post-adoption support services, the cost implications of service development could easily be forecast by adjusting the relevant figures set out in this cost estimation exercise.

As we were interested in understanding more about the costs of post-adoption support, we investigated the different patterns and the cost implications of support. Figure 11.1 summarises the patterns of support for the 69 children.

Thirty-four of the adoptive families (49 per cent) were not receiving any support from SSDs and a further eight (12 per cent) were only receiving an adoption allowance for their child. Seventeen (25 per cent) of the adoptive families were in receipt of an adoption allowance and at least one other form of support from SSDs. Table 11.7 shows the cost implications of the differing levels of adoption support service.

There were still costs to SSDs for those children and families who were not receiving any financial or practical support, due to the costs of facilitating contact with the children's birth families and the associated

Table 11.7

The cost implications of the different patterns of post-adoption support

Pattern of support to adoptive families	Average cost per week
No support (but contact costs)	£4
Adoption allowance only	£80
No adoption allowance but other SSD support	£50
Adoption allowance and other SSD support	£104

time from the adoption planning manager. It is not surprising that the cost, £104 per week, of providing a more substantial post-adoption service, is very similar to the £117 unit cost of supporting children in their adoptive families before the adoption order was made. All of the above costs include contact costs and managerial and administrative costs. Thus, the average cost of £80 per week of supporting an adoptive family with just an adoption allowance is more than the average amount families were receiving in adoption allowances (£66) per week.

The cost implications of the different levels of post-adoption support services could be helpful to local authorities trying to improve and cost their post-adoption support services. In this study, approximately 30 per cent of adoptive families did not want any continued social work support (except for an adoption allowance if they were eligible) after the making of the adoption order. Twenty-five per cent of families were receiving allowances and were also receiving social work support but of these only a third were receiving intensive support. However, what also needs to be borne in mind was that many adopters were unaware of the existence of post-adoption services. As this area receives more publicity, so the demand for these services might grow.

It was also possible to identify the costs for the adopted children in the sample. So far, we have described the costs *per year*, but by examining time taken for matching and the making of adoption orders the average cost for adoption for a child in this sample was £25,782. The vast majority were matched and placed within a year of the best interest decision but the average length of time between placement and the making of an adoption order was 2.4 years. We have assumed that on average the same level of support went into the families in the first and second years.

Within the scope of this study, data were collected which would give the most accurate picture of the resources SSDs were using. Diaries were used by social workers so that time could be allocated appropriately to adoption or fostering activities, rather than be subsumed within the family placement budget. A local authority's legal department also helped collect data to enable an estimate of legal costs. However, because the data were collected with each child as the main focus, this method lost some of the costs of adoption. For example, a great deal of social work time was expended recruiting adopters, but from the many who make initial enquires only a few become approved adopters.

It was not possible to allocate the costs of "drop-out" in this study. Similarly, by building costs per child we may have overestimated the costs when sibling groups needed an adoptive placement. For example, each child had a "matching cost" calculated, but a sibling group of three may not have taken three times the amount of social work time. We were unable within the limitations of this study to compare the costs of single placements versus sibling groups.

Summary of the costs of adoption

- The average cost in 2002 of placing a child for adoption was £12,075, with a range of £9,346 to £29,293.
- The average cost in 2002 of supporting the child in their adoptive home until the making of an adoption order was £6,092 per year, with a range of £1,092 to £13,520.
- The average cost of providing post-adoption support services in 2002 was £2,334, with a range of £71 to around £13,500, assuming respite care was provided.
- The average cost to SSDs for family-finding and supporting the placement until the making of the adoption order for children in this sample was £25,782.
- Forty-nine per cent of adopters were receiving no support services at the time of the follow-up.

12 The lives of the permanently placed children

This chapter follows the placement histories and experiences of the children who found some stability through long-term foster or kinship care. The characteristics of these children are given in Table 12.1.

Table 12.1
Characteristics of the permanently placed children

Characteristic	Percentage (n = 34)
Boys	62
Minority ethnic heritage	21
Mean age at entry to care	4.1 years
Mean age at approval for adoption	7.1 years
Percentage of children matched for adoption	38

Pathways to placement

The children in this group were those who were, at follow-up, in intact long-term foster or kin placements, often as a consequence of a change of plan following the best interests decision or following unsuccessful attempts at adoption. It should be remembered that these children were the ones whose placements had remained intact at the time the study began.

The move to permanence

In the beginning, the adoption panel decision was that adoption was in the best interests of all these children. It was hoped that three would be adopted by their current foster carers, two by kin and the remaining 29 by new families. The search for new families for 13 children was kept within the local authority (LA), sought for six children through voluntary agencies and four were promoted through BAAF. Twelve children in all were matched with a prospective adoptive family. All these adoption attempts disrupted. The majority of matches with strangers disrupted in the early stages, half during introductions, whereas matches with foster carers disrupted much later.[1] For three children, the plan for family permanence was abandoned early on.

Following this, the plan changed to long-term foster care for all bar these three children. Plans changed because suitable adoptive families could not be found, or current carers decided they wanted to foster rather than adopt, or social workers' inactivity or staff vacancies prevented the plan being taken forward. For the three where the plan for family permanence was abandoned, one moved into independent living after a foster care breakdown and another returned home. The third child was placed in a residential facility, as a consequence of severe physical and learning difficulties. This was a stable placement with a stable staff group and with other disabled children needing long-term care. This left 31 children in intended long-term foster and kin placements.

Disruptions

Just over one-quarter of the first intended long-term placements disrupted; three between six months and two years after placement, and five after more than two years.[2] At this point, the children had been in placement for six months to seven years,[3] having been placed when they were between seven and 13.[4] Children whose placements did not disrupt were somewhat younger at placement (mean 7.5 years), but not significantly so. This lower mean age was partly because the age range was wide (from under one year to 12 years).

Six of the children whose placements disrupted were placed again. Half of these had disrupted by follow-up, although their carers continued to look after them until another placement could be found. All had disrupted due the young people's aggressive and unco-operative behaviour. All three were still in frequent contact with their previous carers at the time of the follow-up.

---

[1] During introductions 46 per cent of stranger adoptive placements disrupted v 0 per cent of foster carer adoptive placements. After two years 0 per cent of stranger adoptive placements disrupted v 50 per cent of foster carer adoptive placements.

[2] Mean age at disruption 12.8yrs s.d. 2.1.

[3] Mean 3.4 years s.d. 1.9.

[4] Mean 9 years s.d. 2.1.

Where were they at the follow-up?

At the time of the follow-up the children were living in the following circumstances:

Table 12.2
Whereabouts of the 31 children at the time of follow-up

Type of placements	Number	Percentage n = 31
LA long-term foster care	20	65
Independent living	5	16
Independent foster care	2	6
Kinship care	2	6
Supported lodgings	2	6

Characteristics of the carers

Twenty-one of the foster carers agreed to be interviewed. These included one kinship carer who had a residence order. At the time interviews took place, 20 young people were still living with their carers, although in two cases the placements seemed about to disrupt. Three foster carers were interviewed where the young people had recently left their foster family for independent living or supported lodgings.

Eleven of the carers knew the children before the placement was made. The rest of the carers had responded to advertisements or heard on the foster carers "grapevine" about the children. One-fifth (19 per cent) of the carers were single carers, 76 per cent were white and 40 per cent were also providing short-term and long-term foster care for other children. Long-term foster families tended to be larger than those in the general population (range 1–9 children) and the desire and capacity to care for more children was the main reason given for wanting to offer a permanent home to a child. Interviews were mostly with foster mothers on their own (75 per cent), but 15 per cent were with both carers and 10 per cent with foster fathers only.

The children were on average older at the time they joined their long-term foster family than those who entered adoptive families (on average, seven years versus five years). For some children this was due to delays in implementing their care plans. For 12 others (35 per cent), it was because of failed adoptive placements. Three children had lived with their foster carers since they were 18 months or younger, but the original plan had been to place them for adoption elsewhere. The carers were also older than adoptive parents and, in contrast to adopting families, all the carers had children already in the household, most usually birth children (79 per cent) of the current marriage. Where this was not the case, nine per cent had adopted children and 12 per cent had stepchildren with them.

The carers' experiences

Preparation and matching

All bar one of the carers who did not already know the children attended preparation groups. The one exception was offering to take a sibling of a child they were already fostering. Only 17 per cent had a negative view of this preparation; most enjoyed it but like the adopters (see Chapter 8) they had mixed views of the assessment process itself. The majority thought they been completely truthful in the assessment, but 17 per cent said that they had omitted some information. Some had a rose-tinted view of life as a foster carer (41 per cent) and were unwilling to heed social work advice.

> *I thought I can do this job, I'd had my own kids. I wanted to do things my way, but you don't realise they are damaged children and you have to have different tactics. I had a tunnel mind, I was going to give the kids love and affection and they'd turn out right . . . didn't turn out like that . . . I was gutted when the first foster child didn't want to stay here.*

The carers were generally pleased with the match between themselves and the child, but social work practice varied on how much background history and information they were given and 56 per cent of carers complained of significant omissions. We had expected that social workers would be more likely to work with foster carers than adoptive parents, especially those who had already been caring for the child. However, both the carers who knew the child and those who did not complained of gaps and of information withheld.

> *There wasn't a proper planning meeting, no real in-depth discussions about his needs or concerns or anything like that, it was just the*

practicalities. I would have liked it if we'd talked about how it would impact on all of us, what we needed to do to make him feel safe.

Initially I didn't know she was epileptic or that she had no vision or that she vomited like she did . . . We learnt as we went along.

The decision to offer a permanent home

For those children who were already being cared for within the foster family, the majority (55 per cent) decided that they would become long-term carers because the child had become a part of their family. They could not bear to lose the child and sometimes offered a permanent home when they realised that there was a possibility the child might leave for adoption. Many chose to offer long-term foster care rather than adoption because they needed continuing financial support from the local authority. Other carers were motivated by pity when appeals for an adoptive family brought no response or when adoptions had broken down.

I knew he would just be kicked around the care system, so I discussed it with John (birth child) and he said, 'He's got to come back here mum . . . but . . . does that mean he has to share my room?' He was too old for that by then . . . he was having girlfriends back so I decided to sleep on the sofa so that each of them could have their own rooms.

This carer was still sleeping on the sofa at the time of the follow-up.

Dealing with children's behaviour

As with adoptive families, foster carers gave detailed descriptions of children's challenging behaviour during the first year of their placements.

He had an enormous appetite and would eat every meal like his last . . . he always had his hand down his trousers . . . he would stick out and people would notice and be like 'Look at that little boy' and I would think 'Oh my God, he's not with me!'

Hell, absolute hell, stealing, fighting, suspended from school, lighting fires, swearing, violent, wouldn't sleep . . . He'd had seven years of nothing poured into him and he was empty . . . he was making up for lost time. He knew me and the rest of the family had a lot to give and he wanted every bit of it.

The majority (78 per cent) of the children were able to make a relationship with at least one carer quite early on in the placement. Foster fathers sometimes spoke of feeling more included in parenting than they had been with their own children. Indeed, some children (28 per cent) made stronger or exclusive relationships with foster fathers, which could be a source of tension and marital conflict.

> *He was very anti-women . . . He punished me no end, he wouldn't eat my food . . . wouldn't speak to me . . . And I did think 'Why am I being hated in my own house?'*

Foster fathers felt unprepared for this behaviour. They stated they had been taught during their training that they must be careful of their personal boundaries. They sometimes found themselves "mothering" the children and keeping this quiet, expecting social work disapproval and fearing removal of the child. Foster mothers found the apparent rejection of themselves hard, and felt children were trying to drive a wedge between themselves and their husbands.

> *The thing that was drummed into your head when you go for initial training is that you're a male, so we automatically assume you're a child abuser. You're a male, so if you put your arm around him it will be misinterpreted, if you go out in the car he has to sit in the back not in the front with you . . . It's sad . . . They've been starved of affection and they come into your home and you are so scared . . .*

Family life

All the carers had children living in the household before the arrival of the foster child. They were asked about the impacts on their other children in the first year of the placement and in the year prior to the follow-up interview. Carers saw both positive and negative effects, the majority believing the positives had outweighed the negatives. Three children entered families where one of their own siblings was already living. Their arrival was not always welcomed:

> *Philip didn't like the idea . . . His initial reaction was 'No way!' . . . When she arrived, he found it quite hard sharing his toys with her . . . He didn't like sharing my time with her and he still finds that difficult.*

Sometimes he is glad of the company but it still wouldn't worry him too much if she left tomorrow, to be honest.

On the other hand, others were overjoyed at being reunited:

She had never wanted to be separated from her little brother in the first place and we had always thought it was an injustice that they were. We had wanted them both as a family unit, but . . . Jim was young and they were going to put him up for adoption. But they came back to us with their tails between their legs after his adoptive placement broke down. Lily was thrilled, well, we all were, I can just remember her crying and saying 'Thank you' to me that we were going to take him.

Carers were vocal about the needs of their own children and the importance of the children's role in making the placement successful. They believed their own children were as much a part of the process of fostering as they were and that more should be done for them. They were concerned that their own children had missed out in different ways.

There's nothing there for your own children. Foster children get it all, your own children get bugger all. They can feel very resentful, that's where a lot of breakdowns come, they're sharing their mum.

There were particular concerns about protecting birth children from sexual abuse. Carers felt more attention needed to be paid by social workers to helping carers manage such issues. They spoke of learning as they went along with little help or advice:

He fell in love with Jack (birth child) *so boundaries around bath times, bedtimes, private space, sitting next to people, who can kiss you, etc, all had to be closely monitored and still have to be.*

Other carers, while recognising that their children might have had fewer material goods as a result of fostering, thought they had gained from the experience.

We were initially worried about how they would cope with Sally (severely disabled child) *because she was different. But they held her hand and played with her and always took notice of her as they walked past. I think they did suffer a bit because there weren't as many trips out . . . but they had as much time as we could give them and they knew that. They've also gained a lot by having Sally here.*

Carers thought that children were a source of mutual support. They described situations where the children in the family had intervened to support the foster child and where conversations between children were extremely supportive, listening to concerns and worries. Carers thought that children talked more to each other than to them about their contact arrangements. However, where the relationship between the foster child and birth children was strained or had broken down, disruptions had occurred or were occurring.

The violence has got worse and he takes it out on my wife . . . he has hit her a few times and the girls witnessed it . . . he called her a bitch . . . One of the girls rang me and I came straight back. The girls were in tears. I can't go out and Jenny (birth child) *has turned against him. We reached a decision . . . we couldn't have him any more.*

For most of the families, the carers reported that the relationship between the children had strengthened over the years. They described strong relationships, which they expected to be long lasting, and felt that the positive aspects of long-term fostering outweighed the negatives aspects by two to one. Of course, this was the carers' view. We do not know what the children thought of it. They might not have told their parents what they felt and their parents might have minimised the difficulties to justify their decision to continue fostering.

Relationship between carers and child

Carers were asked how their relationship with the fostered children had changed over the years.

The first year

Closeness: Ninety per cent said that they had been able to get close to the children in the first year, although three foster mothers described serious difficulties in this. Closeness was described in terms of the extent of shared physical affection and in the ways the children showed affection to them, including spontaneous acts of kindness or giving presents. On the other hand, they said that the majority of children had been guarded about their pasts (60 per cent) and about their day-to-day concerns (40 per cent).

Confrontations: Confrontations between the carers and the child were frequent in the first year for 40 per cent of the children, sometimes with screaming tantrums or arguments occurring at least weekly. In most cases, foster carers were able to resolve the conflict, but it had not been possible with three of the children. Twenty-four per cent of foster mothers said they became depressed or anxious because of the child's behaviour and two were prescribed medication. Foster fathers were not reported as having any symptoms.

It is not surprising that half the families found the first year of the placement a moderate or severe challenge for themselves and their families. Interestingly, challenges were most frequently described by those that were already caring for the child or had cared for the child in the past, perhaps because the confirmation that the placement was long-term dashed the child's hopes of a return home and challenging behaviour reappeared.

Positive features: Most carers identified many highlights in the first year, but five (24 per cent) could not. These were the mothers who were having the most difficulty getting close to the child. Nevertheless, only one family felt that neither they nor the child enjoyed each other and that their relationship was very poor.

At follow-up
Confrontations: In the year of the follow-up interview, the degree of confrontation had diminished and was now rare for half the families. Carers said the young people had become more involved in "making up" after a row and had begun to take some responsibility for their actions. Carers thought they had learned how to handle confrontations better or that young people themselves were showing more self-control. But for the other 50 per cent of families, there had been no improvements. Rather, battles were escalating in intensity and frequency. As the young people became older and stronger the level of violence was becoming frightening for some carers.

Although battles were diminishing overall, the majority of carers still found caring for the young person challenging. Despite this, the majority of carers (87 per cent) reported that they were getting along well with the young person, and young people were described as being more open.

Warmth and relationships: The great majority of the carers (87 per cent) spoke warmly about the children.

We do the silly things that mums and daughters do, we have hair sessions and make-up sessions and she'll paint my toe nails.

Only 26 per cent of the young people were said not to be open about how they felt or to speak about their pasts. Where carers said they were not close to the young person, it was clear that the placement was about to disrupt, if it had not already done so. These young people were not the ones that the foster mothers had had difficulty making relationships with at the start of the placement. Rather, they were those whose behaviour had escalated out of control:

When she left we said, 'We love you very much but we're just not tough enough for you. We just don't know what can help you sort you out . . . we hope you can make your way in life.'

Effect on family life and relationships

Foster carers reported fewer changes in their lifestyle than did adopters.

Work and income: None of the foster fathers made any changes to the number of hours they were working or to their type of occupation, but some foster mothers (19 per cent) stopped paid employment and 9 per cent reduced their hours. In comparison with those adopting (5 per cent versus 65 per cent) few reported that they had experienced a substantial decrease in their family income as a result of offering a permanent home. Nevertheless, 14 per cent of families had got into debt in the first year.

Interests and activities: There were both negative and positive changes in their lifestyle. Mothers found that some of their personal interests and activities had to stop, but some stranger long-term foster carers reported that new interests and activities had started. These changes were viewed as an expected consequence of the decision to offer a permanent placement. Lifestyle changes did not have the same impact on the carers as it had on the adopters. Only 14 per cent thought that the changes they had had to make were detrimental, perhaps because they had already made these adjustments during their previous fostering experiences.

Carers' relationships: Marital relationships were on the whole strengthened but a negative impact on marriages was reported in 28 per cent of families. There had been one divorce and two trial separations. Although there were probably many contributory factors, these families were the ones where the child's attachment had been to only one of the adults.

> *He demands so much. He stands between me and my husband and won't let you have any personal space. We're just feeling exhausted because we have put so much into him and we're not seeing any change. John* (husband) *now feels he cannot do anything for him and so I'm feeling like all the responsibility is resting on me and it has become very difficult to function as a family.*

The importance of the support given by foster fathers to their wives was emphasised many times.

> Foster father: *My role has been supportive, the bulk of the work has been on her shoulders. One of the things June has had to do is move mountains . . . if he hadn't had June, he would not be at school. The school has given up on him too many times. You pick up the phone and you hear 'That's it' and it's then that June goes into battle for him and rescues him and she has been fire-fighting for him for years.*

> Foster mother: *My God, when he says supportive he means supportive. He has been my rock.*

In three-fifths of cases, extended families were very supportive and pleased about the decision to offer a permanent placement. Over the years there was little reduction in this support.

Contact

In the first year, 21 (91 per cent) of the 23 children were in contact with parents or kin. By the follow-up, this had fallen to 11 (48 per cent) of the children.

Table 12.3
Contact in the first year and prior to the follow-up interview (n = 23)

Type of contact	Contact in the first year %	Contact prior to the follow up interview %
Face-to-face with mother	50	30
Face-to-face with father	35	17
Face-to-face with both parents	26	13
Face-to-face with siblings	70	74
Letterbox	13	43
Phone	13	70

Contact in the first year

In the first year there was face-to-face contact with birth parents twice a month or more for 21 of the children. All but three face-to-face contact arrangements with birth mothers and five with birth fathers were supervised. As a consequence, there was little letterbox and phone activity. Carers were present at most of the contact meetings and reported that the children's reaction to contact with their parents was a 50/50 split between favourable responses and negative ones. Carers had concerns about contact but were more supportive of the children seeing siblings and members of the extended family. Foster fathers were more negative about contact with birth parents than foster mothers. Concerns centred around the impact and distress caused to children:

> *Contact with birth mother was supervised by the social worker . . . She would slag off social workers during the visit, one time she even slapped the social worker . . . the kids were really frightened . . . I used to dread it. It was terrible to put two children through it.*

Fifty-two per cent of carers reported little or inadequate guidance from social workers about how to manage contact, although a lack of guidance was not associated with more unhappiness with contact arrangements.

Effects of contact on the placement: Despite the misgivings about the level and quality of contact, only 19 per cent of carers thought that it had a negative impact on the child's ability to form attachments within the foster family.

Contact at the time of follow-up

At follow-up, contact arrangements had changed as the children grew older and more independent and more vocal about their own wishes. Face-to-face contact had reduced with both birth parents as had levels of supervised (17 per cent) contact. Nearly all of the face-to-face contact with birth mothers that was occurring was regular contact that had endured over the years. The great majority (88 per cent) of foster carers were supportive of these arrangements because they recognised their importance to the young person. However, these meetings could still be fraught and young people were often extremely difficult before and after the visit. Satisfaction with the level of guidance given by social workers had increased to 75 per cent.

She is always a bit stroppy and mouthy beforehand. It's almost as if she's got to be bad with me before she can go and see her mum. Then she'll come back and it will be 'Do you like my jeans and jacket?' but then a week later it will be 'I know she just stole that stuff anyway'.

No matter what their parents are like, the kids still want to see them . . . sometimes dad would be drunk, Alex would be hyper . . . couldn't sleep, was he going to turn up or not? I wasn't sure who was parenting who . . . whose needs were being met. When I saw them, they were affectionate together. As a professional carer it is easy to think 'What is the point?' but when you see them together you can see the point.

A few carers (12 per cent) felt that they were forced by the social worker to continue face-to-face contact even though the young people continued to be distressed.

It always ends in tears . . . he is always in a terrible state when he comes home . . . Undoubtedly she loves him and has a tremendous amount of guilt . . . but she just sabotages everything else that happens for him . . . Mum has been unable to undermine any progress we have made . . . Some really decisive decisions need to have been made much earlier by SSD.

Re-established contact: There was no support from foster carers for the few (13 per cent) contacts re-established by social workers after many years.

The social worker is determined to arrange contact with his birth mother. She had been stoned out of her head the last time it was organised and didn't turn up. Her social worker's idea was to take the mother and Tony to a café and leave them to get on with it!

Foster carers complained that social workers did not understand that although the young people were adolescent or nearing adulthood, they might need support or protection during contact visits. They could not just be left to get on with it.

Nearly half the children (48 per cent) were no longer in contact or had never had contact visits with birth parents. Some carers (25 per cent) complained that they felt under pressure from social workers to re-establish contact even when young people stated they did not want this and complained that lack of contact was raised at every review. One social worker wrote in the case notes that the young person's refusal to see her mother was 'an affront against the doctrine of the Children Act'. These carers felt they had very little influence on social work decision-making, even though they had cared for the young person for many years.

There had been an increase in indirect contact. Carers thought that young people liked this because it gave them more control and they were more comfortable using their mobile phones to text or talk to their birth parents.

Support

Support to carers is affected by the carer's attitudes as well as the actions of individual workers and of agency policies. Some carers were proud that they could manage without SSD help, others felt a stigma and personal shame attached to asking for help, yet others felt it was their duty on behalf of the child to fight for everything that might be of benefit.

Social work support

At placement: Foster carers were generally appreciative of social work support. At the time the child's placement became long term, the majority (70 per cent) thought that both the child's social workers and their own family placement workers visited at about the right frequency and that they provided good support and advice. There were slightly more positive comments about family placement workers. Where carers were unhappy they tended to describe their relationships with the social workers as poor, to be dissatisfied with the quality of advice and support given and to feel that they were either visited too much or not enough.

There were far more complaints (60 per cent dissatisfied) about the speed at which social workers responded to requests. For example, children missed out on school trips because permission could not be gained in time. Carers were also more critical of the social worker's role in helping them negotiate with other agencies, particularly education and health. There was some confusion about whose role it was to work with these agencies. For example, one carer who set up a meeting with the school after her foster child had been suspended felt she had been "told off" by the social worker, as this was not her job. Others felt left to negotiate with schools by themselves.

There was not enough input when John's behaviour was difficult. I was always dreading the phone going, because it was always the school . . . the social worker was not dealing adequately with it . . . she would just laugh. In the end I said to her, 'What help are you going to give me?'

At follow-up: At the time of the follow-up, most families continued to want help. Sixty per cent of carers reported high levels of satisfaction with what they got from social workers. Only one family consistently felt that they did not want any support at all. The help from family placement workers continued to be more positively valued than that from children's social workers, although the difference was not significant. Most families were still receiving frequent visits from workers. This gave them the opportunity to seek advice and discuss any current issues. Relationships between workers and carers were generally very good. However, 23 per cent of carers said that they rarely saw a social worker and that they were dissatisfied with the service they were receiving.

Social workers were praised for their personal support and advice but concerns were still expressed about the speed of responses to queries and requests for other services. Half the carers reported dissatisfaction with this aspect of SSD provision. Some had chosen to foster rather than adopt believing that it would be easier to get services. Many (43 per cent) found this was not the case. Shared care was part of the support plan for families but this was not readily available and was often not forthcoming when the families needed it the most.

> *They made lots of promises. Nothing ever happened. We felt very let down.*

Help in crises was patchy and services were not able to respond quickly. Carers who were parenting violent and aggressive young men tended to use the police as a support service.

> *Well, where was social services? You call the emergency duty team and they just say, 'Is it that urgent? . . . we'll make a note of it.' If you really need help, forget the emergency duty team, forget social services, ring the police. It's breaking every rule.*

Some thought that SSD services which were available were kept under wraps, so that carers could not find out them.

> *I would have liked a list of available resources because they would say what support do you want? And I'd say, 'Well, what is there?'*

One of the most notable differences, compared with the adoptive parents, was the lack of autonomy felt by the foster carers. They complained bitterly about their inability to take decisions and the bureaucracy to which they were subjected. Some had to ask permission to get the child's hair cut, had to get approval for babysitters, or had no authority to give permissions for school trips or other educational activities. Sleepovers, a very important part of children's lives, were impossible to arrange as SSDs needed weeks to make decisions and do police checks. Consequently, carers were faced with the dilemma of denying the young person the opportunity to lead a "normal life", or lying to the SSD. Many complained that they did not want to be forced into this position.

> *On the one hand you are given all this responsibility . . . but if you make the slightest little decision you got to get the signatures for this, that and the other. We classed him as a member of the family . . . but simple things, like if he wanted to go on a school trip, we needed a signature.*

> *We were allowed to choose somebody who could babysit our own child but not somebody who could babysit David. So the only time we could*

have a break was if social services would "kindly" have him for a couple of hours. We thought that was dreadful.

Another major difference between caring for children in long-term care and those adopted was the planning for the young people around 16 years of age. Some carers felt that the systems that had been set up for looked after children were having a detrimental affect on the stability of the placement. At a time when the young people needed stability and the reassurance that they could stay at home and continue to be educated, carers reported that social workers told young people about the looked after Care Grant and offered to help them set up home independently. The lure of what seemed a large amount of money and "their own place" created tensions:

It's a big issue because he's heard he can get a leaving care grant of £1,000 and all he could think about was leaving, and I desperately don't want him to.

The leaving care grant and compensation make him very vulnerable to exploitation.

We've had loads of social workers and the last one was useless. Their money stops on their 18th birthday and then what . . . I couldn't believe it when their social worker said, 'Well if she wants to live independently we can help her with that.' I said, 'Don't tell her,' but the social worker said, 'I have to, that's my job.'

Expenditure

Just over half the families (52 per cent) thought they had spent and were continuing to spend far more on the young people than they were ever recompensed for. Carers spoke of needing new cars to transport children with severe disabilities, or of needing to replace damaged goods or repair properties. Families felt they had been dissuaded from asking for more than the allowance – 'we were told "you haven't got a hope"' – so they took out personal loans (range £1,000–£10,000) to meet some of the most expensive items. Other families might have been able to claim more than they did but were embarrassed to ask and felt there was a stigma associated with applying for extra help.

199

The allowance didn't begin to cover all the costs. He would chew all his sweaters, there were breakages, he lost loads of clothes. You don't get offered, you find out. Financially we didn't need any help in the first few years but now our circumstances have changed. When he really trashed the place the bathroom was unusable. We spend our lives watching everything we've got gradually get broken. We would spend our lives claiming and what you get back isn't anywhere near what it cost you. But that's our fault really. It was my own fault, I didn't like asking. This child who was really becoming more and more important to you . . . it didn't seem right . . . To have to say, 'Please may I,' or 'It's going to panel to see if you're entitled.' That's just foul.

It was surprising that so many carers complained about the lack of support services, given that this was one of the reasons they had chosen to foster rather than adopt. Some said they had been advised by their social worker not to adopt. As one foster father said:

We agreed to adoption but then our social worker said, 'Don't go down that route because you won't get any support or financial help'.

However, unlike adopters, foster carers did receive a fostering allowance, were recompensed for expenditure on contact visits and 39 per cent of children had transport to school provided by SSDs.

Other support

No carers had bought any private services to help the child, themselves or their families. Three carers (14 per cent) were still attending foster care support groups, but the majority thought they had outgrown them. Informal support networks continued to be strong. Unlike the adopters, who saw their networks shrink, the vast majority of foster carers said that their family and friends had remained supportive throughout the placement. Perhaps this was because parents in the general population develop support networks when they first have a child and all these foster carers already had children in the family.

We got lots of help . . . they (the local community) *all knew about* (the children) *. . . people used to knit for me. One day I got a brand new pushchair left outside the door . . . I don't know who it was from . . .*

Other service use

Health: A significant number of children (61 per cent) had had health problems. Treatment and support had come mainly from paediatricians, occupational therapists, speech therapists and a range of consultants. Children and their foster carers had also been in contact with CAMHS. Although 30 per cent of children had seen a child psychiatrist or clinical psychologist, fewer than half these children had had regular sessions. Most of the contact had been part of an assessment. Art therapy had been used to help 22 per cent of the children.

Education: Half the children had needed or were still receiving support in the classroom from special needs teachers and from educational psychologists. The majority had remained in mainstream schools or in units attached to mainstream schools, with 17 per cent educated at special schools in-county and nine per cent at special schools elsewhere.

Carers' views on how to provide stability

Carers were asked what helped them stick at it when the children's behaviour was difficult or relationships were strained. Different carers emphasised different things but all mentioned the importance of high-quality social work support in which the views of the foster carer were respected.

> *If you've got a constant caring social worker who will listen to the foster carer when she says, 'He needs this . . . we have to fight this corner for him'. Unfortunately, this only comes with experience.*

Others put more emphasis on the fit between the child and carer and the child's own wish to make the placement succeed.

> *This one has worked because we were well matched at the outset . . . nothing was glossed over . . . we've been well supported . . . and the boys wanted a permanent home – they wanted a family.*

A few had a more detached professional approach and could not foresee a time when they would give up on a placement.

> *Even through times of great difficulty it has been a great privilege to see how Mary has changed while she's been in our family and we look forward to a better future.*

Cost estimates

Cost estimates to SSDs were calculated using the cost methodology described previously. The average cost per child from the best interest decision to April 2001 was £129,119 using 2001/2 prices. This rose to an average cost per child of £133,380 when the costs of 12 failed adoptions were divided between the 34 children.

Table 12.4

Cost to social services of caring for the children from the time of the best interest decision until April 2001

	Number of children	Total number of weeks	Cost per week	Total cost
Children supported in their families	3	205	£120	£24,600
Local authority foster care	33	8,704	£318	£2,767,872
Independent foster care	8	1,525	£630	£960,750
Residential care	1	10	£1,646*	£16,460
Independent residential care	3	549	£1,130*	£620,370

* actual cost to SSD

There were variations in costs. Some young people were costing very little by the time of the follow-up, whereas others were in more expensive private placements. Six children were in supported lodgings or living independently. It was not possible to estimate these costs as they were unknown.

Summary for the children in the permanently placed group

- Eighteen per cent had lived with adopters. All had lived with foster carers.
- Fifty-eight per cent of carers who were interviewed said that social

workers had not given them all the information they should have had on the child.

- Where long-term foster care placements had remained intact, the experiences of carers were very similar to intact adoptive placements.
- Face-to-face contact with birth parents had decreased over the years but phone contact had increased. Carers thought that young people liked to keep control of contact arrangements by using mobiles to text or talk with birth parents. Some young people were thought to be being pressured by their social workers to re-establish contact.
- Although the majority of carers were happy with the support they received from their social worker, they were dissatisfied with the responsiveness and speed of SSDs to requests and the lack of inter-agency communication.
- Foster families were less involved than adopters in the educational life of their children.
- Long-term foster carers complained that they had little autonomy and were not part of decision-making.
- Young people were not encouraged by their social workers to remain with their foster families but to leave once they reached 16 years of age.
- Sixty-one per cent of the children had significant health needs.
- Carers thought that placements that remained intact did so because of high-quality social work support, a good fit between the child and the carer and a child who was committed to making the placement succeed.

13 **Adoptive and foster care outcomes compared**

In this chapter we look formally at the outcomes for the adopted children and compare them with the children who went into long-term foster care. Although the study covered all the important areas of the children's functioning and relationships, we did not set out to use standardised instruments, which would provide data that could be compared directly with, say, the recent epidemiological study of the mental health problems of looked after children (Meltzer *et al*, 2003). Nevertheless, our assessments did cover the behaviours used in such assessments and followed the requirement that difficulties should hamper the child's life or development in some way before they could be rated. In this respect they are broadly comparable with standard measures of functioning. In order to preserve the difference between our ratings and these other measures, we have avoided using the term "disorder" unless such problems were formally diagnosed.

This analysis of outcomes is important: firstly, because the sample of children is epidemiologically based; secondly, because we have some measures on the children's functioning at the time of the best interests decision from the case notes, the adoption medical and some psychiatric and psychological assessments; and thirdly, because it is possible to compare the outcomes for the children who went down the adoption route with those who lived in long-term foster care.

Because of the difficulty in identifying the point at which the decision *not* to proceed with adoption was made, we decided to take the best interests decision as the starting point. This gave a common point from which to count subsequent breakdowns and to measure earlier experiences and psychosocial adjustment.[1]

---

[1] All the analyses exclude two severely disabled children who remained in long-term foster case, because most measures of outcome were not appropriate for or calibrated to them. The plans for a further two children changed to residential care following the best interests decision. Both of these entered the unstable care career group and therefore do not appear in these analyses either.

Issues in interpreting the findings

Some caveats about this comparison are necessary. First, the foster care group is not representative of a group of children for whom the plan *from the start* was for long-term foster care. All our fostered children were first considered for adoption. On the other hand, we are in the rare position of being able to ask whether these two types of placement differ in their outcomes and, if they do, whether these differences arise because of children's experiences and adjustment before the placements happened. Even so, the comparison is between the placements in which the children were at follow-up. For this reason, it is not a comparison of children for whom adoption or fostering was the original plan. We know of no data or studies in the UK that would make such a comparison possible at present.

A final note of caution in this analysis concerns who is missing from the follow-up. If there were differences between the groups on some predictive characteristic, such as the extent of problems at the time of the best interests decision, then apparent similarities or differences in the outcomes for the two groups might be inaccurate. This seemed to be part of the picture (Table 13.1). Twelve of the 14 "missing" adoptive children were free of externalising (conduct) problems at the time of the best interests decision (86 per cent), whereas this was true for three of the six children (50 per cent) in the long-term foster group. The comparison of missing and existing cases in the adoptive group was significant. This difference may bias findings against a positive difference in favour of adoption.

Table 13.1
Characteristics of cases missing at follow-up

Externalising problems at "adoption in best interests" decision	Missing foster N = 6%	Foster in follow-up N = 27%	Missing adopted N = 14%	Adopted in follow-up N = 64%
No	50	44	86	61
Yes	50	56	14	39

(exact test, 2 sided, p = 0.027)

Disruptions

Disruption rates are one of the most commonly used measures of outcome, so it is useful to begin with these. Rates can be considered for both groups following the best interests decision and further distinguished for the adoptive group in terms of disruptions during introductions and disruptions following placement.

Adoption disruptions

One hundred and four children got as far as being "matched" with prospective adoptive parents. Eighty (77 per cent) of these intended adoptions were intact at the time of follow-up.

The majority of the disruptions in the adoption group occurred during introductions. This was the case for 15 (14 per cent) of the children. A disruption at this point had a 50/50 chance that the next match would also end in failure, but seven re-matched children went on into adoptive placements. Thus, 96 children altogether entered adoptive households.

The majority of subsequent disruptions occurred early on in the placement: three within six months, eight between six months and the date of the adoption order, and five after the adoption order. Children whose placements disrupted after the order were slightly older at placement than children in placements that did not (six versus five years on average) and were age ten on average when their placements ended. Thus, 17 per cent of placements had broken down by the time of the follow-up interviews. This is not the end of the story. We were aware that some placements were very troubled and that three further disruptions seemed likely.

Foster care disruptions

Twenty-five children had their plan changed to long-term foster care almost immediately following the best interests decision. One later returned successfully to the adoption route following a disrupted foster placement. The plans for a further 22 children changed to long-term foster care following unsuccessful attempts to secure adoptive placements,[2]

---

[2] Nine of these children entered foster care following disrupted adoptive introductions.

leaving 46 who entered hoped-for long-term foster placements.[3] Sixty-four per cent of these placements were with new families, 32 per cent with a previous carer or were short-term arrangements that changed to long-term foster care, and two per cent with kin.

Breakdown in these foster care placements was, not surprisingly, less likely to occur during introductions (4 per cent) but 19 per cent disrupted within six months, a further 11 per cent by two years and 16 per cent subsequently. Thus, 46 per cent of the first intended long-term foster placements disrupted. However, there were marked differences depending on who the new carers were. Sixty-four per cent of breakdowns occurred in "new" families, 36 per cent with carers known to the child and none in the small number of kin placements.

Disruption itself was a predictor of further disruption, as many studies have shown. Eight children who experienced breakdowns then went into residential care and the remaining two into independent living. Over half (55 per cent) of subsequent foster placements broke down, with one child returning home, one going on to independent living and three to residential care.

Thus, long-term foster placements were significantly more likely to disrupt than adoptive ones. Nevertheless, 54 per cent of them were intact at follow-up. These successful placements were made when the children were, on average, aged seven, with a range of 2–12. They were between ten and 18 at the time of follow-up, with an average age of 14. The children whose placements disrupted were significantly older at placement (average nine, range 4–14), their placements disrupting when they were between eight and 15 years (average 11 years). Two intact placements were disrupting at the time of the follow-up.

The adjustment of the adopted children at follow-up

We begin this account of psychosocial outcomes with the adopted children because we had more complete information on them, since it all came from the adopters. In contrast, data on 21 per cent of the fostered children came from their social workers.

---

[3] Apparent small differences in numbers can be understood through careful perusal of the chart of what happened to the children.

The data on psychosocial outcomes follow standard diagnostic principles[4] and the comparison between children with different care careers is based on comparable data. A summary of all the diagnosed conditions of the adopted children on all the outcome ratings is given in Appendix C.

Table 13.2 gives the data on the different areas and the items used in the scales that summarise these. Only those difficulties that were rated as moderate or severe were counted as a problem. This always meant that problems had a definite impact on the children's lives and relationships.

Health difficulties: Only three (5 per cent) of the children had severe physical disabilities and only nine per cent had frequent illnesses and infections.

Education: More children had learning difficulties of one kind or another. Twenty-seven per cent were statemented and, in all, 39 per cent were either statemented and/or a year or more delayed in language or reading. On the other hand, all the children were in education of some kind or had completed their full-time schooling. Seventy per cent were in mainstream schools, two had left school, and six were in vocational or higher education (9 per cent). The remaining 17 per cent were excluded or were in a variety of special day or residential units, on living skills courses or in private boarding schools.

Attachment to carers: Over one-quarter (27 per cent) were rated as having attachment problems according to their adopters, but a higher proportion showed positive features in their relationships, including a willingness to confide (59 per cent) or to disclose important personal experiences (35 per cent). Only six of those with attachment problems were nevertheless able to confide in their parents (35 per cent), compared with 31 of those without attachment difficulties (67 per cent), a significant difference (exact test 0.04).

---

[4] For example: disabilities are only rated if they impaired the child's life in some way; growth and movement delays and impairments had to be medically confirmed; attachment problems included indiscriminate friendliness, marked separation anxiety, stiffness and resistance to affection; conduct problems included opposition or defiance, lying, destructiveness, and physical harm to people or animals.

Table 13.2
Summary scales of adopted children's difficulties

Area	Scale	Frequency % n–62–64	Scale items (all from carers' account)
Disability		22%	Single scale
Learning problems	0	61	Language or reading delay or statemented
	1	20	
	2	9	
	3	9	
Attachment	0	73	Attachment scale, definite or marked problems
	1	27	
Peer relationships	0	14	Sum of: overall scale, doesn't understand feelings, bullied, and follows deviant peers
	1	33	
	2	19	
	3	34	
Emotional problems	0	56	Sum of worried, nervous, performance anxiety, phobias and depression
	1	18	
	2	13	
	3+	14	
Conduct problems	0	39	Sum of defiance, lying, destructive, hurts others, serious rule-breaking
	1	25	
	2	13	
Overactivity, restlessness	0	38	Sum of restlessness, poor concentration, impulsive
	1	27	
	2	16	
	3	20	
Sexualised behaviour		0	Definite or marked problem
Poor self-esteem		42	Definite or marked problem

Emotional ("internalising") problems: A range of emotional problems was apparent, with worrying and anxiety being common. Forty-one per cent of children were either persistent worriers or had performance anxieties or both. Phobias and depressive symptoms were less common, affecting only a small proportion of children. However, it should be remembered that these ratings are based entirely on adopters' views. Rates of depression are known to be higher if children's and young people's accounts are included.

Conduct ("externalising") problems: Behavioural difficulties are, along with attachment problems, known to be among the most potent influences of placement difficulties and disruptions. The children showed high levels of many common problems, including defiance, lying and destructiveness. Indeed, nearly one-quarter (22 per cent) physically harmed other people or animals. Only about two-fifths (39 per cent) of the children were free from any of these behaviours and 36 per cent showed two or more of them. In addition, 13 children (20 per cent) had been involved with the police. The great majority of these were cautions, but two children had been prosecuted.

Overactive and restless behaviour ("hyperactivity"): Overactive and restless behaviour is common among late-adopted children and has been found to be a persistent problem. This sample is no exception. Over a third were restless or had poor concentration and over a half were impulsive. Only 38 per cent of children were without any of these problems and 36 per cent had two or more.

Other problems: Some other problems should be mentioned. Over two-fifths of the children were said by their carers to have poor self-esteem and a small minority continued to have problems with wetting and soiling. None was reported as showing worrying sexualised behaviour, but carers did voice concerns about this for nearly one-quarter of them. This usually involved inappropriate touching. It was not clear to what extent this was sexual in nature. Worrying sexualised behaviour that included open masturbation, more marked inappropriate touching and/or a marked preoccupation with sex did occur in the other placement groups – 11 per cent of the fostered group and 13 per cent of the children with unstable careers.

No adopted children had become pregnant or been accused of sexually harming others. Only four children had problems with personal hygiene or social presentation. There was only one child in the follow-up from a minority ethnic background so it was not possible to examine possible problems in accepting ethnic or cultural heritage.

The overlap of problems

In order to complete this picture, we need to consider the overlap of difficulties so that we can see how many children were functioning well overall or only had minor difficulties and how many were presenting more serious problems. In order to summarise the overlap between problems, we took each of the areas rated above and took two or more problems in each area to reflect definite difficulties. There were two exceptions to this: children with any of the three educational difficulties were rated as having problems; and children with attachment difficulties on the overall scale were rated as definite, regardless of whether there was also confiding and disclosure. The overlap of areas is given in Table 13.3.

Table 13.3
Overlap of problem areas in adopted children

Number of areas	Number of children	Percentage
0	16	25
1 or 2	18	28
3 or more	30	47

Only 25 per cent of the children were free of problems at the time of follow-up. At the other end of the scale, nearly one-half had difficulties in three or more areas. In other words, these children continued to have a wide range of difficulties. Moreover, the method of summarising the data leans towards an optimistic rather than a pessimistic view, since at least two problems in each area were necessary in order to count as definite difficulties.

Summary of the outcomes for the adopted group

The children in the adopted group had had very poor parenting experiences earlier in their lives and carried the consequences of these forward into serious disturbances in behaviour and relationships in their adoptive placements. At the follow-up, substantial proportions of children were anxious and worried and had difficulties in attachments to their adopters and problems in their peer relationships. High proportions showed disturbances of conduct and overactive and restless behaviour and over two-fifths had poor self-esteem. Only 25 per cent were generally free of problems; the remainder had a substantial number of difficulties, with 47 per cent having problems in three or more areas.

The data on disruptions showed that adoption had stabilised their lives compared with those of the long-term fostered group, but in other respects their "outcomes" showed many difficulties.

Adoptive and long-term foster care outcomes compared

We now go on to compare these adoption outcomes with those of the children who ended up in long-term foster care. As detailed earlier, the adoptive group have the advantage in terms of the stability of their placements, but do their outcomes on the other measures show them to be functioning at a better level? The remainder of this chapter looks at this issue in the light of the caveats set out at the beginning of this chapter. The comparison on the summary outcome measures defined for Table 13.2 are given in Table 13.4.

As can be seen from Table 13.4, if disabilities and learning difficulties are put to one side – since we know from Chapter 6 that these are factors that influenced why the children got into these groups – there are no statistically significant differences between the fostered and the adopted children on the outcome areas, apart from sexualised behaviour, although the fostered group showed poorer outcomes on the rating of attachment. Seventy-three per cent of the adopted children had no problems with attachment compared with about half of the fostered children. However, this finding is more complicated than this simple comparison suggests. The reason for this will become apparent when we consider the predictions to outcomes from the level of difficulties at the time of the best interests decision. It will also be remembered that children with fewer problems at the best interests decision were more likely to be missing from the adopted group. This fact may also bias the outcome findings against the adoption.

Table 13.4
Summary scales of children's difficulties

Area	Scale points	Adopted N=62–64 %	Fostered N = 27 %	Statistical significance
Learning problems	0	61	41	
	1	20	3	χ^2 2.df. 10.65 p = 0.014
	2	9	37	
	3	9	11	
Attachment problems	0	73	56	Not significant
	1	27	44	
Poor peer relationships	0	14	22	
	1	33	19	Not significant
	2	19	26	
	3+	34	33	
Emotional problems	0	56	33	
	1	18	37	
	2	13	15	Not significant
	3+	13	15	
Conduct problems	0	39	41	
	1	25	26	
	2	16	7	Not significant
	3+	23	30	
Overactivity/ restless	0	38	41	
	1	27	22	Not significant
	2	16	7	
	3	20	30	
Sexualised behaviour		0	11	χ^2 1 df. 7.35 p = 0.007
Poor self-esteem		42	37	Not significant

For explanation of ratings, see Table 13.2.

Overlap of problems

Table 13.5 looks at the overlap of problems between the groups. We excluded learning difficulties – which were included in Table 13.3 – from this and subsequent comparisons as we knew that this was one factor influencing foster rather than adoptive placement. We did not want to bias the findings against foster care by including learning problems. As can be seen, similar proportions were relatively problem free, but a somewhat higher proportion of the fostered children had problems in three or more areas, although this difference was not significant.

Table 13.5
Overlap of areas of problems[5]

Number of areas	Adopted %	Fostered %
0	27	26
1 or 2	41	30
3 or more	33	44

χ^2 1.73 2.df. not significant

Does this lack of difference mean that adoption has no advantages over long-term foster care? Before concluding this, we need to check whether there were differences between the groups on their experiences and adjustment before they were placed. We know already that this was partly the case for those on whom we did and did not have data. The adopted group was significantly short of the children who had fewer problems at placement. For this reason, the findings will be biased against the adopted group if better adjustment at that time is a predictor of better adjustment at follow-up. Table 13.6 shows the relationship with background factors and higher levels of overlapping difficulty at follow-up, defined as problems in two or more areas. For example, 44 per cent of the adopted and half of the fostered children *without* externalising problems at the time of the best interests decision nevertheless had problems in two or more areas at follow-up.

---

[5] Areas in this analysis are: peer problems, conduct problems, emotional problems, over-activity and attachment.

Table 13.6

Two or more problem areas at follow-up according to background factors at the time of the best interests decision

Rating at the time of the best interests decision		Adopted %	N	Fostered %	N
Age	1–4	56	39	83	6
	5–7	52	23	60	10
	8+	50	2	55	11
Number of areas of abuse prior to best interests	0	67	6	33	3
	1–2	50	26	57	14
	3–4	56	32	80	10
Internalising problems	No	50	48	50	16
	Yes	69	16	82	11
Externalising problems	No	44	39	50	12
	Yes	72	25	91	15
Overactivity	No	50	52	59	22
	Yes	75	12	80	5
Attachment[6] problems	No	42	31	56	18
	Yes	67	33	78	9
Number of areas of difficulty	0	33	21	14	7
	1	36	14	60	5
	2	89	18	100	10
	3+	64	11	60	5

No statistically significant differences within or between groups.

As can be seen from the table above, there were no significant differences either within each group or between the fostered and adopted children in the relationship between individual background factors or a summary rating of all the areas together and outcomes. However, it is clear that the

---

[6] Although the coding attachment problems at AIBI was based on records, this aspect of the children's functioning was systematically assessed by the same specialist paediatrician, who had expertise in this area.

presence of each background adversity was associated with an increase in problems at follow-up. Furthermore, the presence of problems at AIBI appears to be a little less strongly related to problems at follow-up for the adopted group.

The small size of each sample makes more sophisticated analysis difficult. It also cautions us against drawing conclusions from small percentage differences when the statistical tests suggest that these might have arisen by chance. On the other hand, the findings so far may fail to differentiate because the outcome measure is too crude. It may be more informative to look at predictions from the time of the AIBI across specific areas rather than to a summary outcome measure. A series of logistic regression analyses were performed with a yes/no coding of problems in each area used as the outcome measure. The predictor variables were "group" – in order to test for differences between the adopted and fostered group when the background factor was taken into account – and the rating on each area at the time of the AIBI. It should be pointed out that the outcome measures are better than those at the AIBI because these were based on parents'/carers' accounts and on more information, whereas the assessments at AIBI were based on what was written in the case files.

The data from these analyses are summarised in Table 13.7. The odds are the odds of a poorer outcome depending on which group the child is in and the presence or absence of the background factor. Odds above one on "group" point to a worse outcome for the fostered group. However, it is important also to look at the confidence intervals (CI). These show the possible variation in the odds of a poorer outcome. The wider the confidence interval, the more caution should be applied in judging the strength of the prediction.

Generally, the lack of differences between the adopted and the fostered children are confirmed, with one significant exception: the fostered group were significantly more likely to have poorer outcomes on attachment when attachment problems at AIBI were taken into account. For attachment, as for all the other variables examined, the presence of problems at AIBI was a stronger predictor of difficulties in the same area at follow-up than the type of placement in which the child was at follow-up.

These analyses confirm the strong influences of conduct problems, overactivity and difficulties in attachment prior to placement on the functioning of children several years later, regardless of the type of placement in which they end up.

The data on attachment are important for two reasons. First, they show that the adopted group came to placement with more problems in attachment at AIBI (52 per cent versus 33 per cent fostered) and yet had better outcomes on this at follow-up. Figure 13.1 shows the overall effect in both groups of problems before placement but it also shows the adopted group faring better than the fostered group, whether or not there were difficulties at AIBI. Indeed, attachment for the fostered group who did *not* have a history of attachment difficulties was marginally worse at follow-up than for the adopted children who came to their placements with attachment difficulties.

Figure 13.1

Attachment problems at AIBI and attachment at follow-up

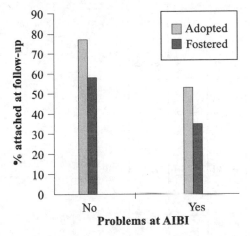

Conclusions

The findings presented in this chapter document the continuing difficulties in both the adopted and the fostered children, a legacy of the problems they brought with them into their placements. There were no differences between the two groups of children on the great majority of outcomes. A cautious reading would lead to the conclusion that adoption

Table 13.7

Problems in specific outcome areas according to the presence of the same problems at the best interests decision

Problems at the time of the best interests decision		*Adopted* %	N	*Fostered* %	N	*Summary of logistic regression analyses*	Odds	95% CI	Significance
Internalising problems	No	19	47	25	16	Group:	2.32	0.89–6.03	ns
	Yes	50	16	36	11	Factor:	1.80	0.70–4.63	ns
Externalising problems	No	26	39	17	12	Group:	0.71	0.26–1.95	ns
	Yes	52	25	47	15	Factor:	3.43	1.37–8.55	0.008
Overactivity	No	27	51	41	22	Group:	1.02	0.38–2.75	ns
	Yes	75	12	20	5	Factor:	2.41	1.36–4.29	0.003
Peer problems	No	47	44	54	13	Group:	1.33	0.53–3.31	ns
	Yes	63	19	64	14	Factor:	0.98	0.91–1.05	ns
Attachment	No	16	31	39	18	Group:	3.11	1.10–8.74	0.032
	Yes	36	33	56	9	Factor:	2.34	1.24–4.41	0.008

had no advantages to foster care as a placement option were it not for two important pieces of evidence and a lack of evidence about the comparative effects into adulthood.

The first piece of evidence concerns the imbalance between the groups on whom we had follow-up data, with the adopted group follow-up missing more data on children who appeared to be functioning at a better level at placement. This analysis was based on the presence of externalising problems, which showed the strongest continuity to difficulties at follow-up of all the variables we looked at. It seems likely that there was some bias against finding good outcomes for the adopted group. The second piece of evidence concerns the findings on attachment, which was systematically explored by the adoption specialist paediatrician prior to the AIBI. Adoption appeared to have advantages over long-term foster care in this area. On the other hand, the analyses were based on small samples and the findings need to be replicated.

The descriptive chapters on the family lives of the two groups suggest that important differences will come into play as the young people get older and reach an age when the transition to adult life becomes an issue. Before a conclusion of "no difference" can be comfortably accepted, we need to know how the young people fare in their mid-twenties when the additional family continuity provided by adoption may result in greater advantages in outcome for the adopted children.

Summary of outcomes

- 104 children were matched for adoption.
- 14 per cent of matched adoptive placements disrupted during introductions.

Disruptions

- A disruption at this point had a 50/50 chance of further disruption, but seven re-matched children went into adoptive placements.
- 96 children entered adoptive placements. The majority (11) of subsequent disruptions occurred shortly after placement and before the adoption order, and five disrupted afterwards.
- 45 children went into long-term foster care. Forty-six per cent of the

placements of children whose *initial* plans changed to foster care broke down, mostly in placements with "strangers", less so with previously known carers (36 per cent) and fewest with the small number of kin carers.

- Over half of the further foster placements broke down (55 per cent) but 34 children remained in long-term foster care, with two disrupting at the time of follow-up.

Outcomes

- Outcome data were available through follow-up interviews with 64 adopters and 21 foster carers. Data on a further six foster children were collected from social workers.
- The adoptive children carried serious and persistent problems forward into their adoptive placements. Only one-quarter (25 per cent) were free of difficulties in learning, emotions, behaviour, relationships and attachment. Forty-seven per cent had problems in three or more areas including learning problems, attachment, poor peer relationships, emotional and conduct problems, sexualised behaviour and poor self-esteem.
- The strongest predictors of problems at follow-up from the time of the best interests decision were conduct problems and overactivity. Abusive experience prior to the AIBI was not predictive, probably because the great majority of children had been maltreated. Age at placement and length of time placed made no difference to outcomes.
- There were few differences in outcome between the adopted and the fostered children, except that the fostered group contained more children with learning difficulties and a higher proportion of children with attachment problems.
- The predictors of poorer outcomes for the fostered children followed the same pattern as for the adopted children, but the adoptive group had made significantly more progress in forming attachments to their new parents.

14 **The lives and outcomes of the unstable care career group**

Finally, in this account of the lives and outcomes of our sample of children, we turn to the children who did not find a stable placement. Chapter 6 showed that these children were different from both the adopted and the long-term permanently placed group. In this chapter we follow the stories of the 16 children in this group from the time the adoption panel made the best interest decision to the time of the follow-up. This is a small group but their stories and outcomes could have been different. For this reason, we give a number of extended case histories at the end of the chapter.

Table 14.1
Characteristics of the children with unstable care careers

	Unstable care careers (n = 16) % or average (mean)
Boys	56
Minority ethnic heritage	19
Average age at entry to care	4.1 years
Average age at approval for adoption	6.7 years
Percentage of children matched for adoption	62%

The information available

Unlike the adoptive and long-term permanently placed groups, there was no one who could be interviewed who was equivalent to a carer or adopter. As with the other two groups, data about the children's histories were collected from case files. Information on their psychosocial outcomes was obtained through interviews with someone whom we hoped knew the child well enough to give accurate information, such as their social workers or residential workers.

Fourteen social workers were interviewed but we were unable to talk to the birth parents of the two children who had returned home. Instead, we got as much data as possible from case files. We had concerns about the comparability of these data (not all data just SDQ scores). Social workers tended, for whatever reason, to choose the middle range for all scores on rating scales, even though this was known to be a particularly troubled group of children. Indeed, one social worker admitted that she would never say that a child had severe difficulties in any area of his or her life, as it "labelled" the child. In addition, where responsibility for the young person was with an adult care or leaving care team, social workers had usually not read the files but relied on a summary provided by the previous social worker. Among the most striking instances of ignorance as a result of this practice was a case where the social worker responsible was unaware that the young person was epileptic.

Efforts to place the children

Initial efforts at placement

Chapter 6 showed that these children had more needs and more challenging behaviour than the other children in the adoptive and permanently cared for groups. This behaviour had been the main factor in the breakdown of placements of 63 per cent of the children prior to the AIBI decision. Indeed, at that time the children appeared to be in a rapid spiral of escalating placement breakdown and exclusions from school. Case records showed that social workers hoped that adoption would arrest this pattern. They believed that the challenging and disruptive behaviour would be reduced if children's anxieties about their futures were removed. There was an optimistic view that if the "right family" was found the child would settle.

This optimism was justified for some of the children in the total sample, but it seemed unrealistic for these children, given the history of persistent and marked difficulties. Some of the behaviours described by foster carers were extreme and bizarre. For example, one child had been self-harming since he was three years old. By the time he was five, he had such a pronounced hand tremor that he could not feed himself.

It is easy with hindsight to highlight undue optimism but as Rogers and colleagues (1992) have commented, the rule of optimism does not simply reflect professional naivety but may also be a response to organisational and service deficiencies. Thus, despite efforts by social workers to get therapeutic help for children, only three of the children were having regular sessions with a CAMHS professional when an adoptive placement was being sought. Optimism could be seen as one way for social workers to defend themselves when making complex decisions without adequate information, assessment and with limited resources.

Attempts to find adoptive placements

Thus, as the 16 children's papers went to the adoption panel it was hoped that they would all be adopted – two by their current foster carers and the remainder (87 per cent) by strangers. The children for whom new families were sought were featured at least once locally and through *Be My Parent*. Television campaigns were also used for three of the children. The agencies recognised that these children would be hard to place so more publicity attempts were made for them than for those who ended up in adoptive or permanent family placements. Placement teams looked for adoptive families who would be willing to support high levels of direct contact with the birth parents and kin of nine children or a previous foster carer of five others. Face-to-face contact with siblings was planned for all the children.

Publicity brought no response for three of the children. For a further three, social workers on extended sick leave, staff vacancies or failure to follow up expressions of interest meant that possible families dropped out.

Concerns grew over the effects on the children for whom no adoptive families were found. There were distressing descriptions on case files of the emotional impact on the children . . . 'inconsolable crying disabling his whole body', or a child who put his fingers down his throat '. . . so I will die'.

Adoptive placements and their fate

Adoptive families were found for ten of the children, four with previous foster carers and six with new families. It was clear from the files that there were reservations about the suitability of some of the foster care placements. Indeed, half of the foster carers who applied to adopt were not approved wholeheartedly. For some, there were concerns about their ability to parent the child. However, in one case they fitted the bill because they were offering unlimited parental contact and in the other provided an ethnically matched placement. For these reasons, other concerns were put to one side. Later in the file, one social worker recorded that they were treated like "gold dust".

All these adoptive placements disrupted – six before the adoption order and four after the order was made. The placements of children into new families disrupted more quickly than those matched with previous foster carers – often during introductions or the early months of a placement. There was a second attempt to place two of the children with an adoptive family but both of these disrupted during introductions.

Disruptions occurred primarily because of children's challenging behaviour and the impact of unregulated contact. Adopters reported that children's behaviour was often violent and/or sexualised. Birth parents ringing throughout the day or threatening the adoptive family also contributed to placement breakdowns. Ill-thought out contact plans, especially restarting contact after a gap, and high levels of face-to-face contact just before moving into an adoptive placement, contributed to 40 per cent of the placement disruptions. For example, one child saw his mother fortnightly and was re-introduced to his father eight days before moving into an adoptive placement. This placement disrupted two months later.

At the other end of the scale, four children lived with their adoptive families for some time before the placement disrupted (mean 5 years s.d. 2.7). Two of these disrupted as the children reached adolescence and their behaviour became too difficult for the adopters to manage. The other two were foster care adoptions where there had been the initial concern about the suitability of the placement. These concerns were catastrophically substantiated in later evidence that one child had suffered years of sexual and emotional abuse and the other years of physical abuse. Concerns were only acted upon when the abusive behaviour spilled over outside the immediate family into the neighbourhood. The belief that the placements were like "gold dust" had overridden all normal child protection procedures and practices.

Changes of plan and their failure

With the failure to find adoptive placements or the disruption of those that were found, plans for 13 of the children changed to long-term foster care. One of the remaining children had run back to her birth mother and been allowed to stay and two others had been placed in residential care.

SSDs began advertising again but now for long-term foster carers, which were found for all 13 children, the majority being strangers who responded to advertising. Only one was linked with a carer who knew the child. But these placements had no more success. The carers could not contain the children's behaviour and all the placements disrupted, most during introductions or within the first six months. A second attempt was made to place three of the children but these too disrupted.

Without an adoptive or long-term foster care placement, the 15 children's subsequent placements broke down at an increasing rate, some only lasting a few days. Case recording showed increasingly desperate attempts to find a placement that would "hold" the child and offer stability. Children went through a series of short-term foster placements (mean 4 s.d. 2.9) until this resource too was exhausted. At this point, a decision was often made by a social work manager that a child was unable to live within a family and that a residential placement should be found.

Unfortunately, local authority group homes and specialist residential care were no more stable than other placements for these children. Thirteen children experienced in total 54 different residential placements, an average of four per child (s.d. 3.0). In addition, five children spent at least one period in a local authority secure unit. Some children had an extraordinary numbers of placements. For example, one child had ten foster placements, 20 respite placements, 11 residential placements and two spells in a secure unit, all within a five-year period.

Even residential units with staff ratios of 3:1 and where the study child was the only resident were not always able to contain the violent behaviour that some of these children were showing. For example, one young person was described as creating an air of menace and an expectation that something was about to happen. All visits outside the residential unit involved four members of staff in case restraint was necessary. In other cases, there were descriptions on file of police in riot gear being called out or all general hospital admissions having to be stopped as a young person rampaged through a hospital.

Funding was sought and gained for 13 of the children to be placed in specialist therapeutic units or EBD schools outside county boundaries. Only five of these placements were still intact in 2001. Inevitably, with the number of placement changes this group of children experienced, their school careers were also disrupted. Changes of school were frequent and educational progress was severely limited. At the time of follow-up, descriptions (from case files and interviews) of the young people's behaviour were of very challenging behaviour with little optimism for future progress. Data was incomplete for the two young people who had returned home. The mean age at follow-up was 15 years, with a range of 11–18 years.

The children's psychosocial functioning at follow-up

Education (n = 16): At follow-up, six young people had left school, were no longer receiving any education and had never had a job. Vocational courses, such as hairdressing, were being taken by two of them and one young person was receiving life skills training in a college. Three young people were receiving education in special schools and two were just being contained within mainstream education. A further two children were currently excluded.

None of the 16 children had or were regularly attending school. Half had been or were regular truants while the other 50 per cent had spent long periods excluded. It appeared to be particularly difficult for social workers to find a school that would accept young people who had sexually abused other children. These children were excluded for long periods. None of the unstable care career group of children obtained any educational qualifications during their school careers.

Learning difficulties had affected eight of the children, with three of these being assessed as moderate. The rest were thought to have IQs within the average range and four had IQs in the range 110–125. Young people were described by teachers as '. . . incapable of learning' or their severe emotional and behavioural difficulties got in the way of progress . . . 'academic skills . . . are thwarted by his extremely short attention span and need to be the centre of attention'.

Health (n = 16): Many of these children were in poor health. Chronic health conditions and frequent illnesses were reported for 20 per cent of the group. For some, the effects of foetal alcohol syndrome had become more apparent as they grew up and two were now developmentally affected by the condition. Other young people seemed completely unaware of their bodies or their own health. Workers commented that the young person would not know if they were bruised or had a broken bone. This was particularly concerning for those young people living independently.

Emotional and behavioural difficulties (n = 16), conduct problems and violence: These young people showed high levels of violence directed at carers, carers' animals, other children and other adults. This behaviour was, not surprisingly, a potent cause of disruption as the children attacked carers, killed their pets and caused tremendous damage to property. Psychiatric reports described 'major conduct disorders with episodic aggressive outbursts' and one foster carers stated:

> . . . *every day is like a battlefield.*

Nearly three-quarters of this group showed conduct disorder and 50 per cent had received this diagnosis formally. A quarter had been arrested for crimes of violence against a person, an attempted murder, criminal damage or fire-setting. The following foster carer's description of trying to care for one of them illustrates the multiple difficulties the young person displayed:

> . . . *Tries to get under people's skin and find their weakness. He pushes boundaries to the limits and never stops talking. He is in your face all the time, dogs avoid him. He sets animals up deliberately . . . like leaving the gate open . . . There is nothing rewarding about caring for him . . . He tries to lure other children . . . He sets himself up . . . like wanting braces and glasses and needing neither.*

Over-activity and restlessness: Ritalin had been prescribed for the five young people with a diagnosis of ADHD, but only two of these were actually taking the medication. Another two were described as having a great deal of difficulty concentrating and were impulsive, restless, fidgety and overactive.

Anxiety and depression: Concerns about the degree of anxiety and depression were also reported. Fourteen of the young people were described as worrying excessively and three psychiatric reports linked high levels of violent behaviour with underlying depression. Six young people were diagnosed as suffering from depression, with three of these also being described as hyper-vigilant, watchful and suspicious. They listened at doors and were scared of the dark, having to sleep with the TV and lights on.

. . . Is a highly disturbed boy and the extent of this disturbance is extreme . . . deals with his uncertain world and the experiences of breakdowns and rejection in a very primitive way. (Psychiatric report)

Social relationships: The early difficulties in making relationships reported as the children had entered care continued. They were described as indiscriminately friendly with strangers, particularly those with dogs. Few had any friends. They seemed not to be able to understand another person's point of view or that other people had feelings. Only two had any interest or hobbies outside their home base.

Self-harm and substance abuse: Four of the young people were already heavy drinkers and were combining alcohol with cocaine and/or cannabis use. Another four had made a serious attempt at harming themselves. Some of these attempts were bizarre, such as attempted electrocution or swallowing nails. One had attempted to overdose on his Ritalin medication.

Elimination problems: Enuresis and soiling continued well into adolescence. At the time of follow-up, four young people were still troubled by this problem. For one young girl, this had only ceased after the birth of her own baby.

Sexualised behaviour: As the children grew older there were increasing concerns about sexualised behaviour. At least eight were known to be currently sexually active; four of the seven girls in the group had had a pregnancy. Half had kept their children, there had been one termination and one baby was placed for adoption. There were concerns that the young people were at risk of sexual exploitation and fears that some were sexually abusing other children. Aggressive sexual behaviour from young women as well as young men was noted, with two having been arrested for indecent assault. A further two had sexually abused other children but had not been prosecuted.

All the young people had moderate to severe difficulties in more than one area, reflecting the complexity of their combined needs. For each of the 14 young people on whom we had follow-up information from social workers (i.e. not including the two young people who returned home), we counted how many of the following 11 difficulties they were presenting to a moderate or serious degree: attachment problems; anxiety; depression; self-harm; violence; conduct problems; over-activity and restlessness; peer problems; alcohol abuse; substance abuse; and sexualised behaviour. The results are presented in Table 14.2.

Table 14.2
Number of overlapping moderate or severe difficulties presented by the young people at follow-up

Number of difficulties / 11	Number of young people (n = 14)
8	1
7	3
6	4
5	2
4	1
3	2
2	1

Ten of the 14 young people (71 per cent) were showing at least five overlapping difficulties at a moderate or severe level by the time of follow-up. There were few commonalities between the young people in the patterning of these difficulties, reflecting the highly individualised nature of their problems. Only depression and self-harm were significantly correlated across the whole group (r 0.70, p<0.01).

Where were the young people at follow-up?

Details on the current whereabouts of the children and young people are given in Table 14.3. Two had been returned home but not to changed circumstances. Factors involved in the original removal of the child were still present. Parents refused social workers access and Schedule 1 offenders were still in the home. In both cases this caused concern but, because there were no other placements, there was a certain amount of relief that the "problem" of placement had been solved. Neither young person was receiving support from a SSD (see case histories).

Table 14.3
Where the young people were at follow-up

Placement	Number of children
Long-term secure facility	4
Specialist residential care	5
Independent foster care (short-term placements)	2
Independence-training unit	1
Returned home	2
Independent living	2

Two young people were living independently, one successfully, the other not so (see case histories). One young person who had "gone off the rails" when her adoptive placement had ended turned her life around after having a baby of her own. This stabilised her risk-taking behaviour and reports said that she was a good mother to her child.

Four young people were in specialist secure facilities and were expected to remain there, at least until adulthood. Five young people were living in specialist residential care and another in a residential independence-training unit. Two had new placements through an independent foster care agency and social workers were hoping that these might contain them.

Contact with family had diminished greatly over the years. The high levels of contact planned at the time adopters were being sought were not happening at the follow-up. This group of looked after children had *the least contact* with family members of all the children in the sample.

Cost estimates

It is not surprising that, as the children's behaviour became more challenging, so the costs of caring increased. The average cost per child of providing placements from the time of the best interest decision (1991–1995) to April 2001 was £471,070. If the cost of disrupted adoptions is added for those who were matched, the average cost rises to £478,616.

By 2001, SSDs were continuing to incur a range of costs. Some young people who were living at home and whose birth parents had excluded social workers were costing SSDs virtually nothing. Other young people were living in very expensive secure accommodation at an average cost of £3,000 per week. However, these figures are not the total cost of care for these young people. Many other services, especially health care, were providing support. We were not able to estimate these costs due to lack of accurate information on social work files.

Table 14.4

Cost to social services from the time of the best interest decision until the follow-up

	Number of children	Total number of weeks	Cost per week	Total cost
Children supported in their families	5	467	£120	£56,040
Local authority foster care	16	2,264	£318	£719,952
Independent foster care	9	435	£630	£274,050
Residential care	7	593	£1,646	£976,078
Independent residential care	12	1,837	£3,000	£5,511,000

Unlike the majority of children who were adopted or those placed in other forms of permanent care, the majority of these young people's costs rose with age and were expected to continue to rise. There was only one young person whose social worker talked positively about her future prospects. The remaining young people were expected either to need continuing mental health provision and/or to enter the criminal justice system.

Case histories

Robert

Robert was his mother's second child. She had learning disabilities and had been sexually abused by members of her own family. During her pregnancy she vacillated between wanting to keep the baby and asking on several occasions that the child be adopted. After the birth she continued in the same pattern: asking for adoption and then changing her mind. There followed several years of numerous house moves, periods of homelessness, and several maternal suicide attempts. Mother began a new relationship and a third baby was born. There were growing concerns as Robert failed his two-year development check and allegations were made by his mother that her new partner was physically and sexually abusing him. Robert was increasingly cut out of the family, spending eight short periods in foster care before the age of five. His mother refused all help offered and was abusive to social workers. There were numerous written agreements but she never kept any of them. Robert began school but was suspended after one term due to highly sexualised behaviour, head banging and attention seeking.

Robert became a longer-term looked after child at the age of seven after his mother demanded he was removed. The initial plan was for rehabilitation to the birth family. His first placement lasted five months before his crude language, soiling and unpredictable outbursts resulted in a disruption. His next foster placement had a care plan of "shared care", living with foster carers but with high levels of contact with his mother. The team manager was against adoption because he believed there was "an intense emotional bond" between mother and child. Mother had unrestricted contact and this eventually ended the placement.

The plan changed again to adoption but Robert's behaviour by now was very challenging. He had sleep disturbance, nightmares, soiled and smeared, and ate all kinds of objects including leaves. His carers described his behaviour as "animal like" as he licked and sniffed people's bodies. He often regressed into baby talk, walked like a toddler and sucked his fingers.

A new team manager took over and pushed through the adoption plans quickly. The descriptions on the Form E were bland and lacked a detailed analysis of Robert's history and difficulties. A freeing order was sought but the child's guardian argued successfully that contact should not be reduced as mother had remained in touch throughout Robert's life. No family could be found and the plan changed to long-term foster care. A family was found, but again the placement broke down because the carers were bombarded by unrestricted contact and phone calls from mother. Robert moved through a series of five residential placements, each breaking down either because Robert made allegations that he was being physically abused or his own levels of violence were too high for staff to contain. After absconding from the last of these when he was 13 years old, he ran back to his birth mother's home and SSD decided to leave him there. Mother blocked all social worker attempts to visit, but rang the police for help when Robert became violent. Robert was described by psychiatrists as a 'highly disturbed young man'. He was self-harming, offending, hyperactive, and very violent. At the end of the case file review, Robert was receiving no support from any service.

Philip

When Philip was four years old a place of safety (now an emergency protection) order was taken by the police and social worker who stated that they had never seen such awful conditions '. . . There was no light; mattress in the hall, the living room was littered with rubbish, a dustbin in the centre of the room. The stench was appalling, as bad as I have ever experienced. The children had no clothes on . . . very slowly the children dressed, having to take matches upstairs to find clothing.' On entry to care, Philip could not walk, had no speech, no social skills and was used to eating from a rubbish bin. He received no therapeutic help while in care; neither did his foster carer receive advice on parenting a child who had experienced such gross neglect. All the professionals who came into contact with the family remarked on the extreme nature of the children's early deprivation.

Philip's birth father and his new wife were keen for Philip to come and live with them and he moved in after a year in care. His stepmother struggled to manage his very difficult behaviour. He soiled day and night, was binge eating and was seen as a bully. Philip was returned to care as his stepmother could no longer cope and she believed he would get therapeutic help in the family group home where he was placed. His behaviour was highly sexualised and he spent a lot of time rocking and looking at walls. The SSD plan was to find a long-term foster care placement but planning was confused '(child is in) despair . . . not knowing what arrangements are being made to safeguard his long term future . . . as it has not been possible to find a suitable long-term placement with a family for Philip, application is now being made to the adoption panel.' At this point he was 11 years old.

Contact was maintained for a short while but was then stopped by the family. Publicity began and one family appeared suitable. The approval process was very quick but not related specifically to the child's difficulties. Philip was very keen and started moving in favourite objects (e.g. teddies) and after pressure from the adopters it was agreed to speed up the process. Philip moved in but within a month the adopters rang the SSD asking for him to be removed immediately.

The plan changed to finding long-term foster carers. He moved to a specialist foster care placement but very soon they were asking for help with his behaviour. He was referred for and began psychotherapy. However, the carers felt excluded from this and did not feel it helped them contain his difficult behaviour. They struggled on, but three years later gave notice. Philip moved into supported lodgings. His attendance at college was erratic, his personal hygiene was poor and he was increasingly isolated. He ate for comfort and was very overweight; he had problems remembering instructions and could not make decisions; he was indiscriminately friendly, attaching himself to strangers with dogs. He preferred to spend all day in his room watching TV and seemed to be recreating his family home in his lodgings. It was not until he had left school that an educational psychologist assessed his difficulties. He was diagnosed as dyslexic and with a high IQ. Philip's verbal ability had contributed to the depth and degree of the impact of his early experiences on his development being underestimated.

Summary for the children in the unstable care career group

- Fifty per cent of this group had lived with adopters, 81 per cent with foster carers. By the time of the AIBI decision, many had entered a spiral of escalating placement breakdowns and school exclusions.
- Social workers clearly hoped that adoption would arrest these children's damaging patterns of behaviour, a level of optimism that, with hindsight, appeared unrealistic but which may also have been based upon an expectation that other therapeutic resources could be harnessed to help the children and their adopters. In reality, despite the strenuous efforts of the social workers, only three of the children were having regular sessions with a CAMHS professional when an adoptive placement was being sought.
- Most adoptive placements disrupted either before or soon after placement, primarily because of the children's challenging behaviour and the impact of unregulated, problematic contact. By follow-up, however, the children in the unstable care career group had the least amount of family contact of all the children.
- These children ultimately exhausted not only all the adoptive and fostering placements found for them, but also a host of other residential, therapeutic and secure resources. By follow-up, none had achieved any educational qualifications.
- Their outcomes were very poor across a range of measures. Three-quarters were exhibiting violent behaviour and 50 per cent had been diagnosed with a conduct disorder. At follow-up, ten of the young people (71 per cent) were showing at least five overlapping difficulties at a moderate or severe level, reflecting the complexity and extreme nature of their individual needs and challenging behaviours. Overall, these were very damaged young people. Social workers were pessimistic about all but one young person's prospects of remaining in the community as an adult.

SECTION V

Policy and practice implications

15 Summary and policy and practice implications

Sample and data

Sample

This study capitalised on the opportunity to follow up a complete epidemiologically-based sample of 130 older children for whom a best interests decision had been made in the 1990s. A catch-up prospective design was used to track the care careers of the children aged 3–11 years at that time and who were aged 7–21 years at follow-up. Case files were read and current carers (80 per cent of adoptive parents and 74 per cent of foster carers) were interviewed. Ninety-six of the children had been placed with an adoptive family and 80 of these were still with their adoptive families at follow-up, which was, on average, seven years after placement. Of the remaining children, 34 had had long-term foster care placements or other permanent placement and 16 children had had numerous moves and disruptions, with no stability of care. These three groups formed the basis of analysis of outcomes. This gave the study particular strengths and enables the "success" of adoption to be more accurately portrayed, as the pathways of all the children could be charted, rather than, as is more usual, examining outcomes for children already in adoptive families.

Quality of case file data

There has been little up-to-date information on the birth families and early histories of older children who are now placed for adoption. This study tracked the children's histories from the time the child was referred to a social services department (SSD), through the planning and interventions that subsequently took place and up until the placement and psychosocial outcomes for the children in 2001/2. Every case file (range 4–27) was read, except for one child's whose files had been lost. For this case, information was gathered from siblings' files. Many previous studies have found, as did we, that getting information from case files was extremely time consuming. Recording was often poor, with information sometimes seemingly entered randomly. Case chronologies were generally absent.

This made the task of understanding planning decisions difficult, especially when events happened without explanation. The impact on social workers was also evident. Social workers taking over a case rarely read all the files and, without a chronology, they often relied on a handover summary. These were brief and concentrated on the present circumstances. This left some young people very vulnerable and social workers ill-informed in making key decisions. For example, a young person was about to be moved into independent living with the new worker unaware that the young person was epileptic.

Poor recording also affected the cost element of this study. We had intended to estimate a unit cost of adoption, but instead were only able to provide the unit cost of adoption to SSDs. Other service provision could only be described. Information on file might suggest that a child had been referred to another agency, for example, for speech therapy, but not whether the referral was accepted, whether the child attended, or for how many visits. Without knowing who provided a service and over what length of time, it was not possible to assemble the basic building blocks to estimate a unit cost for all agencies. However, adopters and foster carers gave good information on service use since the start of the adoptive/foster placement.

Standardised measures

Standardised measures – particularly the Strengths and Difficulties Questionnaire (SDQ) – were completed but were not used in the comparisons between the different "care career" groups. This was because social workers had to fill in the questionnaires for some of the fostered children but often felt unable to answer the questions. They had much higher thresholds than the carers for describing behaviour as severe, and some were reluctant even to use the "definite" point, as they believed this was "labelling" the child. This compromised our ability to compare SDQ scores across our three groups.

Sampling issues

The advantages of this sample have been pointed out but two issues limit some analyses and conclusions. First, the different pathways children took led to some small groups and limited the statistical analyses. Secondly, practice may have changed since the adoption decisions made for this sample in 1991–1995. If this is so, we may have found more delay than would be the case today. The emphasis in 1991–5 (immediately after the Children Act 1989) on ensuring children remained within their birth families may have led to greater reluctance to consider children for adoption. We chose our sampling period to ensure we were examining social work practices after the Children Act but also to ensure that children had been in their placements for some time by the time of follow-up. The introduction of National Standards and Public Sector Agreement (PSA) targets has reduced the time taken to complete adoptions. On the other hand, we do not know if agencies still place children who show the level of difficulties described for this sample, or whether concerns about meeting targets have changed the characteristics of children for whom adoption is the plan.

Why were some children successfully adopted and others not?

This study began by asking why some children were more easily adopted than others. All the children had a best interests decision, but from an early point in the study we knew that not all the children had been placed, and that still fewer had achieved stability in adoptive placements. By the time of follow-up, 80 children (62 per cent) were still in adoptive families (83 per cent of those actually placed), 34 (26 per cent) had been in long-term foster care or other permanent placements, and 16 children (12 per cent) had had very unstable care careers with numerous disruptions of foster placements and many moves between educational, residential, therapeutic and secure environments.

The reasons why plans for adoption did not come to fruition for some children were complex. Nevertheless, the study was able to identify a number of statistically significant differences between the three outcome groups in the study sample. These reflected both the children's attributes and family histories and the needs and difficulties that were evident at the time of the best interests decision.

At the point that the children entered the care system, there were already differences that related to the children's later care careers.

Unsurprisingly, as much other research has found, the children in the successfully adopted group were younger when they entered care (mean age 2.6 years) than those in the other two groups (mean age 4.1 years). Delayed decision-making prior to entry to care (identified for 68 per cent of the children) was clearly a linked issue. Both age at entry to care and the length of time between entering care and having a best interests decision were found to be significant predictors of not being adopted, with the odds of not being adopted increasing 1.8 fold for every extra year of age on entry into care. In the permanently placed (i.e. fostered) group, the odds of not being adopted also increased by 1.6 for every extra year of delay in reaching a best interests decision.

Practice decisions and legal uncertainties clearly have a marked influence on a child's age at entry to care and on delay in addressing their needs both before and after entering the care system. Our research underlines the importance of current policy efforts to achieve early and rigorous risk assessment and swifter decision making for children.

Children with learning difficulties and chronic health conditions were more likely to be in the permanently placed group, as were those of black or black mixed ethnicity. Seven of the ten minority ethnic children in the sample were in this group at follow-up.

The children in the unstable care career group were differentiated from the other children across a range of attributes. Maternal mental health problems were significantly more common in this group, and parents were nearly four times more likely to have been sectioned under the Mental Health Act. This study was unable to answer questions about how mental illness and the involvement of adult services affected judgements about the capacity to parent a young child and delayed entry to care. Children in the unstable care career group had also been exposed to more kinds of abuse than children who were adopted or permanently placed, and it appeared that this abuse had often taken a sadistic form. Perhaps unsurprisingly, given these features of their histories, children who followed unstable care careers were more likely than children in the other two groups to have emotional and behavioural difficulties when they entered care.

These children were also more likely by the time of the best interests decision to have experienced attempted reunifications and disruptions of placement than the children in the other two groups. By the time of the AIBI they had significantly more difficulties in attachment, social relationships, and displays of sexualised behaviour. In general, there were indications that overt sexualised behaviour by young children (aged less than three at entry to care) significantly reduced the likelihood of them being adopted, possibly because carers found this behaviour especially worrying and difficult to address in such young children. The other significant predictors of an unstable care career were: older age at entry and showing violent behaviour towards others or animals. The odds for these children of not being adopted increased 3.4 for every stepped increase in the level of violence they showed at the time of the best interests decision (on a scale from 0–3).

The impact on children's subsequent care careers of violent behaviour, which was already causing concern by the time of the adoption best interests decision, and of sexualised behaviour by very young children, does not necessarily suggest that adoption was the wrong choice for them. It does have implications, however, for the level and type of therapeutic input that children with these difficulties need as permanency plans are made.

The early experiences of the 130 children

Life at home
The childhoods of the children's birth parents often involved abuse, neglect and periods in care. Sixty-three per cent of birth mothers and forty-eight per cent of birth fathers had been in care and 32 per cent had already had a child/children looked after or adopted. As parents, they

had multiple overlapping problems, where drug/alcohol abuse (46 per cent), mental health problems (31 per cent) and domestic violence (86 per cent) were common difficulties. A Schedule 1 offender was living in or frequently visiting 32 per cent of the children's homes and, of these, 80 per cent of offenders had attached themselves to a mother with learning difficulties. Concerns about the parent's capacity to care for a new baby began before or shortly after birth for 63 per cent of the children.

Parental roles in birth families were often only fleetingly described and where mothers had more than one partner, children were often returned home without a careful assessment of the new family unit. This made the children vulnerable to further episodes of abuse. Birth father's information was also missing from Form Es, even when it was available. This had consequences for adoptive families when children later asked questions about their histories.

During the early years, children moved around a great deal. Thirty-nine per cent spent short periods in care, 34 per cent had lived with other family members and 29 per cent had a period of homelessness. The extent and severity of abuse and neglect that the children suffered was considerable. Ninety percent of the children were abused and neglected and 68 per cent of children experienced multiple forms of abuse. Abuse was suspected in far more cases than could be evidenced by visible signs. Forty-nine per cent had very clear evidence of injuries, such as broken bones, bite marks and cigarette burns. Sexual abuse was confirmed for 15 per cent of the children, with the average age of sexually abused children being three. A significant number of children (51 per cent) were rejected by their parents to some degree, with 15 per cent completely so. The majority of rejected children were boys and had been physically abused and neglected, but none were sexually abused.

Lack of assessment and planning in the children's early lives

Although the full extent of abuse was often not known until the child had been looked after for some time, there was little social work or any other type of evaluation of the parents' capacity to care for the child. There were plenty of descriptions of parents' circumstances, of their drug and alcohol abuse for example, but this was rarely used to assess the impact on the child. It was only by reading family support workers' accounts of visits to families or nursery nurses'/teachers' reports that a picture of the child began to emerge. Despite the fact that many families had intensive visiting by health visitors, their observations as recorded on the files were limited to height and growth calculations. We were left wondering, for example, how a child and family could have been visited for years without anyone looking at the child's bedroom. This might have ensured that some of the more sadistic and cruel practices were stopped.

Stevenson's (1998) and Tanner and Turney's (2003) overviews of neglect and emotional abuse have tried to pull together recent knowledge in the area. In this study, the term "neglect" was variably and imprecisely used. Social workers and other professionals used "neglect" to cover a variety of circumstances. For example, cases where neglect and deliberate cruelty were combined were described as neglectful, as were cases where parents neglected themselves as well as the children, or where families singled out one child for rejection. Quinton and colleagues (1998) and Rushton and colleagues (2001) have pointed to poorer outcomes for rejected children but social work practice often failed to take into account the consequences of neglect and did not recognise or intervene effectively in these situations.

Family support

Social workers tried to keep families together by providing nursery places and nearly three-quarters of the families had a family support worker. Social workers realised quickly that thresholds of significant harm had been reached for 32 per cent of the children and acted to have them looked after. For the remaining 68 per cent, assessments were poor and plans unfocused, giving no clear indication of what changes were being aimed at and within what timescales. Few families (9 per cent) had a comprehensive assessment and interventions were not targeted. There was little evidence of agencies providing a co-ordinated response, even though many other agencies were involved with the families. SSDs do not want children entering care unnecessarily but too many of these children were left at home in worsening and abusive circumstances for, on average, 2.7 years (range 21 months to eight years) from the date of the first referral until they entered care.

The introduction of the Assessment Framework should improve the quality of social work assessments, but attention also needs to be given to helping social workers analyse the mass of complex and sometimes contradictory information collected. There was plenty of information in the case files but it was rare to see this information converted into a clear plan. Interventions were unfocused and continued without it being possible to evaluate their success. This contributed to delayed decision-making.

Reasons for delay

Delay in removing children was due to a number of factors. Drift caused by lack of social work assessment, planning and action accounted for 53 per cent of delay, although 15 per cent of this was due to staff vacancies or sickness. Legal delays were responsible for 22 per cent of delay, because of concerns about insufficient evidence to meet thresholds of significant harm, or guardians/psychiatrists insisting that more work be undertaken with the family. Birth families also created delay, by pretending to comply with plans or moving locations when they thought the children would be removed. Every move meant a new social worker was allocated and referrals to family centres for assessments started all over again. Many of these families were violent and social workers were intimidated, and in a few cases physically assaulted.

Entry to care

The general level of concern about the children was heightened just before entry to longer-term care. Concerns centred on the severity of abuse for 73 per cent, and for 20 per cent, the parents refused to look after the children any longer or abandoned them. As they entered care the children were, on average, aged three (range 12 months to ten years), 24 per cent had been on supervision orders and eight per cent were the subject of care orders. Forty-seven per cent entered after an EPO was taken.

Developmental progress at the time of entry into care

The children had development delays in a number of areas when they entered care. Only 15 per cent had no recorded physical health problems. Forty-three per cent had growth delay on at least one measurement. Although only 28 of the children were old enough to attend school, eight of those were already being made subject of a statement of special educational needs and five children had had exclusions. Emotional and behavioural problems were also evident. Sixty-one per cent of the children had problems making friendships. Other children were said not to want to sit next to them at school and nursery. They often smelt, had sores on their bodies (32 per cent) and were described as bullies (20 per cent). Delayed speech and poor language skills (54 per cent) contributed to difficulties in school and with peers.

Extremely poor and abusive earlier experiences certainly contributed to these deficits. Many of the children were described as having poor self-esteem or distorted self-concepts, as less friendly, more aggressive, and more isolated than other children. All these difficulties have been associated with the longer-term impact of abuse (Bolger *et al*, 1998).

Active learning requires curiosity, yet many had been punished for exploration, for asking questions and for moving around. They were locked in rooms or tied down. There were comments from social workers on several files about the children being kept as "babies" and not allowed to walk. A number of primary school reports remarked that a child had "no curiosity" and that the lack of childish wonder at the world had saddened teaching staff.

The children become looked after

Eighty-nine percent of the children were first placed with foster carers, 10 per cent with kin and one per cent in residential care. There were rehabilitation attempts for a quarter of the sample. Some of these attempts were the results of court directions while others were social work decisions. An aim of any child welfare system is to ensure the safety of the children within its care. It seems perverse that, in order to prove (during care order proceedings) that rehabilitation would not be successful, it had to be attempted, even when the risks to the children were high. For three-quarters of the children where rehabilitation was attempted, it was known or there were strong suspicions that further abuse had taken place.

Stability of first placements

Thirty per cent of children remained in the same placement from the time they entered care to the best interest decision, with two being the average number of placements (range 1–7). Failed rehabilitation attempts and planned moves produced some instability as children re-entered new foster placements. Forty-seven children also had between them 67 disruptions, with the majority of disruptions due to the child's challenging behaviour. Other factors influencing disruptions were the detrimental effect on the foster carer's own children (20 per cent) and the behaviour of birth parents (18 per cent). Unregulated unsupervised contact where the birth parents threatened carers, abused children or bombarded carers' homes with phone calls or visits were frequently mentioned as contributing to disruptions. Parental behaviours also disrupted 70 per cent of the kin placements.

Remedial help

The severity of the children's early experiences indicated that they needed intensive nurturing experiences as they entered care. This did not happen. Children were placed with foster carers who were given no additional help or training in working with them.

The provision of ongoing therapeutic services was sparse. At the time, CAMHS policy was to provide no services to children who were not in a stable placement. Although this practice has now changed in our sample authorities, we are aware that CAMHS practice varies in this respect across the country. While psychotherapy may not always be appropriate, there is a range of other possible interventions. We found it unacceptable to read accounts of children's distress, with help refused from health agencies. Social workers' increasing concerns about the child were often matched by a scatter-gun approach to getting help. Letters were fired off to a range of agencies and individuals with little assessment of whether the interventions on offer were appropriate or worked. Each child's social worker seemed to go through the same process of sending for information from agencies and then trying to evaluate their appropriateness. There was no central information point. We suggest that children would be better served if all authorities had a "bank" of approved services that were provided by national and local agencies.

There is an urgent need to review the mental health services and therapeutic services for looked after children. Only seven per cent of this sample received ongoing support from CAMHS whilst they were looked after, although the need was far greater. Many children were exhibiting distressed and distressing behaviour at school and in their foster placements.

Permanency planning and implementation

How delayed was permanency planning after the children became looked after? We defined delay as a lack of active care planning after the child had been looked after for longer than 12 months. There were no delays in making a permanency plan for the majority (59 per cent) of children. The delays that did occur were due to an acceptance of the status quo in 53 per cent of cases, for example, because the children were safe in foster care and there was little urgency to make plans and move on. Legal hold-ups accounted for 34 per cent of planning delay, with social workers reluctant to make plans without a care order. Professional disagreements about whether there should be more rehabilitation attempts also contributed to delay. For a small group of children whose behavioural difficulties were becoming very challenging, delay was caused by concerns about the appropriateness of the plan. Fifty-three children waited more than a year before a plan was in a place (mean 2.7 years), with a range from just over 12 months to eight years.

Delay was also examined from the time adoption had been confirmed as the social work plan to the date of the best interests decision made by the panel. Fewer children (31 per cent) were subject to delays at this point but 11 per cent waited more than two years before their papers went to panel. Finding adoptive families for older children is very difficult and delay reduced the opportunities to do so. Delay also affected children's self-esteem, their sense of security and their behaviour.

> The National Standards (Adoption) state that a child's need for a permanent home will be addressed at the four-month review and, once adoption has been identified as the plan, the panel will make recommendations within two months. Findings support the Standard's aims in reducing delays in planning and also highlight the multiple ways delay affects children.

There were very few comments on case files about the children's own views, but the effects of delay were noted by teachers and carers. Children took their fears to school, where they were reported as writing plaintively of their need for a new family and asked why no one wanted to look after them. Other children accosted strangers and asked if they wanted to be their mummy or daddy. Delay also brought other insecurities for them, as long delays allowed parents to mount further legal challenges, which affected children's behaviour detrimentally in foster placements.

The best interests decision and the children's subsequent careers

Special needs at the time of the best interests decision

Ninety-five per cent of the children had at least one special need by the time adoption was recommended by the adoption panel. Special needs included developmental delay, sexualised behaviour, emotional and behavioural problems, attachment difficulties, poor concentration and hyperactivity and disability. The extent and complexity of needs was marked. More than half of the children had four or more of these special needs. Not all were old enough to have started school but of those who were in school, 31 per cent had been or were in the process of being made subject of a statement of special educational needs. The children carried severe and persistent problems forward into their permanent placements.

Matching and placing

Not all of the 130 children were matched with a prospective adoptive family. For 27 children, the plan changed very quickly to long-term foster care or residential care and different approaches were taken to find suitable placements.

Of the 104 children who were matched, 15 experienced disruptions during introductions. If a disruption was experienced at this point, there was about a 50/50 chance that the next match would not be successful. In the end, 96 were placed for adoption, of whom 80 were still with their adoptive families at follow-up.

These 80 children were placed with 66 families, with just over a quarter adopted by their foster carers, four by kin and the remainder adopted by families not known to the children (stranger adopters). Children adopted by foster carers were usually adopted on their own, by non-professional families, and where there were already children. Stranger adopters were not a homogeneous group. Around a quarter already had children. These adopters tended to take older children with more complex abuse histories and more special needs. Childless stranger adopters were more likely to take younger sibling groups with fewer special needs.

Ethnicity

There were only ten black/minority ethnic children in the sample and therefore this study cannot make any recommendations for practice or policy as far as minority ethnic children are concerned. However, there were some worrying comments on files. Injuries to two children were not spotted when they first presented in hospitals, due to paediatricians stating they lacked training in identifying burns on black skins. SSDs did try to match children according to their ethnicity but there was also a concentration on skin colour. For example, one child's identity needs were thought to have been met simply because she was placed with a black carer. She was from an African background while her adopter was from Jamaica. This girl grew up believing she was Jamaican and knew nothing about her own culture. Only one of these minority ethnic children had a successful adoption placement, but five had good long-term foster placements.

The adoptive placements

Stability

Previous studies have found that adoptions by foster carers are less likely to disrupt and are more successful that stranger adoptions, perhaps because foster carers are more likely to have realistic expectations and because their relationship with the child is already developed. In this study we found a more complex picture, perhaps because of the longer follow-up. Stranger adopters were quicker to give up, with most disruptions occurring during introductions or in the early months of placement. In comparison, foster carer adopter disruptions occurred after the child had been in placement from two years or more. Of course, foster adopters had already got through the introductions phase so, if disruptions at introductions are excluded, 47 per cent of foster care adopters subsequently disrupted in comparison with 25 per cent of stranger adoptions. There were only 15 foster care adopters in this study, so care needs to be taken about over-stating findings. However, this pattern of disruptions was repeated in those who had offered long-term foster care placements, with stranger carers disrupting earlier than those with known foster carers. This suggests that there is not one type of family that is more likely to be successful than another.

Challenges of adoption

In the first year of the placement, only seven per cent of families had a relatively trouble-free time. These parents found the child easy to care for and reported many rewards. This positive picture was more common at follow-up, with 28 per cent of adopters reporting happy, settled placements with few conflicts. For another third of adopters, family life at follow-up was described as a mixture of struggles and conflicts, but also rewards, with real progress evident. For the remaining third, their descriptions of family life were of problems in many spheres, with few or no rewards and with behaviour difficulties escalating or showing no signs of progress.

In the first year of placement, in spite of difficulties, the majority of adopters thought that relationships had developed well and 45 per cent described themselves as being as close to the child as they could be. Foster carer adopters described the most closeness, most confiding and least conflict of the families. Mothers who were unknown to the child but who had children of their own were the least likely to describe themselves as being close to the child and this may be because they had divided loyalties, or the children placed tended to be older. By the follow-up, this had changed and these differences were no longer apparent. There was no relationship between the child's age, type of family, and the quality of the parent–child relationship at that time.

For all adopters, it was the child's difficulties that affected relationships. Some of these children were said to have shown no warmth and were also aggressive and defiant. For example, one adopter said that she had no idea whether her son loved her, he had never sent a birthday card or present, and had never hugged or expressed love in any way. He had never been invited to another child's birthday party and was now often in trouble with the police. For the third of families who were really struggling with these children, the couple's relationship was strained. The child's behaviours also had an impact on the couple's relationships with kin, neighbours and friends: 41 per cent thought that some or all of these relationships had been adversely affected.

Role of male carers

Many studies from a range of disciplines have highlighted the marginal-isation of fathers in studies of parenting. This study also found that fathers had not received sufficient attention. Only 26 adoptive fathers were interviewed but they believed that there was an assumption by social workers that they would play only a minor and supportive role in the placement. When support groups were being run by SSDs, it was invari-ably adoptive mothers who attended while adoptive fathers were left at home to babysit. Male and female parents/carers emphasised the import-ance of the father's role in providing emotional support to their partners and in taking over more of the parenting tasks with birth children to ensure jealousies were minimised. Due to the demands of parenting adopted children who had had such a poor start, many fathers were far more involved in parenting than they had been with their own children and most enjoyed this role. Others were confused when they took over not just the fathering role but also the mothering role, as some children refused to allow adoptive mothers to care for them. Some children refused to eat food prepared by adoptive mothers or be bathed and put to bed by them. This was unexpected. Fathers felt unprepared for this and were fearful that social workers might think that they too were abusers if this was revealed.

Far more attention needs to be paid to assessing the role male partners play within birth families. Fathers have an important role to play in foster and adoptive families and they need to be included in training and support groups. Consideration needs to be given to the parenting style of substitute parents and the attachment history of the child.

There was also some indication that adoptive fathers responded to contact with birth parents differently from their partners. They were less supportive of contact arrangements and were less likely to feel close to children who were having contact. They also seemed to find parenting boys with conduct disorder or ADHD especially difficult.

Placements in families where other children were present

Adopters (and foster carers) emphasised that assessments and support to families also needed to include the other children. The parents' view was that their own children benefited from the experience of adopting and thought these benefits outweighed the negative aspects by two to one. However, this was the parents/carers' view and the children might have reported differently. As other studies have found, where the adopted child and birth children were in conflict, placements were disrupting. Parents reported that conflicts were not because of jealousies but because of birth children's wish to protect their parents from the behaviour of the adopted child, or anger at the way behaviours were affecting their friendships and school-life.

Parents thought that their children had been supportive in innumerable ways and offered adopted children an important friendship. As other studies have noted, parents also found that techniques that had worked with their own children did not necessarily work with the adopted child and they had to learn new strategies. Where adopted children were placed in very large families, parents thought it had benefited them because they were *not* the centre of attention and could fit in gradually.

Contact

Contact with birth parents began to reduce from the time children became looked after long term. Abuse during unsupervised contact visits, children's disclosure of abuse while living at home, parental rejection and the realisation that the children would not be returning home all contributed to contact with birth parents diminishing. By the time of the best interest decision, 52 per cent of children were in contact with their birth parents.

Contact plans were often not well thought out. There was an assumption by social workers that in the long run contact would be good for the child. High levels of contact and re-establishing contact just before the move into an adoptive placement contributed to many early disruptions.

Plans for contact were made as children moved into their new families but there was a lack of attention to the process. Twenty children from the 64 children's families who were interviewed had face-to-face contact during the first year of their adoptive placements. The majority of adopters were supportive of this contact but some complained that levels of contact were set at a frequency that did not allow the child to settle in their new family. Far more were supportive of sibling contact than of contact with birth parents.

The majority of adopters had little guidance in managing contact. Children's behaviour was often very difficult before and after contact visits and the after-effects could last for several weeks. Far more attention needs to be paid to the process, including considering the impact of contact on the child in school.

Contact at follow-up

Of the 103 children for whom information was available at follow-up, 61 per cent had had no contact at all with a birth parent in the previous 12 months and 26 per cent had no kind of contact with their family or previous carers. There had been a reduction in face-to-face contact with birth parents for all the children. Table 15.1 shows the changing patterns of contact over time among the three groups.

As the follow-up for this study was on average seven years after the children had been placed, most of the children were adolescent and their own wishes in relation to contact were becoming more prominent. Parents/ carers described how the young people themselves were taking over the management of contact arrangements. Many young people had mobile phones and could text or ring whoever or whenever it suited them. They were making their own choices. Sometimes this involved trying to re-establish contact and sometimes refusing to continue contact arrangements. This did not always please adopters or social workers. It is interesting that, for those adopted or in long-term foster care, contact with others outside the nuclear family increased over time.

The young people's lives were also very busy so that, although they had had less face-to-face contact with siblings during the previous 12 months, parents/carers stated this was mostly because it had been difficult to arrange. They also said that young people seemed to prefer to text or to talk to siblings by phone. Sadly, the children who had had unstable care careers had the least contact of all the groups. This group had the highest planned levels of contact at the time of the best interest decision but as their behaviour became more concerning and their placements became more specialised and distant from their birth families, contact with everyone diminished. The unstable care career group may also have had less access to mobile phones and have had less autonomy about whom they contacted.

There has been very little practice guidance on working with young people and adoptive families where contact has been re-established after many years. Adopters thought that current practice expected young people to display far greater maturity and emotional stability than was reasonable to expect.

Table 15.1

Comparison of recommended contact patterns at the time of the best interests decision and actual contact at follow up

	Successfully adopted		Permanently placed		Unstable care career	
	BI decision n = 64	Follow-up n = 64	BI decision n = 23	Follow-up n = 23	BI decision n = 16	Follow-up n = 16
Face-to-face with mother	20%	11%	50%	30%	38%	13%*
Letterbox or phone with mother	17%	19%	6%	26%	19%	0%
Face-to-face with father	16%	11%	35%	17%	13%	13%
Letterbox or phone with father	11%	9%	3%	9%	6%	0%
Face-to-face with siblings	53%	34%	71%	69%	56%	31%
Letterbox or phone with siblings	11%	36%	6%	52%	0%	0%
Face-to-face contact with others (kin, previous foster carers)	23%	26%	35%	30%	6%	6%
Phone or letterbox with others (kin, previous carers)	13%	23%	12%	21%	25%	0%

* placed at home

Costs

This study was able to provide SSD unit costs for the adoption process and placement of a child into an adoptive family. It was also possible roughly to cost the children's care careers and to cost the whole of SSD involvement with the 130 children. The table below brings together information from this report.

Table 15.2
Average cost per child of social services involvement from the child's first referral to 2001/2

Children	Supported in family	Looked after	Adoption costs	Total per child
Adopted n = 80	£13,680	£36,252	£25,827	**£75,759**
Permanently placed n = 34	£22,440	£181,811	£4,261	**£208,512**
Unstable care career n = 16	£20,002	£513,682	£7,546	**£541,230**

As well as delay affecting children's life chances, it is also clearly associated with increased costs. The children who did not find a stable placement cost seven times more than those who were adopted. This raises difficult practice and policy issues about whether it is possible to identify earlier the small number of families where support and intervention will make little difference and simply delay the inevitable removal of the child.

Adoption costs were calculated using data mainly from the largest local authority and should be used with caution because of likely inter-authority variations, although these figures were checked wherever possible with the other authorities' costs. We also searched for other sources with which to make comparisons. A Californian study (Allphin *et al*, 2001) estimated that adoption activities cost public agencies $19,000 per adoption in the financial year 1998/9, but that there were huge variations between counties. For example, the home study report in the USA was completed in three hours in one county while another county took 33 hours, giving an adoption unit cost range of $6,000 to $28,539. We would not expect adoption agencies in England to have the same extreme variations in service delivery, and therefore in costs, but nevertheless we do not know how much variation there is across England and Wales. However, because we have been explicit in the way unit costs have been calculated, different activity hours could be inserted easily to calculate each authority's unit cost.

The Californian study and this study are not strictly comparable. Allphin's study was designed to find out how much time social workers spent on adoption activities but did not examine the costs of placing a particular group of children. Payments to carers and higher management costs were excluded from the Californian study. These were included here, but we were unable to estimate the costs of "non-activity" – where adopters dropped out or where contact arrangements did not take place, etc.

This study calculated the cost of finding a new family and placing a child for adoption as £12,075 and a further unit cost was calculated for supporting the child in their adoptive placement until the making of an adoption order as £6,092. This gives a total of £18,167. We also calculated the adoption activity costs for children in this sample. This cost was £25,827. It was higher than the unit cost because children lived with their adopters, on average, for two years before the adoption order was made.

It is possible to compare our unit cost of £18,167 with charges made to local authorities by voluntary agencies. In 2002, inter-agency rates as published by BAAF were £14,931 for the placement of a child. The fee represents the cost of family-finding and placement but does not include, as our study did, other costs associated with adoption, such as visits to the adoptive family by the child's social worker.

The cost to SSDs is only part of the story of the costs for adoption. From the date of the adoption order, only 17 of the children's adoptive families received support from social workers and an allowance. Instead, they used their own resources and turned to other agencies.

Supporting adoption

Social work and other services

Prior to the making of the adoption order, all the families had been visited by at least one social worker and the majority by both a family placement worker and the child's social worker. All were aware of adoption allowances but there was a lack of knowledge of any other services available post adoption. The general view was that they had been discouraged by social workers from thinking that help might be available. In the early days, half of the families did not want additional help, they wanted to be free of SSDs and get on with their lives. But one in eight had purchased private services, such as additional educational help and speech therapy, when these had been unavailable publicly.

Adopters singled out some social workers for particular praise. These were workers who were seen to be champions for the child and who listened respectfully to the carer's views. They also understood the reality of how difficult parenting could be and offered concrete advice and support.

After the adoption order was made all social work visiting ceased for the majority of families. This left many adopters feeling they had been abandoned. At follow-up, 54 per cent of families had no social work support and 13 per cent were receiving only an allowance. Far more families wanted help but thought they had to be in real crisis before SSDs would provide other services. The children's difficulties were such that parents had to look beyond social workers for help. Forty-seven percent of the children had problems in three or more areas, which included learning difficulties, attachment, poor peer relationships, emotional and conduct problems, sexualised behaviour and poor self-esteem. Indeed, 22 per cent had physically harmed other people or animals, a behaviour associated with the more serious manifestations of conduct disorder.

At follow-up, 67 per cent of children were receiving additional educational support, 59 per cent had seen a health specialist and 55 per cent had been seen by a CAMHS professional. There was considerable overlap of service provision with one in five children involved with health, education, CAMHS and police services.

We were surprised at this level of service use, as adopters complained that they had difficulty accessing services and that services were often unresponsive. The general message was that services were "too little, too late". Adopters complained that services had little understanding of the needs of adopted children. Although many children had been seen, far fewer were receiving ongoing support – for example, only 16 per cent of the children referred to CAMHS received anything more than an initial consultation.

The need for adoption support changed throughout the adoption placement. Some families settled down, while others began to experience problems as difficulties emerged. At any one time, about one-third wanted no support other than the allowances to which they were entitled, a further third wanted support and advice, and a further third wanted multi-disciplinary assessment and interventions.

Role of the foster carer in the transition to adoption

The task of supporting adoptive placements begins long before the child actually moves in with a new family. The support that families are going to need should begin with a thorough assessment of what the child and the new family are bringing to the placement. The child needs to be prepared for the move. In this study, adopters commented on the key role foster carers played in being a bridge to the adoptive placement. Where this was done well, the placement got off to a good start. Adopters felt that they could ask carers what it was really like caring for the child, details that were missing from social work accounts. Information from previous carers could ease the transition for the child, for example, when the adopters knew the child's favourite food or their bedtime routines. In other cases, foster carers did not support adoption plans and did not meet with adopters.

The need for information

In many previous studies the lack of accurate background information has been noted as an issue. Recent practice guidance has highlighted this as an area that should be improved. Writing the background section of

Form Es is quite an art. We read excellent reports but also ones where the history had been sanitised to such an extent that the effects of the child's earlier maltreatment was not explicit. Fifty-six per cent of long-term foster carers and 68 per cent of the adoptive parents interviewed stated that they had *not* received all the information on the child that they thought should have been given.

However, there was also an acknowledgement by some adopters and foster carers that they had not always "heard" the information that social workers tried to give them. This information was often given when the adopters/carers were thinking about being parents to the child (at matching) or when the child was actually moving in. These are exciting and busy times for adopters and they may not be ready or able to absorb difficult information. They may also be reluctant to ask professionals questions about the child's background or be unaware of what they ought to know.

It was only as time went on that the adopters, and later children, began to ask questions about the past. Interest was often re-awakened by emerging health or behavioural problems and in some cases concerns were awakened about genetic factors. Other parents wanted to have more background information to help them understand the child's behaviour and the response of the child to them or, more negatively, to apportion blame for current problems to what had happened in the past. Information was also wanted in relation to positive attributes. Finally, as the majority of the children were reaching adolescence, they too wanted to understand more about their own histories.

For many years, background information has been given at the time of placement when the agencies' responsibilities in this respect were seen to have ended. We believe that this approach needs to change. Helping adoptive families get and understand information should be a key post-adoption service. Families may need to know when there are gaps in information that no one can fill. In this case both they and the child may need help to live with uncertainties. This raises questions about whether agencies should have a continuing responsibility to pass new information on after an adoption order is made. For example, one child went for his regular hospital check-up only to be informed by the nurse that his sister was upstairs. He and his adopters had no idea that his mother had had another child.

The need for background information and understanding its impact continues throughout a permanent placement. The search for understanding is not a one-off event but a process that starts before the placement begins and continues into adulthood. At first, the new parent wants to understand the characteristics and behaviour of their child but as the child grows older they too want to know more about how they came to be adopted. Agencies need to consider how to help parents and children access and make use of the information that is available. Agencies should consider whether help with this should be a key part of their adoption service.

Need for behaviour management advice

Adopters and foster carers also wanted information about how to handle difficult behaviour. For some, the social worker's reassurance that they were doing a good job was sufficient. Others found this frustrating if the child's behaviour did not improve or became more challenging. Social workers looked to CAMHS to provide help, but reactions to CAMHS interventions were mixed. It seemed particularly difficult to get help for children with conduct disorders and/or attachment difficulties – the two most common problems. For those parenting children who had severe difficulties in these areas, the adoptive placements were in crisis. Social workers and adopters were searching for possible counsellors or treatments that might help.

There is a lack of information on interventions that have been shown to be effective with permanently placed children who have attachment difficulties and conduct disorders. Lack of evidence ensures that adopters and social workers do not know who or what to recommend.

Need for financial support

Historically, there has been a view that adopters do not need financial help. In this study, adopters described the kind of expenditure they incurred and the pressures on their family income. All had become aware of the existence of allowances. For foster carer adopters these had been an important factor in their decision to adopt. Adopters complained about the severity of means testing – testing that took no account of the needs of the child.

Adoption had an impact on family work patterns and income. Forty-eight per cent of mothers and 10 per cent of fathers had changed their working patterns in the first year of the placement. Many mothers stopped work all together. As well as finance being squeezed as income reduced, expenditure also increased with spending over and above what parents might normally expect to incur. Some children arrived with just a few clothes in a black plastic bag, so that adopters felt they had to start from scratch with clothing, toys and other personal items such as beds, car seats, etc. Others wanted to compensate for the children's early deprivation through buying expensive toys designed to stimulate and/or educate. Half of those interviewed thought they had struggled financially and a fifth had run up overdrafts or were in debt as a consequence of adopting. Other families had relied on their savings until they were used up.

By the time of the follow-up, only 30 per cent of adopters were receiving allowances but 44 per cent said they were struggling financially. A third of the adoptive mothers had been unable to return to work, either because of the child's ongoing medical needs or because of frequent school exclusions. Some also had much larger household bills because of the child's continuing emotional and behavioural problems such as enuresis/encopresis. The second income they had anticipated had not materialised and, with savings exhausted, 26 per cent described themselves as in debt. Some adopters felt really angry that, on top of everything else, they had had to deal with financial worries that were a consequence of the adoption. Expenditure remained high. A fifth of adopters were still buying private health and education services. Adopters also picked up the bill for replacing items damaged by the young person or for recompensing neighbours for damage or theft.

Need for high-quality, multi-disciplinary support

The children continued to have a wide range of overlapping difficulties. Forty-seven per cent had problems in three or more areas including learning problems, attachment, poor peer relationships, emotional and conduct problems and low self-esteem. Adopters wanted the opportunity to request a multi-disciplinary assessment and to have access to services that could address these problems holistically.

Adopters wanted social workers to take more responsibility in helping them work with other agencies, for example, if the child had educational or health problems. Post-adoption support services need to have a multi-disciplinary focus to provide the support that older children placed for adoption might need.

In summary, adopters identified the following factors as placing the family under the most stress and putting the placement in jeopardy.

- Child's behaviour
- Changes in their own lifestyle, including financial pressures
- Impact on family and friends
- Lack of support and service provision

Outcomes

As discussed earlier, the children went down different care-career routes following the best interests decision. The children's difficulties were persistent whichever type of placement was found, but most severe for the unstable care-career group.

Outcomes for adopted children

Adopted children's lives were more stable and suffered fewer disruptions that those in other kinds of placement. Nevertheless, only a quarter of the children were free at follow-up from difficulties that were interfering with their lives and development in some way. The strongest predictors of difficulties at follow-up were the extent of conduct problems and overactivity at the time of the best interest decision. Problems at placement were the strongest predictors of problems at follow-up, but the adopted children showed better attachments than the fostered children, even when attachment problems prior to placement were taken into account.

In this study, neither age at placement nor the length of placement were related to outcome, although the follow-up was not over a standard period or made at comparable ages. Only a longer follow-up can resolve some of these questions and related important ones, in particular, whether adoption is likely to provide much greater support and continuity into early adulthood than other forms of family placement. The fact that so many adoptions have survived is very encouraging in this context.

Outcomes for children in long-term foster care

Long-term foster placements were not as unstable as in some previous studies (e.g. Sinclair *et al*, 2004a, 2004b). Although 46 per cent disrupted, 20 per cent of these were children who had already had a failed adoption. The views of long-term carers were very similar to those of adopters, with two notable exceptions. First, was their frustration with a system that gave them the responsibility for caring for a child for years, but did not allow them to make the kind of decisions that every parent needs to make. Unlike adopters, who quickly realised that they had parental responsibility and used this authority to do what they believed was right for the child, long-term foster carers were left unsure of how much authority they had. Should they be ringing the school? Whose role was it to communicate with other agencies? Did they have any say in the amount of contact with birth parents? Could they agree to a sleepover?

It was expected that with the introduction of the Children Act 1989 long-term carers would be given more authority. There was very little evidence of this. Social workers wanted to control what was happening in the children's lives (maybe because of child protection fears) but the consequence was that young people were said by their carers to feel very different from their peers, and where consent was needed (e.g. school trips), bureaucratic delays resulted in children missing out.

The introduction of special guardianship orders will allow long-term carers more freedom in decision-making, but inevitably there will continue to be long-term carers who do not become special guardians. The needs of these children and carers to have some autonomy should also be considered.

The second difference was in what was happening in the young people's lives as they reached 16 years of age. The long-term carers were concerned that the social work plan was for the young people to move on. Most carers did not want the young people to leave, but thought that the system was set up in such a way as to make it very difficult for them to go on caring. There was concern about where the young person would go. In most cases independent living was being planned. It is ironic that young people were being encouraged to live independently when written permission had been required for sleepovers with friends at a time when monitoring by carers was possible. The few children in the sample who had moved out were not doing well. One was pregnant and the others unemployed.

Both differences suggest that there might be a link with the poor educational performance of children who continue to be looked after. At a time when many young people are worrying about GCSEs, those in long-term foster care also had to think about where they would live. Lack of clarity about professional roles also served to make communication between school and home difficult, with some carers concerned that social workers saw this as solely their role. Consequently, there was often a lack of adult oversight of the children's educational progress, with the carer not having day-to-day responsibility for educational links. In comparison, the majority of adopters were not thinking about the young person leaving home and were involved in the minutiae of school life.

Less parental responsibility and the lack of future security might also explain why long-term foster carers believed the children were not as closely attached to them as did the adopted parents.

Factors in the stability of long-term foster placements and adoptive placements

Adoptive parents and long-term foster carers identified the following as crucial to the stability of placements:

- *The child's own wishes.* Children could make or break a placement depending on whether they wanted the placement to succeed. There was little evidence that children had been engaged in a *dialogue* (not just a quick consultation) about what they wanted.
- *The child's relationship with the carer's birth children.* Birth children were seen as having a key role to play in the success of placements. They provided support and mediated between family members. Where relationships between the children were strained, there was a strong likelihood the placement would disrupt.
- *Accurate assessment of the child's abilities and developmental needs.* Social workers over-estimated the remedial impact of environmental influences on children where parents were known to have significant learning difficulties. This led to disrupted placements as adopters found their expectations unfulfilled and birth children were less accommodating of the adopted child's behaviour.
- *The child's behaviour.* Carers found conduct problems and difficulties in making relationships the hardest thing to live with. There was a view expressed by many that they could cope with most behaviours as long as the young person showed some concern and affection. It was when there was no progress *and* difficult, aggressive, disruptive behaviour *and* a lack of affection that parents/carers wanted to give up.
- *Quality of support from social workers.* The social workers most appreciated by carers were those who understood the reality of trying to care for very challenging children, who offered concrete advice and who listened to and respected the views of carers.

The unstable care career group

It might be thought that the descriptions of the lives of the children in the unstable care-career group given in the main body of the report have been selected to highlight the more extreme cases. Unfortunately, this was not the case. Indeed, details were omitted that would have identified these young people who, because of the difficulties they continue to create, are well known in their local authorities. Reading these case files was distressing. Fourteen of the 16 had been referred to an SSD at the time of their birth. Decision points that might have changed their pathways were identifiable. Of course, this comes with the benefit of hindsight, but there were reports on file of attempts by teachers and carers to draw attention to the child's plight but little specialist help was forthcoming. Inadequate assessments played a major role in failing to identify specific conditions. At an early stage, the behaviours exhibited were either unusual or extreme and merited a thorough investigation. One young person did not have such an assessment until very recently when he was 17 years old and only then did he begin receiving appropriate help.

The educational needs of this group of children had not been attended to. Half had been excluded for long periods and the other half had been truants. Over a quarter of the children were of above-average intelligence, yet none of those who had left school had any qualifications. It was difficult for social workers to find a school that would accept a child who had sexually abused another child.

It is striking that, despite the mayhem these young people caused, they had had so little assessment and diagnoses in comparison with the other children. Their current levels of violence (including the use of violence in sexual attacks) and their current residential or institutional placements lead us to assume that their futures are unlikely to be in the community. It is difficult not to conclude that they were already "lost" or in such severe difficulties by the time the best interests decision was made that only exceptional help and support could have had a chance of turning their lives round. Adopting children with this degree of early adversity needs very substantial support.

Nevertheless, predicting who will have successful adoptions and who won't is an inexact science and thankfully, some children and young people surprise by their resilience. Making decisions primarily on the basis of predictors might exclude from the adoptive route children who would really benefit (but might never get the chance). One boy with a history of multiple sexual abuse, rejection, neglect and who was not taken into care until he was 11 years old had a very successful adoption. Now a young man, he strode into the room as the researcher was talking to his adopters and announced that he wanted her to know that this (adoption) was the best thing that had ever happened to him. One young woman in the unstable career group had a baby in her teens and, despite all concerns, appeared to be a competent young mother.

Research and the factors it uncovers is important in providing guidance to practitioners on what should be taken into account and what needs to be done in the way of assessment, inter-agency working and support. We hope that this study goes some way to providing more information to help those who have the difficult job of finding and placing and supporting children in permanent substitute families.

Appendices

Appendix A
Costing methodology

The costs of supporting the children in their families and the costs of their care careers were estimated using national and local cost data. National cost data were taken from *The Unit Costs of Health and Social Care 2001* (Netten *et al*, 2001). Local data were obtained from the 2000 Children in Need Census and a Best Value Review conducted by the largest local authority in the sample. In addition, three adoptive placement unit costs were calculated.

- **The "adoption process" cost:** The cost to social services of placing a looked after child for adoption. This cost is not time specific.
- **The "post-placement" cost:** The cost to social services of maintaining a looked after child in an adoptive placement prior to the adoption order. This cost is time specific and has been calculated as a cost per year.
- **The "post-adoption" cost:** The cost to social services of providing adoption support services to adoptive families after the adoption order. This cost is also time specific and has been calculated as a cost per year.

The adoption process and post-placement unit costs were both calculated using case file data about the resources used to place and initially support in placement the 96 children who moved into adoptive homes. The post-adoption unit cost was based on information collected at interview about support services received. Good information about social services resource use was also available on file for the five children whose adoptive placements disrupted after the adoption order was granted. The decision was therefore taken to include these five cases in the post-adoption unit cost sample so that a representative unit cost, including both intact and later disrupted placements, was derived. The post-adoption unit was therefore based on a sample of 69 children, 38 boys and 31 girls, who had been adopted for between two and ten years (average six-and-a-half years). Chapter 2 presents details of how the data were collected. This chapter gives details of the method of analysis and calculation of these costs.

Methodology

We had hoped to be able to estimate the costs to all welfare agencies and to families themselves. This, however, was not possible using the retrospective data available. Data on resource use were gathered from social services' case files and from carers at interview. Whilst the case files gave sufficient data to estimate the costs to social services departments (SSDs) in most cases, recording was generally not detailed enough to estimate the costs to the other agencies. For example, a referral might be made for speech therapy but there was no indication whether the referral had been accepted and how many sessions had taken place. Carers at interview were able to remember significant events, but more routine forms of care could only be recorded as received or not. For these reasons, a full analysis of the costs of the children's entire care careers has not been possible. We report instead the costs to SSDs of supporting the children in their families, of the children's care careers and the costs of adoption. We have taken averages across all children for whom applicable data were available.

Unit cost definition: A unit cost is the monetary cost of an identifiable component (a "unit") of activity. A unit of activity can come in many forms; it may be an hour of social worker time, it may be the cost of a day's care in a residential home, or it may be the cost of a process not defined by time, for example, placing a child for adoption.

Estimating unit costs from the Children in Need Data: The national Children in Need (CiN) data collection exercise, among other things, calculated the average cost to SSDs per week of a looked after child (CLA) and of a child being supported in their family or independently (CSF/I). It did not divide these unit costs into more specific categories, such as children looked after in residential care or in-house foster care. CiN data from the largest authority in our sample were therefore re-analysed to give unit costs for specific groups of children, such as children looked after in in-house or commissioned foster or residential care. This authority's unit costs were compared with a benchmarking exercise undertaken in another of the sample authorities and were found to be very similar.

To re-analyse the data, the standard CiN categories were used. These were *Staff and Centre Costs, Ongoing and Placement Costs* and *Miscellaneous Costs*. Staff and Centre Costs were calculated on the basis of all centre and staff time for intake and referral, initial assessment and ongoing work with each child during the census week. Ongoing and Placement Costs included all regular payments such as placement costs (e.g. fostering/boarding-out allowances) and other continuing payments (e.g. services to children in need). Miscellaneous Costs encompassed all non-regular payments made during the census week (e.g. one-off expenditure on aids and adaptations).

The Ongoing and Placement Costs and Miscellaneous Costs were extracted from the largest authority's database for each sub-category of CLA or CSF/I. Extracting Staff and Centre Costs by sub-category was more complex. The total number of hours of staff time or centre time for each sub-category of CLA and CSF/I could be recorded manually from the database. However, to calculate the average cost per child, the unit costs per hour of staff or centre time, and the total number of children in each category, were also needed. The total number of children in each category was available on the database, but unit costs of staff and centre time were not.

We solved this problem by using unit costs published by the personal social services research unit (PSSRU) in *The Unit Costs of Health and Social Care 2001* (Netten *et al*, 2001). The unit costs were £31 per hour of team manager time and £23 per hour of client-related work. This latter unit of measurement apportions all activities, such as team meetings, training and supervision, which are not directly related to the client but are necessary for the social worker to undertake their role. This is considered a more appropriate measure than using a simple per hour cost of social work time (Beecham, 2000). We compared these unit costs with estimates from other local authorities and found they were very similar.

Using this approach, we were therefore able to generate unit costs for children supported in their birth families, for children looked after in in-house or commissioned residential or foster care, and for children in secure/therapeutic accommodation. We have not given a description of the services or shown the calculation of the costs, as these methods are standard and described in Beecham (2000) and supporting documents for the CiN census. Twelve months later, the largest authority in our sample conducted a Best Value Review of looked after children. They used the re-analysed CiN data and method to build more accurate financial information of their own spending. These latter unit cost estimates have been used to calculate the children's care careers. Table A.1 below gives the cost estimates used in this study.

Table A.1
Source of unit costs

Activity	Source	Average cost per week
Child supported in their family	National CiN census	£120
Local authority foster care	Best Value exercise of largest LA in sample	£318
Independent foster care	Best Value	£630
Local authority residential care	Best Value	£1,646
Independent residential care	Best Value and actual cost for sample children	£1,100–3,000

Mean values mask a range of costs. For example, the local authority foster care unit cost includes allowances, recruitment, assessment, training, support and overheads. But it masks the cost of "fostering plus" carers who receive an additional fee in recognition of special skills in caring for children with the highest level of need. We could have used this latter figure for estimating the cost of foster care but as only 38 per cent of the children's carers were receiving an enhanced allowance it was more appropriate to use the average figure.

Independent agencies, on the other hand, charge different amounts and provide different services as standard. Some include therapy and educational support and provide more support to carers than the local authorities in this study. They argue that their costs reflect the true cost of providing foster care services to children who have higher levels of need.

Similarly, the average in-house residential care unit cost hides variation between independence units, which have low costs, and admission and assessment units with much higher costs. Independent agency costs also show variation between basic residential provision at £2,000 per week and residential schools with education at £4,000 per week. Many of the latter type of placement are funded jointly with education and health and therefore the whole of the cost is not met out of social services budgets. For this study, it was possible to calculate the cost to SSDs of purchasing the placement but not the unit cost, as it was not known, for example, how often the social worker visited the residential school and other associated costs, particularly when the school was at a distance.

Making comparisons between costs is difficult. In this study, we were not attempting to compare the costs of different types of provision but to estimate the cost to SSDs of the children's care careers. Therefore, averages have been used but these caveats need to be borne in mind.

Estimating the costs of the children's care careers

Using the figures in Table A.1 above, the cost of each stage of the children's care careers were estimated as follows. From the case files the number of weeks each child spent in the different types of provision was recorded. The cost was then calculated by multiplying the number of weeks by the appropriate unit cost. So, for example, Child A spent 104 weeks being supported in the family (104 × £120) and 64 weeks in local authority foster care (64 × £318) before the best interest decision, giving a total cost of £32,832.

Estimating the adoption process, post-placement and post-adoption unit costs

A number of recent government initiatives, for example, local authority Best Value Reviews as well as the Children In Need Census, have required the estimation of social care unit costs. To aid local authorities in this endeavour, a guide to estimating unit costs for children's social care (Beecham, 2000) was published. The recommended methodology, clearly detailed in this publication, was followed to calculate the three adoptive placement unit costs. This takes a four-stage building block approach to unit cost estimation as follows:

1. **Describe** the ingredients of the "service"
2. **Identify** the activities and a unit of measurement
3. **Estimate** the cost implications of the service elements
4. **Calculate** the unit cost

First, all the components of the service were described. This involved describing both the direct services (services at the point of delivery) and the support and management services necessary to sustain the service delivery setting (higher-level services). For our unit cost calculations, the main service delivery setting was the family placement team. Direct services delivered by the family placement team included, for example, social worker visits, the provision of respite care or a sessional worker. The support and management services sustaining this service delivery setting were many, but included an adoption planning manager and more generic support services such as finance, personnel and information technology. The term Direct Costs is used to refer to all expenditure on resources directly associated with service delivery, while the term Support Service and Management Costs is used for all higher-level costs. It was necessary to *describe* in detail not only all the components of the adoption service, but also something of the structure of our largest local authority, in order to follow this approach to unit cost estimation.

A bottom-up approach was employed to ascertain the direct services used to place and to support in placement our sample children. Once the adoption services were thus described, a unit of measurement was *identified* for each service component. As actual service use and cost data had been collected from case files and interviews, many of the units of measurement had already been determined (e.g. adoption allowances in pounds per week, respite care in weeks).

It was then possible to *estimate* the costs of each service component. For the direct costs, this was relatively straightforward and involved identifying an appropriate cost estimate for each service element not already in pounds per week. Data supplied by our study local authorities were used wherever possible (i.e. our foster care unit cost per week was used to cost a week of respite care). This was supplemented with national data or information from other agencies where necessary. For example, the costs of the identified staff inputs were estimated using costs per hour taken from *The Unit Costs of Health and Social Care 2001* (Netten *et al*, 2001). If relevant data were not available in this publication, the standard *Unit Costs* format was used to adjust appropriate salary information and calculate a derived cost per hour. These costs are referred to in the text as "derived unit costs". So that the direct cost estimates reflected prices in the same base year, our actual cost data were replaced with 2001/2 costs as far as possible (for example, for inter-agency fees). They were also adjusted, where appropriate, to take account of inflation and changes in law and social work practice since our sample children were approved for adoption. For example, an element to cover Consortium membership, not in existence at the time our children were placed for adoption, was included to reflect present-day practice and costs. In the interests of transparency, all cost estimations are described in detail with clear reference to the data source.

Estimating the costs of the support and management services proved more complex for two reasons. First, because an element for all management and administrative overheads had already been included in the PSSRU methodology there was a risk of double-counting and second, because adoption services did not constitute a service delivery setting in their own right but instead formed part of the broader services provided by the family placement team. To have accurately estimated the adoption costs would have involved apportioning all the family placement team support service and management costs (SSMC) between each of the various services delivered by the team. To do this, detailed information about allocation of staff time and resources to each of the services would have been required. As not all of this information was available, the decision was taken to assume that the management and administrative overheads element, already included in the PSSRU methodology, was sufficient to cover the support service and management costs. It was felt that the weakness of this approach, i.e. that it lacked the accuracy of the top-down approach, was compensated for by the fact that it safeguarded against double-counting. Where information was available about the support service and management inputs, these were described as fully as possible. Moreover, the methodology employed and the data used to estimate the costs are clearly set out and so any of the components could be adjusted to reflect more accurate data if this became available.

In the final stage of the unit cost calculations, all data were input onto an Excel spreadsheet and the cost estimates for each of the identified staff and resource inputs added together for each child and then averaged across all children to give the unit costs for the adoption process, post-placement and post-adoption support. These results are found in Chapter 10.

Appendix B
Adoptive parents' wish list of desired services

Three-fifths (58 per cent) of adopters had felt inadequately supported by the available services at some point since their child was placed with them. We asked what adoption support services adopters would have liked. For ease, we have split adopters' responses into three categories: a) educational and informational services; b) therapeutic and personal support services; and c) financial help.

Educational and informational services
Adopters complained that they had received just the bare facts or key dates in their child's history. Some had never received any written information about the child. Their suggestions included the following:

- Children should complete **life story books** as they progress through the care system. These could capture stories and photos from the child's life and act as a record of important events and people and the stories carers remembered about their lives. Life story books completed retrospectively often failed to capture this detail. If social workers had changed, the memories that they held of the child's early life were lost.
- Adopters should receive **full written information** about the child and his or her history including the reasons for being in care, all placement changes, full medical information, details of all birth family members, the child's educational records and a record of all recorded emotional/ behavioural difficulties. Some adopters also wanted to know when other children were born to the birth family.
- **Clear explanation** of terms such as "learning difficulties" and a balanced assessment of the lifelong impact should be provided.
- Adopters should have the opportunity of **additional training**. Preparation groups had dealt with problems in the abstract but what adopters wanted once a child was placed with them was clear advice about ways to help *this* child. Behaviour management training would have been

welcomed by the majority of adopters. Faced with difficult behaviour, even the adopters who already had children were often at a loss to know how to handle it or whom to go to for help.

- **Adopters should be given briefing notes** on common problems and suggestions for parents, especially advice about behaviour management, i.e. what has worked for other people and references for further reading, especially about issues relevant to their child.
- A **directory of support services** was suggested that would be given to all adopters. This would specify statutory and voluntary agencies where help or advice could be sought. Details about local and national adoption help and advice lines and support groups would also be included.

Therapeutic and personal support services

Many adopters experienced lifestyle changes and relationship difficulties both within the immediate family as well as with extended family and friends. For some adopters, life was a constant struggle and some suffered episodes of depression. Children also continued to experience emotional and behavioural difficulties. Adopters wanted:

- **wider recognition** of the impact of adoption on new families and an acknowledgement that services are needed for adoptive parents as well as for the children;
- SSD-run **adoption support groups** with childcare provision to enable both adopters to attend;
- a **mentoring scheme** with an experienced adopter assigned to each new adoptive family as a source of support and advice;
- a **24-hour adoption crisis line** run by staff with adoption expertise who could listen and give sound advice about how to manage the problem, but who could also suggest whom to turn to for further support:

> *Something like NHS Direct would be useful. A 24-hour contact line that you could call, fully to deal with adoption, so that you've got one number and then they can channel it out to whoever is the best person to deal with your problem at that point.*

- support through the provision of **short-break and childminding/ babysitting** services and help with domestic chores if desired;
- SSD-facilitated help accessing health and education support services;
- the opportunity to request a **multi-disciplinary assessment** at any point in the placement;
- **therapeutic services** appropriate for adopted children with more specialist services for children with attachment difficulties and conduct disorders.

Financial services

A recurring theme from the interviews was the extent of unexpected expenditure adopters incurred. This was particularly associated with three things: the initial expenditure necessary to equip a child with all the things they needed; problem-related expenditure where children were destructive or stealing; and special needs-related expenditure, for example, to help a child with developmental delay catch up. Adopters suggested:

- fair allowances that reflected the special needs of the children and were not means tested;
- financial help with initial expenditure and with buying a larger car or making home adaptations if necessary;
- flexible use of allowances to meet the child's needs.

Appendix C
Diagnosed conditions

Table C.1

Number and percentage of children with formal diagnoses: Adopted group

Diagnosis	Number (n = 64)	%
No formal diagnosis	32	50%
Mild learning difficulty	19	30%
Moderate learning difficulty	11	17%
Dyslexia	8	13%
ADHD	7	11%
Asperger's syndrome	3	5%
Autism	3	5%
Epilepsy	3	5%
Hearing impairment	2	3%
Visual impairment	2	3%
Word-finding problem	2	3%
Severe learning difficulty	1	2%
Cerebral palsy	1	2%
Mobility problems	1	2%
Praeder-Willi syndrome	1	2%
Angelman's syndrome	1	2%
Narcolepsy	1	2%

Note: Percentages rounded to nearest whole number;
9 children (14 per cent) had 3 or more formal diagnoses:
(6 children had 3 diagnoses; 2 children had 4; 1 child had 6).

Table C.2

Number and percentage of children with formal diagnoses: Permanently placed group

Diagnosis	Number (n = 29)	%
No formal diagnosis	9	31%
Moderate learning difficulty	13	31%
Severe learning difficulty	4	14%
ADHD	4	14%
Mild learning difficulty	2	7%
No speech	2	7%
Dyslexia	1	3%
Epilepsy	1	3%
Asperger's syndrome	1	3%
Autism	1	3%
Attachment disorder	1	3%
Visual impairment	1	3%
Blind	1	3%
Cerebral palsy	1	3%
Foetal alcohol syndrome	1	3%
Post-traumatic stress disorder	1	3%
Childhood schizophrenia	1	3%
Developmental delay	1	3%
Type C brachydactyl	1	3%
Club foot	1	3%
Kleinfleter's syndrome	1	3%
Quadriplegic	1	3%

Note: Percentages rounded to nearest whole number;
4 children (14 per cent) had 3 or more formal diagnoses:
3 children had 5 (1 child had 3 diagnoses;).

Table C.3

Number and percentage of children with formal diagnoses: Unstable care career group

Diagnosis	Number (n = 14)	%
No formal diagnosis	5	36%
ADHD	5	36%
Mild learning difficulty	4	29%
Moderate learning difficulty	3	21%
Attachment disorder	2	14%
Epilepsy	1	7%
Hearing impairment	1	7%
Foetal alcohol syndrome	1	7%
Disassociative disorder	1	7%
Sexual arousal disorder	1	7%
Tremor	1	7%
Episodic dyscontrol	1	7%

Note: Percentages rounded to nearest whole number;
3 children (21 per cent) had 3 or more formal diagnoses:

Table C.4

Number and percentage of children with formal diagnoses: All outcome groups

Diagnosis	Number (n = 107)	%
No formal diagnosis	46	35%
Moderate learning difficulty	27	21%
Mild learning difficulty	25	19%
ADHD	16	12%
Dyslexia	9	7%
Severe learning difficulty	5	4%
Epilepsy	5	4%
Asperger's syndrome	4	3%
Autism	4	3%
Attachment disorder	3	2%
Hearing impairment	3	2%
Visual impairment	3	2%
Cerebral palsy	2	2%
Foetal alcohol syndrome	2	2%
No speech	2	2%
Word-finding problem	2	2%
Blind	1	1%
Post-traumatic stress disorder	1	1%
Childhood schizophrenia	1	1%
Developmental delay	1	1%
Type C brachydactyl	1	1%
Club foot	1	1%
Mobility problems	1	1%
Angelman's syndrome	1	1%
Disassociative disorder	1	1%
Sexual arousal disorder	1	1%
Kleinfleter's syndrome	1	1%
Quadriplegic	1	1%
Praeder-Willi syndrome	1	1%
Tremor	1	1%
Episodic dyscontrol	1	1%
Narcolepsy	1	1%

Note: Percentages rounded to nearest whole number;
16 children (15 per cent) had 3 or more formal diagnoses:
(7 children had 3 diagnoses; 5 children had 4; 3 children had 5; 1 child had 6).

Appendix D
Problems of adopted children at follow-up

Problem	% with problem N = 63–64
Health	
Frequent illness	9
Chronic	5
Growth	8
Overweight	6
Co-ordination	8
Were dependent on adults because of physical disability	2
Education	
Learning disabilities	17
Reading problems	5
Language delay	16
Statemented	27
Truanting	6
Exclusion	16
Relationships	
Prosocial behaviour	41
Poor understanding of others' feelings	34
Too self-reliant	14
Babyish	33
With adults	
Attachment problems	27
Does not confide in parents	42
Does not disclose to parents	65
With peers	
Difficulty making friends	54
Bullied	57
Follows deviant peers	39
No outside activities	28

Problem	% with problem N = 63–64
Elimination	
Eneuresis	17
Encopresis	9
Problems with self-image	
Low self-esteem	42
Eating disorder	11
Emotional/internalising	
Psychosomatic	13
Nightmares	9
Worried, anxious	29
Nervous, highly strung	19
Performance anxiety	25
Phobias	9
Depressive	11
Conduct/externalising	
Self-harm	13
Showing off	39
Defiant	34
Lies, fantasies	44
Destructive	27
Physically harms	22
Rule-breaking	9
Overactive/restless	
Restless, fidgets	34
Poor concentration	33
Impulsivity	5
Situational overactivity	23
Other risky behaviour	
Drinking	3
Substance abuse	5
Trouble with the law	20
Running away	6
Sexualised behaviour	0

References

ACE, *The Effects of Childhood Experiences on Adult Health and Well Being*, www.acestudy.org Accessed 2005

Allphin, S, Simmons, B and Barth, R P (2001) 'Adoption of foster children: How much does it cost public agencies?', *Children and Youth Services Review*, 23, pp. 865–891

Baker, D, Morris, S and Taylor, H (1997) *A Census Comparison to Assess the Representativeness of the ALSPAC Sample*, unpublished report: University of Bristol

Barth, R (1997) 'Adoption policy and special needs children', in Avery R (ed.) *Public Adoption Policy*, Westport CT: Greenwood Press

Barth, R and Berry, M (1988) *Adoption and Disruption: Rates, risks and responses*, New York: Aldine de Gruyter

Barth, R and Berry, M (1994) 'Implications for research on the welfare of children under permanency planning', in Barth, R, Berrick, J and Gilbert, N (eds) *Child Welfare Research Review*, New York: Columbia University Press

Beecham, J (2000) *Unit Costs – Not Exactly Child's Play: A guide to estimating unit costs for children's social care* (Report), London: Department of Health, PSSRU & Dartington Social Research Unit

Berry, M and Barth, R (1990) 'A study of disrupted adoptive placements of adolescents', *Child Welfare*, 69, pp. 209–225

Bohman, M and Sigvardsson, S (1980) 'Negative social heritage', *Adoption & Fostering*, 10:1, pp. 25–31

Bolger, K, Patterson, C and Kupersmidt, J (1998) 'Peer relationships and self-esteem among children who have been mistreated', *Child Development*, 69, pp. 1171–1197

Brodzinsky, D and Schechter, M (eds) (1990) *The Psychology of Adoption*, Oxford: Oxford University Press

Brown, G (1983) 'Accounts, meaning and causality', in Gilbert, G and Abell, P (eds) *Accounts and Action*, Aldershot: Gower

Cadoret, R (1990) 'Biologic perspectives in adoptee adjustment', in Brodzinsky, D and Schecter, E (eds) *The Psychology of Adoption*, New York: Oxford University Press

Castle, J, Beckett, C and Groothues, C (2000) 'Infant adoption in England', *Adoption & Fostering*, 24:3, pp. 26–35

Cleaver, H (2000) *Fostering Family Contact*, London: The Stationery Office

Collinshaw, S, Maughan, B and Pickles, A (1998) 'Infant adoption: psychosocial outcomes in adulthood', *Social Psychiatry & Psychiatric Epidemiology*, 33, pp. 57–65

Dance, C, Rushton, A and Quinton, D (2002) 'Emotional abuse in early childhood: relationships with progress in subsequent family placements', *Journal of Child Psychology and Psychiatry*, 43, pp. 395–407

Department for Education and Skills (2004) *Children Act Report 2003*, Nottingham: Department for Education and Skills

Department for Education and Skills (2005) *Children Looked After in England 2004–5*, National statistics SFR, Issue 01/05, January 2005

Department of Health (1998) *Adoption Achieving the Right Balance*, Department of Health Circular LAC98, London: Department of Health

Department of Health (2000a) *The Children Act Report 1995–1999*, London: Department of Health

Department of Health (2000b) *Adoption: A new approach: a White Paper*, London: Department of Health

Department of Health (2002) *The Children Act Report 2001*, London: Department of Health

Department of Health (2003a) *The Adoption Support Services Regulations*, London: Department of Health

Department of Health (2003b) *The Children Act Report 2002*, London: Department of Health

Erich, S and Leung, P (1998) 'Factors contributing to family functioning of adoptive children with special needs: long-term outcome analysis', *Children and Youth Services Review*, 20, pp. 135–150

Fergusson, D, Lynskey, M and Horwood, L (1995) 'The adolescent outcomes of adoption: a 16 year longitudinal study', *Journal of Child Psychology and Psychiatry*, 36, pp. 597–615

Fisher, P, Gunnar, M, Chamberlain, P and Reid, J (2000) 'Preventive intervention for maltreated preschool children: impact on children's behavior, neuroendocrine activity and foster parent functioning', *Journal of the American Academy of Child and Adolescent Psychiatry*, 39, pp. 1356–1364

Goodman, R (1997) 'The Strengths and Difficulties Questionnaire: a research note', *Journal of Child Psychology and Psychiatry*, 38, pp. 581–586

Goodman, R (1999) 'The extended version of the Strengths and Difficulties Questionnaire as a guide to child psychiatric caseness and consequent burden', *Journal of Child Psychology and Psychiatry*, 40, pp. 791–801

Groze, V (1996) *Successful Adoptive Families: A longitudinal study of special needs adoption*, Westport CT: Praeger

Hart, A and Luckock, B (2004) *Developing Adoption Support and Therapy: New approaches*, London: Jessica Kingsley Publishers

Haugaard, J, Wojslawowicz, J and Palmer, M (1999) 'Outcomes in adolescent and older child adoptions', *Adoption Quarterly*, 3, pp. 61–69

Hodges, J and Tizard, B (1989a) 'IQ and behavioural adjustment of ex-institutional adolescents', *Journal of Child Psychology and Psychiatry*, 30, pp. 53–75

Hodges, J and Tizard, B (1989b) 'Social and family relationships of ex-institutional adolescents', *Journal of Child Psychology and Psychiatry*, 30, pp. 77–97

Holloway, J (1997) 'Outcomes in placements for adoption and long-term fostering', *Archives of Disease in Childhood*, 76, pp. 227–230

Howe, D (1996) 'Adopters' relationships with their adopted children from adolescence to adulthood', *Adoption & Fostering*, 20:3, pp. 6–15

Howe, D (1997) 'Parent-reported problems in 211 adopted children: some risk and protective factors', *Journal of Child Psychology and Psychiatry*, 38, pp. 401–412

Howe, D (1998) *Patterns of Adoption: Nature, nurture and psychosocial development*, Oxford: Blackwell Science

Howe, D, Sawbridge, P and Hinings, D (1992) *Half a Million Women: Mothers who lose their children by adoption*, London: Penguin

Ivaldi, G (2000) *Surveying Adoption: A comprehensive analysis of local authority adoptions 1998–1999 (England)*, London: BAAF

Kadushin, A (1970) *Adopting Older Children*, New York: Columbia University Press

Lambert, L and Streather, J (1980) *Children in Changing Families*, London: Macmillan

Lowe, N, Murch, M, Borkowski, M, Bader, K, Copner, R, Lisles, C and Shearman, J (2002) *The Plan for the Child: Adoption or long term fostering?*, London: BAAF

Lowe, N, Murch, M, Borkowski, M, Weaver, A, Beckford, V and Thomas, C (1999) *Supporting Adoption: Reframing the approach*, London: BAAF

Maluccio, A and Anderson, G (2000) 'Future challenges and opportunities in child welfare' (special issue), *Child Welfare*, 79, pp. 1–124

Maughan, B and Pickles, A (1990) 'Adopted and illegitimate children growing up', in Robins, L and Rutter, M (eds) *Straight and Devious Pathways from Childhood to Adulthood*, Cambridge: Cambridge University Press

Meltzer, H, Gatward, R, Goodman, R and Ford, T (2000) *Mental Health of Children and Adolescents in Great Britain*, London: The Stationery Office

Meltzer, H, Gatward, R, Goodman, R and Ford, T (2003) *The Mental Health Needs of Looked After Children*, London: The Stationery Office

Nelson, K (1985) *On the Frontiers of Adoption: A study of special needs adoptive families*, Washington DC: Child Welfare League of America

Netten, A, Rees, T and Harrison, G (2001) *The Unit Costs of Health and Social Care 2001*, Canterbury, Kent: PSSRU

Parker, R (ed.) (1999) *Adoption Now: Messages from research*, Chichester: Wiley

Partridge, S, Hornby, H and McDonald, T (1986) *Legacies of Loss, Visions of Gain: An inside look at adoption disruption*, Portland, ME: University of Southern Maine, Human Services Development Institute

Perry, B (1995) *Maltreated Children: Experience, brain development and the next generation*, New York: W.W. Norton

Peters, B, Atkins, M and McKay, M (1999) 'Adopted children's behaviour: a review of five explanatory models', *Clinical Psychology Review*, 19, pp. 297–328

Performance and Innovation Unit (2000) *The Prime Minister's Review of Adoption*, London: The Cabinet Office

Plomin, R (1995) 'Genetics and children's experience in the family', *Journal of Child Psychology and Psychiatry*, 36, pp. 33–68

Quinton, D and Rutter, M (1988) *Parenting Breakdown: The making and breaking of intergenerational links*, Aldershot: Avebury

Quinton, D, Rushton, A, Dance, C and Mayes, D (1998) *Joining New Families: A study of adoption and fostering in middle childhood*, Chichester: Wiley

Reid, W, Kagan, R, Kaminsky, A and Helmer, K (1987) 'Adoptions of older institutionalized youth: social casework', *The Journal of Contemporary Social Work*, 68, pp. 140–149

Rogers, W, Hevey, D, Roche, J and Ash, E (1992) *Child Abuse and Neglect*, London: Batsford Open University, p. 163

Rosenthal, J (1993) 'Outcome of adoption of children with special needs', *The Future of Children*, 3, pp. 77–88

Rosenthal, J and Groze, V (1992) *Special Needs Adoption: A follow-up study of intact families*, New York: Praeger

Rosenthal, J, Schmidt, D and Connor, J (1988) 'Predictors of special needs adoption disruption: an exploratory study', *Children and Youth Services Review*, 10, pp. 101–107

Rowe, J, Cain, H, Hundleby, M and Keane, A (1984) *Long-Term Foster Care*, London: Batsford

Roy, P, Rutter, M and Pickles, A (2000) 'Institutional care: risk from family background or pattern of rearing?', *Journal of Child Psychology and Psychiatry*, 41, pp. 139–150

Rushton, A (1999) *Adoption as a Placement Choice: Arguments and evidence*, Unpublished manuscript, London: Maudsley Discussion paper

Rushton, A and Dance, C (2002) *Adoption Support Services for Families in Difficulty: A literature review and UK survey*, London: BAAF

Rushton, A and Dance, C (2004) 'The outcome of late permanent placements: the adolescent years', *Adoption & Fostering.* 28:1, pp. 49–58

Rushton, A, Dance, C, Quinton, D and Mayes, D (2001) *Siblings in Late Permanent Placements*, London: BAAF

Rushton, A, Quinton, D and Treseder, J (1993) 'New parents for older children: support services during eight years of placement', *Adoption & Fostering*, 17:4, pp. 39–45

Rushton, A, Treseder, J and Quinton, D (1995) 'An 8 year prospective study of older boys placed in permanent substitute families', *Journal of Child Psychology and Psychiatry*, 36, pp. 687–695

Rutter, M (2000) 'Children in substitute care: some conceptual considerations and research implications', *Children and Youth Services Review*, 22, pp. 685–703

Rutter, M, Silberg, J, O'Connor, T and Simonoff, E (1999) 'Genetics and child psychiatry: II empirical research findings', *Journal of Child Psychology and Psychiatry*, 40, pp. 19–55

Sack, W and Dale, D (1982) 'Abuse and deprivation in failing adoptions', *Child Abuse and Neglect*, 6, pp. 443–451

Schofield, G (2003) *Part of the Family: Pathways through foster care*, London: BAAF

Sedlak, A and Broadhurst, D (1993) *Study of Adoption Assistance Impact and Outcome. Final report*, Rockville MD: Westat Inc

Seglow, J, Pringle, M and Wedge, P (1972) *Growing up Adopted*, Windsor: National Foundation for Educational Research

Sellick, C and Thoburn, J (1996) *What Works in Family Placement?*, Barkingside, UK: Barnado's

Sinclair, I, Baker, C, Wilson, K and Gibbs, I (2004) *Foster Children: Where they go and how they get on*, London: Jessica Kingsley Publishers

Skinner, H, Steinhauser, D and Santa-Barbara, J (1983) 'The family assessment measure', *Canadian Journal of Community Mental Health*, 2, pp. 91–105

Smith, S and Howard, J (1991) 'A comparative study of successful and disrupted adoptions', *Social Services Review*, pp. 248–265

Social Services Inspectorate (SSI) (1996) *For Children's Sake: An inspection of local authority adoption services*, London: The Stationery Office

Social Services Inspectorate (SSI) (2000) *Adopting Changes: Survey and inspection of local councils' adoption services*, London: The Stationery Office

Stevenson, O (1998) *Neglected Children: Issues and dilemmas*, Oxford: Blackwell Sciences

Tanner, K and Turney, D (2003) 'What do we know about child neglect? A critical review of the literature and its application to social work practice', *Child & Family Social Work*, 8:1, pp. 25–34

Thoburn, J (1990) *Success and Failure in Permanent Family Placement*, Aldershot: Avebury

Thoburn, J (1991) 'Survey findings and conclusion', in Fratter, J, Rowe, R, Sapsford, D and Thoburn, J (eds) *Permanent Family Placement: A decade of experience*, London: BAAF

Thomas, C, Beckford, V, Lowe, M and Murch, N (1999) *Adopted Children Speaking*, London: BAAF

Triseliotis, J (1980) *Growing up Fostered*, London: Social Sciences Research Council

Triseliotis, J (2002) 'Long-term foster care or adoption: the evidence examined', *Child and Family Social Work*, 7, pp. 23–33

Triseliotis, J and Hill, M (1990) 'Contrasting adoption, foster care and residential rearing', in Brodzinksy, D and Schechter, M (eds) *The Psychology of Adoption*, Oxford: Oxford University Press

Triseliotis, J, Shireman, J and Hundelby, M (1997) *Adoption: Theory, policy and practice*, London: Cassell

Westhues, A and Cohen, J (1990) 'Preventing disruption of special-needs adoptions', *Child Welfare*, 69, pp. 141–155

Index

Compiled by Elisabeth Pickard